MW00975340

The Wonder Of It All

A New System of Belief
To Sustain Human Life

The Wonder Of It All

A New System of Belief to Sustain Human Life

Peter Bearse PhD

Shoestring Book Publishing

Maine, USA

The Wonder Of It All
A new system of belief to
sustain human life

Paperback

ISBN: 9781943974436
Second Edition

Published by: Shoestring Book Publishing

Copyright 2020
By, Peter Bearse PhD

All rights reserved.
Printed in the Unites States of America
No part of this book may be reproduced, stored in a Retrieval system,
or transmitted in any form, Electronic, mechanical; or by other means whatsoever,
Without written permission from the author, Except for
The case of brief quotations within reviews and critical Articles

Layout and design by Shoestring Book Publishing

For information address:

Shoestringpublishing4u@gmail.com

www.shoestringbookpublishing.com

To one of my mentors,
the great scientist and humanist,
Jacob Bronowski.

To: Beth, with warm
regards & best wishes.

Peter

Acknowledgements

For the thoughtful and careful comments
and editorial help of Kathy LaFrance,
Helen Cleaveland [love of my life]
my dear old friend, Carmine Gorga,
and Dana Taff.

Table of Contents

Foreword

This book has been written to advance a vision – to foster the nurture and sustenance of human life on the precious biosphere we call "earth," our one and only home. Any vision without foundation is vacuous. So, what is our foundation? – only two basic assumptions about human nature: (1) That we all have spiritual qualities; and (2) That our spirits aspire to reach and attain states of being, qualities of life and other things that are higher and better for ourselves and our families. It is an unerring focus on LIFE, one that builds on its relentless force in each of us, reaching for the stars.

This focus was sharpened by the thinking and writing of Michael Shermer, rendered just as this book was being brought to term. He reported on the results of a line of research recently completed by Clay Routledge and colleagues at North Dakota State University on connections between extra-terrestrial intelligence [ETI] and religious belief. They found an inverse relation between religiosity and ETI beliefs. That is, those more religious were less likely to believe in the existence of intelligence way outside of earth. Less belief in the latter, more religious.

The key intermediate factor here, however, is a search for meaning in life by the irreligious. Most view the possibility of ETI as the likely existence of life elsewhere in the universe. ETI is definitely not viewed as supernatural. Thus:

> "...subjects who self-identified as being either atheist or agnostic were...more likely to report believing in ETIs than those who reported being religious...presence of meaning and higher search for meaning

were associated with higher belief in ETI...ETI beliefs showed no correlation with supernatural beliefs."[1]

And so, this book is for all who, religious or not, are:

Searching to deepen a sense of meaning in their own lives specifically and for the sake of life more generally, in all its richness and potential; and

Open to the possibility of a new system of belief that would help us to be better able to sustain human life on the earth that sustains us as we learn how better to nurture the earth that contains us.

Throughout, our focus needs to be brought and kept down to earth even while we seek to recognize, relish and enrich our spirituality. For many who count themselves as religious, the shift in focus may be difficult, unwelcome and perhaps even impossible. It is a shift away from an external god-in-heaven that has been a product of human imaginations through the ages. This, so-called "God," however, has now become a needless distraction away from our true mission as human beings – the nurture and advancement of life in all its dimensions. The focus needed simply (!) to sustain human life needs to unerringly be brought to bear on a real god – the god of earth, nature and life; indeed, a God of Life.

To set forth the need and ways of this refocused vision is the purpose of this book. Let our spirits rise to the occasion even while, like mussels adhering to the rocks of the ocean shore, they are firmly tethered to the rootedness of our lives on earth.

---

[1] Shermer, Michael (2017), **"Sky Gods for Skeptics," SCIENTIFIC AMERICAN** (October), commenting on Routledge, Clay, et al. (2016), **"We are Not Alone," MOTIVATION and EMOTION** (an academic journal).

Introduction

I was listening to the news on the radio. A suicide bomber was reported as having detonated his bomb after seeking refuge in a family's apartment, killing nearly everyone there. My friend June exclaimed: "Why did he do that?" I yelled: "Because he thought he would go to heaven!" This jibes with the sadly and increasingly numerous reports of other mass-murderers being similarly motivated, including the latest as of this writing [11/5/17] – that of the young Uzbeki man who used a rented truck to mow down folks along a bike path in lower Manhattan. Suicide bombers' and other killers' trainers or religious leaders hold out the promise of paradise with sixteen virgins awaiting them.[2] One editorial remarked:

> "They know exactly what they are doing and exactly what they want. They want me, and everyone like me, to walk around terrified that instant death is...a moment away. And they think it's all for the glory of God. Well, they can go to hell."[3]

Nothing reveals more sharply the perverse incentive built into religious beliefs in life-after-death. A life wishing to die before its full term is up? The very phrase "life after death" is a contradiction in terms. What does a religion value more, life or death? Ambivalence over such a choice suggests a death wish. Any belief system that fails to be four-square for life looks at least

---

[2] Failure to mention the killer's name here is deliberate. May he forever remain nameless, and may media reporting follow suit as it has now begun to do so.

[3] Hennessey, Mathew (2017), "As Terror Strikes Again, New Yorkers No Longer Wonder Why," **WALL ST. JOURNAL** (November 2). Hennessey is an Associate Editor of the Journal. There have been many other mass murder events since. Is our sense of the preciousness of life being deadened by their frequency?

implicitly for fulfillment in death. Life is a struggle. It needs to be sustained by a belief system that provides unqualified support for it.

Let us recognize, however, that excising life-after-death from the coda of those religions that rely on it need not necessarily spell the death of those religions. In the case of Christianity, for example, one could still revere Christ as one of the greatest prophets and teachers of the human race even if most Christians were to declare that life-after-death is not fundamental to their system of belief or if they were to adopt the New System of Belief that this book outlines and advocates [hereafter abbreviated "NSB"]. As indicated earlier, our spirituality can and should be rooted in the reality of life on earth.

Proof of the rooting is the subject of long, detailed chains of argument and evidence. Each chain constructs one of the frames upon which the new system is built. The main frames are four (4):

1) The Universe, revealed to provide localized homes for the gestation of life.
2) The Human Brain as a Complex Adaptive System [CAS] from which consciousness and spirituality emerge;
3) Evolution, grounded not only upon natural selection but also upon self-organization and emergence.
4) Emergence: The ability of a CAS to generate new forms that are different from the parts entering into the evolutionary process.

The result of such a complex process arose over billions of years. It is: US! – human beings endowed with faith, hope, love and, above all, spirituality, the subject of most chapters. This is the great punchline of this book. The process is still ongoing. Thus, please try to bear with or, if you wish, selectively ignore the most difficult chapters, Chapters 3 and 5 being chief among them.

Chapter 1

Science, Soul, God and Belief

in the Context of Our Universe

SOUL: Definition [4] --

1) **The immaterial essence, animating principle, or actuating cause of an individual life; regarded as a distinct entity separate from the body, and commonly held to be separable in existence from the body; the spiritual part of humans as distinct from the physical part** ["Descartes' Error"].

2) The spiritual part of humans regarded in its moral aspect, **or as believed to survive death; arguing for the immortality of the soul.**

2a : The spiritual principle embodied in human beings, all rational and spiritual beings;

3) The disembodied spirit of a deceased person.

3a: A person's total self.

---

[4] **OXFORD ENGLISH DICTIONARY**, 11th Edition (2008), p.1378.

NOTE: Those marked above in **bold** are FALSE, as many authors have shown in light of science, as careful readers shall see herein. Nevertheless, #2a above is underlined because it underlies much of what follows. Why? -- Because spirituality is fundamental to any system of belief. Soulfulness is its counterpart. We will see in what ways #3 can be true in due course. Now let us turn to discuss "soul" in light of science.

We live in an age in which science is the greatest source of discovery, development and progress. Why – Because science is a discipline dedicated to discovery grounded on truth-seeking procedures and empirical evidence drawn from the real-world – not a mythical, supernatural world.

A scientific hypothesis must satisfy two criteria, that it is:

> (1) testable, empirically, in light of replicable experiments and data; and

> (2) falsifiable. Any statement or concept that cannot satisfy these criteria is not scientific.

"Intelligent creation" is one; life-after-death is another. Such statements characterize religious belief. To which Bob Pirsig delivers a sacrilegious retort: "When one person suffers from a delusion, it's insanity; when many...it's called religion."[5] Go to nearly any church, synagogue or temple and you will find the clergy there trying to support an archaic concept of the universe vs. the discoveries of science. Yet science has steadily defeated the claims of religion over 500 years.

The existence of a soul in human beings has itself been a subject of debate for centuries. The most important bone of contention here, however, is not the existence of soul or soulfulness per se but claims of the soul's immortality. One wonders why, in this scientific age, claims such as the latter continue to prevail in so many minds. One of the most powerful, sworn to be true by

---

[5] Pirsig, Robert, **ZEN and the ART of MOTORCYCLE MAINTENANCE.**

Christians world-wide, is the resurrection story. The fact that it cannot be proven to be false is what sustains its belief. So many people wish it to be true. It is the lodestone of faith and hope in the Christian system of belief. It extends from the distant past to the present of now to the ever-distant future: That Christ will rise again – "as it was then, as it is now, as it shall ever be..."

What follows at the end? – "World without end. Amen." Unfortunately, not true. Science says otherwise on the grounds of decades of research documenting the life cycles of stars. So, our world will end, says science, in about 3.5 billion years. And human life? "Since moons decay and suns decline, how else should end this life of mine...?"[6] There is already speculation that it might continue on another planet. Fortunately, there is time to plan so that the end of our world does not necessarily mean the end of life and time.

However, the soul itself has never lacked for believers, including 90% of the American public, according to pollsters.[7] As authors Baker and Goetz observed:

> "Most people, in most times, in most places, at most ages have believed that human beings have some kind of soul."[8]

Is it possible that the high percentage of believers owes in some significant degree to the association of soul with life after death? Yes, because the percentage of Americans who believe in the afterlife has been consistently

---

[6] Poem by John Masefield, "The Passing Strange," on page 1115 of the **OXFORD BOOK OF ENGLISH VERSE.**

[7] Hameroff, Stuart, MD and Deepak Chopra MD (2014), Can Science Explain the Soul?, **THE BLOG** (5/25).

[8] Baker, Mark, and S. Goetz (2011), **THE SOUL HYPOTHESIS: Investigations Into the Existence of the Soul**. New York, N.Y.: Continuum International Publishing Group.

high, hovering around 75% (3/4) for decades, since 1944. Later in this book, we'll review the evidence favoring the likelihood of life after death, to conclude that it is zero = nill, nix, null. Nevertheless, belief in the immortality of the soul was featured in the Oct. 15, 2012 issue of **NEWSWEEK** as a cover story entitled "Heaven is Real: A Doctor's Experience of the Afterlife."

> "Belief in heaven has stayed over eight in ten since the late 1960s...A 1986 **ABC/Washington Post** poll that asked...if heaven was a real place found 81% saying "Yes"...among these, 82% said it was a place where people existed only spiritually."[9]

The drift of scientific research, however, is providing insights that run against the prevailing grains of mainstream media, religious belief and public opinion. Prof. of Psychology Julien Musolino sees the confrontation directly:

> "Trust science, not myth. Religious hucksters with claims of souls are lying. Let's embrace reality."[10]

The phrase quoted earlier, citing "heaven" as a place "where people exist only spiritually..." is quite problematic – as to HOW. Indeed, how can anyone so 'exist' after death if the essence of their life, their spirit; indeed, their soul, is not recognized and carried forward by living souls in present and future generations? The further implication is that "heaven" can exist only here on earth, populated by living souls to the extent that they are willing and able to build it out. As Ella Fitzgerald and Louis Armstrong sang: "I'm in heaven...when we're out together dancing cheek to cheek." For Ella and Louis, heaven is soulful love right here. It's certainly not the kind of heavenly

---

[9] Weldon, Kathleen (2016), "Paradise Polled: Americans and the Afterlife," **THE BLOG** (June 15).

[10] Musolino, Julian (2015), **THE SOUL FALLACY: What SCIENCE Shows We Gain by Letting Go of Our Soul Beliefs.** Prometheus Books, Amherst, N.Y.

"Kingdom" evangelistic preachers love to preach, especially to those who may not yet have discovered their own souls.

One scientific attempt to eternalize consciousness and soul is that of Hameroff and Penrose. Their theory allows for "information" about a conscious being to live on somewhere else in the universe, even though not allowing for any other "life-after-death" of the deceased.[11] It is "a quantum theory of consciousness" led by Hameroff's provocative, controversial statement that "cognitive decisions are best described by quantum mathematics." The theory claims that our souls are contained within very tiny (nanometer scale) protein-polymer "microtubules" that reside within a brain's neurons. Consciousness arises from quantum oscillations in these microtubules, vibrations which entangle, interfere, 'collapse,' resonate, control neuronal firings, generate consciousness, and ultimately connect to 'deeper order' ripples in space-time geometry.

The two scientists have speculated that, at time of death, the microtubules lose their quantum state, yet the information they contain is not lost; it returns to the universe. How is this speculation testable? Might it relate to the debate over whether information is lost within black holes? Anyway, in some sense as yet undetermined, the soul – **if** it can be defined by informational bits and bytes (very doubtful, as we shall see) – might somehow live on. Even if so, there is no apparent way to retrieve it beyond the obituaries, memories and other memorials that people leave behind so that others can and might actually retrieve something of the meaning and value of lives lived. See Chapters 5 and 6 for more, but beware: Chapter 5, which traces complex networks within the brain on the basis of the most recent scientific research, may be hard reading for some. If so, feel free to skip much of 5 and proceed

---

[11] Hameroff Stuart and R. Penrose (2014), "Consciousness in the universe – Review of the 'Orch OR' theory," **Physics of Life Reviews** 11(1):39–78. Hameroff explained the theory at length in the Morgan Freeman-narrated documentary **Through the Wormhole**, aired in the U.S. by the Science Channel.

directly to 6 on "Emergence" – a key to understanding how spirituality can arise.

The fact that "information" is the stock-in-trade of both minds and computers has led many to go astray. George Johnson, for example provides a sophisticated but incomplete case for seeing conscious minds as no more than advanced computers.[12] It is worth noting that his review pre-dates Penrose's more recent book as well as that of Kaufmann – two books that provide strong support for the thesis of this one.

An alternative view supporting the existence of the human soul and soulfulness has been provided by the Australian biologist Jeremy Griffith. It is worthy of consideration because of being well-grounded in biological science and human evolution. Thus, it seems far more realistic than a theory grounded in quantum mechanics where there is still much work to be done to connect the dots between the sub-micro level of physics and what we know to be the immanence and transcendence of human consciousness. Griffith argues that the growing length of time in human infancy, coupled with maternal love, establishes both individual and collective subconsciousness (souls) of selfless love. This view has been doing battle with the set of competitively selfish and aggressive instincts observed over tens of thousands of years. He describes the battle as a conflict between two "learning systems"; one, a nerve (neuron)-based system – a conscious intellect unique to humans – the other, our unconscious, a gene-based system – our instincts – a learning system we share with other animal species – consciousness vs. instinct.

The neuron-based learning system has slowly but surely gained over our instincts until now, it is foreseeable that education and training can generate a selflessly well-behaved, cooperative society. The latter, in turn, would

---

[12] Johnson, George (1999), "New Mind, No Clothes" (a review of Penrose's **THE EMPEROR'S NEW MIND**), in **THE SCIENCES** (March/April).

increasingly serve to generate a moral soul. Evolved genes would follow and reinforce the positive development process. [13]

A third perspective on the origin and development of consciousness and soulfulness is provided by Jaynes. [14] Though admitting that the earliest evidence based on archeologically unearthed tables from Mesopotamia and other ancient places is not conclusive, he submits that it provides sufficient basis for thinking that the minds of ancient human species were "bicameral." By this he means that they were divided, not just in two parts, physically – the right and left lobes of the brain -- but that they were divided mentally and somewhat independently as well. His arguments in favor of this thesis are very well documented on the basis of research completed up to the time of his writing. His method is scientific.

As Jaynes documents and others have acknowledged, the origin and evolution of consciousness have been influenced by major changes and challenges arising from the environments to which we early humans have had to adapt or perish. The lives of our earliest, "bicameral" ancestors were dominated by "auditory" communications during cataclysmic events that occurred throughout three millennia B.C. Only those survived whose minds succeeded in synthesizing the signals thereby provided into a nascent and evolving consciousness. These highlights of Jaynes' research and thinking are all to brief. We'll find opportunities to see more of them further on.

So, we have before us three lines of science-based evidence for the development of our consciousness, the basis for soul and soulfulness. Science has at least taken these out of the realms of religious myth, the supernatural and huckster hype. Griffith states that his view represents a "demystification

---

[13] This paragraph has drawn from "Science at Last Explains Our Soul," in **ZME Science** [www.zmescience.com/science/science-explains-our-soul]

[14] Jaynes, Julian (1976), **THE ORIGIN OF CONSCIOUSNESS IN THE BREAKDOWN OF THE BICAMERAL MIND**. Boston: Houghton Mifflin.

of religion," though he also says that the works of art, philosophy and religion that have "resonated through the ages" have done so, "not because they were survival tools but because they contained profound truth(s) about our condition." For example, he cites two great English poets, Blake and Wordsworth.[15]

Griffith's optimism over the evolution of "the human condition", however, needs to be tempered by some other, related areas of research. He has been criticized for omitting or downplaying evidence of violent, aggressive behavior among the Kung! and other African tribes in his analysis of archeological evidence. His views would also need to be modified on the basis of a broader view of how relatedness affects the evolution of altruism" and cooperation: "group selection cannot always be reduced to kin selection."[16] The reduction of inter-group conflict may prove critical in the realization of the positive evolutionary process he paints. The process is likely to be very bumpy and take much longer than anticipated. It may even fail if the human species cannot avoid destroying itself through nuclear war and/or environmental collapse.

Contending mythologies are playing a tiresome but potentially destructive game. The main problem is that they have very little relevance to the fundamental problem of contemporary life -- that we need to recognize that we're all passengers on the same "spaceship earth," as Buckminster Fuller called it. In-group / out-group attitudes of retaining love and admiration for your own group and projecting disdain and aggression towards others are archaic, self- and other-destructive attitudes.

Nevertheless, Jaynes' views on the development of our consciousness and Griffith's view of the evolution of soul and soulfulness provide at least some bases for hope. They also provide many lines of testable theories that have

---

[15] **ZME Science**, op. cit., p.2.

[16] Vladar, Harold P. and E. Szathmary (2017), "Beyond Hamilton's Rule," (5 May).

help to move the discussion of soul forward, out of speculations grounded upon supernatural belief. The key question remains: **What is the nature and content of a belief system sufficient to the sustenance and nurture of human life** over a multitude of millennia [at least 3.5 million of them]?

The challenge of this question is daunting. After all, the great belief systems of our time are no more than two millennia old, merely a tiny scratch in time – 1/1,750,000th of 3.5 billion. The very fact that the question can be raised with credibility is a sign of our times. We are now living in the midst of a millennial cusp [discontinuity, disjuncture – pick your own word]. We can look backwards and ask where advances in technology are taking us. The danger is that there may be little or no advance. Technology is a double-edged sword. It can cut and thrust for good or evil.

The lead question of belief systems, already noted, begs that an implicit assumption be made explicit, for implicit assumptions can be dangerous. This is that, necessarily, we humans will not, willfully or otherwise, act to destroy so much of our world that our species, along with so many others, becomes extinct. In order that this not be so, ever, four major possibilities need to become real:

- ❖ Not only a ban on the use of, but total destruction of nuclear weapons stockpiles;
- ❖ The end of war as an instrument of international competition;
- ❖ Comprehensive recordings and digital storage of human genomes, cultures, knowledge [17]and histories along with seed banks and genomes for all other species of life.[18]

---

[17] These four are the first in a larger set of implications of a NSB. See the final chapter on "Implications of...."

[18] An example of a comprehensive seed bank is found in Norway – the Svalbard Global Seed Bank. Another kind, gene banks "are underfunded worldwide." See Williams, Maxwell (2016), "Hope in the Permafrost," **GOOD** (Fall), plus other references with regard to species death.

❖ The International Criminal Court be strengthened in its ability to punish crimes against humanity.

There is little sense in even imagining a new system of belief to sustain human life if the subjects are all dead. Rather, let us adopt a view that assumes the continuation of human life:

> "When we are as Nineveh, our white columns thrown and scattered...Our words, our music, who will build a dome to hive them? In whose belly shall we come to life? A new life, Beyond submergence and destruction..."[19]

Another proviso (the 5th) is also needed: That the belief that there is life-after-death is adverse to the continuation, nurture and development of human life [the human species: homo sapiens] Unfortunately, life-after-death is a fond hope for so many that it is unrealistic at this point to proscribe the belief. Nevertheless, there is a growing body of evidence contrary to the "fond hope." The example cited at the outset is but one of a steadily increasing number. It is time to face the fact that suicide bombers and other mass-murderers are not only motivated by an assumption that their cause is righteous but also by the belief that their act will deliver them to a paradise of life-after-death. See Chapter 4, on LIFE, for more.

At the same time, we need to recognize that science is an incomplete source of truth.[20] Man is not only a scientific but a spiritual creature. This fact, however, by no means necessitates a conflict between science and religion. Both are animated by a sense of awe and wonder. The latter, in turn, "makes

---

[19] Lowell, Amy (1925),"The Congressional Library," in **WHAT'S O'CLOCK**. Boston: Houghton Mifflin Co.

[20] A point that is recognized and discussed by Nobel Laureate in Physics Richard A. Muller in his 2016 book **NOW: The Physics of Time**. New York: W.W. Norton & Company.

us more spiritual."[21] This is especially so as we contemplate the growing knowledge of our universe gained through the science of cosmology. Every discovery makes us realize how much we don't know and may never learn. According to physicist Freeman Dyson, the universe is a source of awe and wonder "infinite in all directions."[22] Increasingly, research points to the universe as also being a source of life. Then why should not the universe be a candidate for real, natural rather than super-natural godship?

The fundamental premise of any "God" is undeniable: That we need an elevated point of reference to which we can repair. Man's god is an unending source of awe, wonder and life. So, we could imagine the Universe as God. This would resonate with man's spirituality. Except that the Universe is not, nor ever can be, a personal god – one we pray to and turn to for help, understanding and forgiveness. Nor is the behavior of the Universe completely benevolent or a surfeit of goodness. On balance, it seems largely the opposite – a maelstrom of violence and birth – of stars aborning, colliding and exploding and of galaxies centered on black holes. How could this be considered a model for a God?[23]

How not? We have invented a theoretical God synonymous with the best in human nature. Why not an actual God also exhibiting the full range of the features of our surrounding natural and physical environment, from worst to best? Does this range not reflect the spectrum of features that also characterize human society? The drawbacks are obvious. We cannot talk to the Universe-as-God or, even if we tried, could we expect there is anyone

---

[21] As noted by Hutson, Matthew (2017), "Awesomeness of Everything," **THE ATLANTIC** (Jan./Feb., p.15).

[22] Dyson, Freeman (1988), **INFINITE IN ALL DIRECTIONS**. New York: Harper.

[23] Stuart Kauffmann has grappled with this issue at length in his 2008 book **REINVENTING the SACRED**, suggesting that we could recognize and worship a "creative universe" as God.

listening or get a response in return? Tough. That's why we have media and politics. Can one expect a real, really all-powerful God to pay attention to a puny single one of a vulnerable species? Though each of us is singularly unique, we have to fight to get the attention of our own species, let alone some distant god.

The major and perhaps only significant problem with Universe-as-God is that that it appears to be entropic. Entropy is an index of systemic disorder. The expansion of our universe is accelerating. Arguably, this could lead to a universal death of cold, empty worlds alien to life. The only anti-entropic forces, even now, are localized. There's a paradox here: A universe full of heat and light that has been an undeniable origin of life, heading inexorably towards universal death. Such a universe could not be viewed as the God of Mankind. Or might it be?

One basis could be the exquisitely fine-tuned set of parameters requisite for life on earth that have emerged from the evolution of our universe.[24] And yet, "multiverse" cosmological theories have been put forth that deny this basis, as we shall also see. While alternative theories of "God" are debated back and forth, let us be humble. There's still so much that we don't know, such as the nature of the "dark" matter and energy that comprise as much as 84% of the universe.[25] While awaiting further insights from cosmological research, we still need to be toasting L'Chaim ["to life"] and relentlessly building frameworks and institutions to nurture life. A New System of Belief [hereafter, designated NSB] would help.

---

[24] A very impressive set, indeed, defined and discussed in Chapter 4. This statement is the latest version of the "Anthropic Principle" – that the universe has been specially tailored to enable the emergence of human life.

[25] Some discoveries on this may begin to arise from the Axion Dark Matter Experiment described in Rosenberg, Leslie (2018), "Searching for the Dark," **SCIENTIFIC AMERICAN** (January), pp. 50-57.

Chapter 2

Belief, Life and Living-in-Action:

Introduction of a New System of Belief

So, what system of belief is needed to go along with a realistic concept of a god new and true? A system that is, first, pro-life and anti-entropic. What we know about our universe is that it has fostered localized subsystems that foster life. So far, cosmology has not found life elsewhere in the universe. Even though it is highly likely [inevitable, I believe] that life be found in other solar systems, the number of which is huge, we have all the more reason to see how very special is the blue orb of our planetary world shown floating in what appears to be empty space. How we need to cherish and nurture life on this earth! How we need to construct sub-subsystems to facilitate and foster all anti-entropic creations and nurture pro-creations!

What does "anti-entropic" mean? First, let us be clear about what entropy means. The concept is probabilistic, connoting random and unstructured distributions such as gaseous molecules in a box. Anti-entropic is the antithesis. It connotes structure: Nonrandom patterns of both existence and change. Many scientists, observing increases in the entropy of the universe overall, have come to call entropy "the arrow of time," though Muller challenges this view in his 2016 book.

Meaningful time markers appear to derive from entropy decreases, but these are local, not overall. Note one of Muller's examples: A teacup knocked off a table. The cup shatters. That provides a slight increase in entropy, the index of disorder. If the pieces are put back together, that is a slight decrease in entropy – an increase in order. Humpty Dumpty might have provided a more colorful example except that "All the King's horses and all the King's men couldn't put Humpty together again."

Next to life, the most fundamental anti-entropic feature of any human system is that of human values. These are proscriptive, starting with the 10 Commandments. Others are fundamental to the ordering of peoples' interrelationships for their common good. These include mutual caring, sharing, communication, cooperation, collaboration, curiosity, creativity, empathy and truthfulness to guide the being and becoming of human life. Recall 1st Corinthians: "There is faith, hope and love but the most important of these is love:" love of life, love of self and love of and for others: Human life lived by the Golden Rule.

Another major feature of the anti-entropic is locality, or de-centralization relative to a larger universe. This means enabling a large scope for variability across localities in beliefs, cultures, institutions, races, ethnicities, activities and innovation in human life. Indeed, worldwide, we see contexts of peoples' lives characterized by increasing divisions, separations, segregations and inequalities. Excessive variability within localities without internal communication, cooperation and coordination among the parts may impair development {increase entropy}. Shared values and goals spell community – people better together – anti-entropic.

Like other shared values, spirituality serves as an anti-entropic integrator. In the human context, we see brains featuring dense local connectivity and a few very long connections between neurons and regions: small-world or scale-free networks which have many local interactions and a smaller number of inter-area connections. Localized systems with emergent properties or structures may appear to defy entropic principles (and the 2nd Law of Thermodynamics) because they form and increase order despite the lack of a command and control system. Why? --- Because open systems can extract information, energy and order from their environment(s). Localization runs contrary to quantum action-at- a-distance – an inference from quantum mechanics that has been mistakenly used to justify an external God-at-a-distance.

A 4th anti-entropic feature is leadership. Though everyone is a potential leader, the qualities of leadership are unevenly distributed and so they constantly need to be nurtured. These qualities include self-confidence, initiative, charisma, and, above all, life-long learning – not only from one's own studies but, at least as important, from others and from our life experience, knowledge of others, delegation, and innovation.

A 5th is closely related to leadership: entrepreneurship, meaning leadership in new enterprise formation, processes of innovation and/or in leading change within existing organizations or institutions. Curiosity, creativity and innovation help to start, but other characteristics will influence whether an enterprise grows or fails. These include tenacity, team building, patience, persistence, foresight and mindfulness.

A 6th is learning and teaching. These are two sides of the same coin: A thirst for knowledge and search for truth. The best teachers learn as they teach, and the most important feature of their teaching is showing their students how to learn and how to develop their own critical and creative faculties.

Notice the overlaps in the preceding among values, goals and means of their expression and implementation – mixtures of thought and action. For a system of belief is more than just a statement of ideals. It is also a guide to living-in-action and action-for-living. This points to a host of people whose lives embody and represent the values-in-action. These include teachers, mentors, pastors and best friends. What is lacking, however, are venues for young people to join the learning by doing. There are few or no apprenticeships to learn the art of the matter and experience how to manage inevitable conflicts between values and work. When we confront the question of how a new system of belief might be introduced, we seem to confront an impossibility: As yet, there are no venues [churches or pastors] for its teaching, let alone for the joining of belief and action.

But here we start to run ahead of ourselves. In light of the foregoing, we need to begin to construct a new system of belief. Its focus is the maintenance, development and nurture of human life ever after. In so doing, we need to look, not to any external god-in-heaven but to the life force within ourselves, because each of us is a unique being, and to our brethren, because we can and must be "better together" if the human race is to survive altogether.

We should start by realizing that those things that our lives have in common outweigh those that pull us apart. What are they? Focus on the days of our lives. For most people, a day in the life of can be viewed as a life in the day of. Every workday most of us get up, get dressed, make and have breakfast, go to work, come home, make and eat dinner, spend some time with spouse and kids, get ready for bed and go to sleep. Weekend days, for those that do not have to work 6-7 days a week, vary only in nature and timing of activities – those devoted primarily to family and/or friends and to recreation.

Any cataloging of hopes, desires and expectations also reveals essential commonalities throughout the world. What do most adults want?-- A...

- ❖ **Job** at a rate of pay that enables them to sustain themselves and others in their care.
- ❖ **Home** that they own and/or can occupy with some semblance of security.-
- ❖ **Spouse** or life-partner with whom a life can be built and shared.
- ❖ **Community** with some good neighbors and security for themselves and their family.
- ❖ **Education** that is good for their children, if any.
- ❖ **Good health** for themselves and those who rely on them; and last but by no means least...
- ❖ **Government(s)** that are trustworthy and democratic and that provide some assurance that the foregoing will not be denied.

Above all, the prime, everlasting common denominator is the LIFE we share, with all its quirks, miracles, mysteries, puzzles, problems and conundrums.

7+1 common desires. Is this too much for any man or woman to ask? I think not. These are the basics. Separately and overall, they represent crucially important aspects of human life – of human well-being. The keyword and focal point of any new system of belief [hereafter, abbreviated NSB], therefore, is LIFE – generally, all life. For human life is inextricably bound up with all others in a "great chain of being," as the great scientist/humanist Jacob Bronowski reveals in his book **THE ASCENT OF MAN**.

Prayer has an essential role in any NSB. To whom? For what? In light of the woof and web of interrelationships that link us, prayer would be more for one and all, not just one – as in "One for all and all for one." As for the singular, each of us can and should be praying frequently to understand, to be understood, and for the 3C's of togetherness – communication, cooperation and collaboration. Prayer has several relatives, including mindfulness meditation, contemplation and reflection. Prayer is not simply a singular exercise in silence. Some of the best sermons are prayers. Whether spoken or silent, to or for others, prayer should help us plumb the depths of life and life forces in ourselves and others.

Prayer can also help us confront and overcome our limits. "Limits are what we are inside of."[26] So, prayer helps us go outside of ourselves. Prayer is inherently spiritual. We should renounce prayers of commoners pleading to a King for aid, as in "Our most gracious, heavenly father..." Recognize that such honorific appeals to an external, "heavenly" God are fruitless but for the little more than good-feeling that leads so many appellants to believe in what is truly unbelievable. They yearn for a god that listens to each of them. But what would such a god hear from above – nothing but noise – the sound of billions talking at once – the Tower of Babel realized with a vengeance.

In recently published research on Carmelite nuns, a working group at the University of Montreal identified specific areas of brain activation associated with contemplative prayer. These patterns, however, were quite distinct from those associated with hallucinations, autosuggestion, or states of intense emotional arousal. Instead, they resemble the manner in which the brain processes real life experiences. Thus, the ability of prayer to help us "go outside of our-selves" is rooted in real life, not hallucinations of/or the

---

[26] Olson, Charles, **MAXIMUS POEMS**

supernatural, again pointing to the sacredness of everyday life. See the next chapter for more.

Places of worship (e.g., churches or temples) are a common feature of any religion and could continue to be so if representing a NSB. The main reason has little to do with religion per se. It is that a church is not only a place of worship; it is also a social institution enabling people to get together at least once a week. If such a place was to carry a NSB label, many church attendees might presume to call it "secular." Not so. For as recognized in the Bible, "when two or three are gathered together...", the Holy Spirit will infuse the gathering and suffuse the space. Even atheists feel the need of such a place, as I learned when, during my national tour, I visited a Humanist Society church.

Thus, without reference to or need for an external god, we have found sound bases for a NSB in this chapter. They include the foundations of our physical existence, shared values, learning, soulfulness, prayer and places of worship.

Chapter 3

The Human Brain:

Where and How Does Spirituality Emerge?

Let us try to decipher the structure of the brain in order to try to identify those parts and processes of the brain that may figure in the spirituality of the human species. First, however, a note of caution is in order. The amount of research on the human brain and related neuroscience has grown tremendously over the past generation, yet there is still so much that we don't know to help answer our title question. This chapter and the one to follow will address many relevant questions, those both answered and unanswered.

The Cerebral Cortex: Introduction[27]

The cerebral cortex is the most important part of our brain. It is what makes us human. The cerebral cortex is a densely packed sheet of "gray matter" -- neurons covering both lobes of the brain. You were born with more neurons

---

[27] This and subsequent sections on the structure of the brain in this chapter rely heavily on Carter, Rita (1999), **MAPPING the MIND.** Berkeley, CA: University of California Press. In addition to subsequent footnotes, parenthetical notes also reference pages of Carter's book that this chapter has relied upon.

in the cortex than you have now, but then they were young and inexperienced. As we get older the neurons learn to work together forming what we call neural networks. Recall, for example, when you were a kid and your parents taught you how to wipe your own butt. The first time you wiped it was awkward, you probably wiped poo everywhere and had to concentrate really hard to clean yourself. The neurons in your cerebral cortex were firing in the pattern of butt wiping for the first time. Every time you wiped your butt afterward gave the neurons practice. Pretty soon that bunch of neurons that fire whenever you have to wipe your butt form a butt wiping team – a neural network. Today you probably do not even have to think when you wipe yourself because your neural network has become such a cohesive team that it has joined the subconscious.

The cerebral cortex is full of wrinkles. These are called fissures. If you ironed out all of the wrinkles, the cortex would be as big as a large pizza. The cortex is divided into two hemispheres- left and right. For the most part the two exhibit what we call "contralateral control." The left hemisphere controls the right side of out body and the right hemisphere controls the left. In general, right-handed people (those with a stronger LEFT hemisphere) seem to be better at logical and sequential tasks. Left-handed people (those with a stronger RIGHT hemisphere) are better at spatial and creative tasks.

Between the two hemispheres is a band of nerve fibers called the corpus callosum. The job of these fibers is to help the two hemispheres communicate with each other. In some cases of people with severe epilepsy, the corpus callosum is surgically removed and seizure activity decreases. However, these people lose the ability of their hemispheres to communicate to each other. So, they are called split brain patients. It is like having two separate brains inside their head. One of them has no idea what the other is doing. For example, for most people the ability to see comes from the left hemisphere, which controls the right field of vision. Thus, if split brain patients see an elephant in their left visual field, they will not be able to say what they see, but they can write it with their right hand (not their left hand). Through processes facilitated by the brain's plasticity, most split-brain patients will compensate and find ways for the hemispheres to communicate.

Lobes of the Cerebral Cortex

Our cerebral cortex is divided up into four lobes, areas as shown in Fig. 1, below. More specifically, we really have eight lobes because each lobe has a right and left side. The cerebral cortex is contra-lateralized! Neurons on the left side of the brain influence or control what happens on our right sides, and vice-versa.

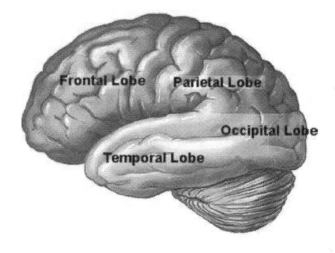

Fig. 1

Frontal Lobes of the Cerebral Cortex

The frontal lobes are located at the top part of our brain behind our eyes. The frontal lobes are where most of our personality hangs out. They are involved in the ability to control our emotions; also, in the generation of abstract thought. The latter may include spirituality. Here we find the primary areas of memories and a host of other ingredients that figure, directly or indirectly, in spirituality, including consciousness, language, dreaming, and thought. Carter wrote:

"The frontal cortex is the part that mushroomed most dramatically during our transition from hominid to human and it makes up about 28% of the human brain, a far larger proportion than in any other...animal...The frontal lobes are where ideas are created, plans constructed; thoughts joined with their associations...it is here, too, that mystics have traditionally placed...the gateway to highest points of awareness."[28]

The neuroscientific identification of multiple memory systems related to different brain areas has challenged the idea of memory as a literal reproduction of the past. Neuroscientific analyses support a view of memory as a generative, constructive and dynamic process relying on the connectivity of neurons in various portions of the brain.

Frontal Insula (FI)

❖ This is one of two areas of the frontal cortex that is home of a relatively rare but highly important type of neuron – the Von Economo, named after its discoverer, a Viennese anatomist, Christian von Economo, in 1926. These neurons evolved from a common ancestor of the great apes about 13 million years ago. They are "particularly active" when we experience emotion or are "self-monitoring." The FI has a:

"specific role in generating social emotions such as empathy, trust, guilt embarrassment, love – even a sense of humor...where the brain monitors and reacts to "gut feelings" within a social network."[29]

---

[28] Carter, op.cit., p.180 (Intro. to Chapter 8: Higher Ground"). Subsequent page references are also to Carter.

[29] For more, see Chen, Ingfei (2009), "The Social Brain," SMITHSONIAN (June), pp. 39-43, from which Fig. 2 is also drawn.

Von Economo neurons are also found in the anterior cingulate cortex, discussed further on and shown in Fig. 2.

Fig. 2

Prefrontal cortex

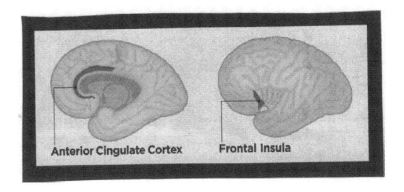

According to Carter, this is:

> "The area of the frontal lobe most closely associated with the generation of consciousness...also responsible for our conscious perception of emotion and our ability to...focus. Most important...it endows the world with meaning and... a sense of purpose... (It is) the only part of the brain that is free from the constant labor of sensory processing. It is an area concerned with "controlling impulses and planning actions...When something unusual happens... or "when we actually think rather than day-dream, the pre-frontal cortex springs into

life and we are jettisoned into full consciousness as though from a tunnel into blazing sunshine."[30]

In other words, the prefrontal cortex takes our brain from the physical to conscious mentality.

Dorsolateral prefrontal cortex

The area for "The nuts and bolts of thinking – holding ideas in mind and manipulating them..."

Orbito-frontal Cortex

This "has rich neural connections to the unconscious brain where drives and emotions are generated...the area of the brain that bestows a quality that we call free will. It serves to "inhibit inappropriate actions, freeing us from the tyranny of our urges..." (p.182).

Motor Cortex

Located in the back of the frontal lobe this thin strip of tissue sends signals (via motor neurons) to tell our body to move. Parts we move more (such as fingers) have more space devoted to them in the motor cortex than the parts of us we do not move as much (toes). The top of the motor cortex controls the bottom of our body and the bottom of the cortex controls the top of our body.

If that is too confusing, just know that every time you voluntarily move your body, you are using the motor cortex in the frontal lobe

Broca's Area

This is located in the left frontal lobe (at least for most people). In some left handed people, Broca's area is on the right side; more specifically, in the front

---

[30] Carter, op.cit., p.181 & 182. Quotes to follow have been drawn from the same source.

of the right side of the neocortex – see Fig. 3, below. This area controls the muscles in our mouth involved in speech. Speaking is a complicated task. The brain has a whole area devoted to just talking. With severe damage to Broca's area, one is unable to talk. The medical term for such damage is called "Big Broca's Aphasia" to distinguish it from lesser damage to the area. Patients suffering the latter "usually recover after a few months."[31]

Fig. 3:

Broca's and Wernicke's Areas

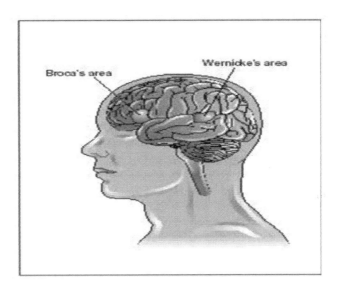

---

[31] From an article offering much more on this subject in **THE SCIENCES** (Nov./Dec., 1997). p.23, entitled "Peak Capacity: Speech and thought inextricably linked."

Parietal Lobes

The parietal lobes are located in back of the frontal lobes on the top of our head. Most of the parietal lobes are made up of what are called "association areas" – those associated with specific bodily functions [See Fig. 4, below]. There are several structures to note, as follows.

Sensory Cortex [2]

Located in the front of the parietal lobe (directly behind the sensory cortex in the frontal lobe), this structure is responsible for us feeling touch sensations from our body. Every time you feel a type of touch sensations (pleasurable or painful), the information is sent by sensory neurons to the thalamus and up to the sensory cortex so we can feel it. It is set up the same way as is the motor cortex. The bottom of the cortex is responsible for the top of our body and the top of the cortex responsible for the bottom. See Fig. 4, below.

Focusing attention on the important physical appendages and other flesh and blood features of the human body should in no way detract from our focus on spirituality. The error of Descartes' view has already been recognized. The spiritual world cannot and should not be viewed as somehow separable from the physical world. Note that major parts of the human body are connected to corresponding locations in the human brain. Also note the great tactile sensitivity of the body parts identified in Fig. 4. These sensitivities have been celebrated in poetry and song.

Erotic sensations are best known, especially to lovers. Yet the human body, both male and female, is responsive to a broad tactile spectrum of touching and physical closeness. These generate a range of feelings approaching spirituality, from excitement to rapture to other-worldly transport.

Fig. 4 Occipital Lobes

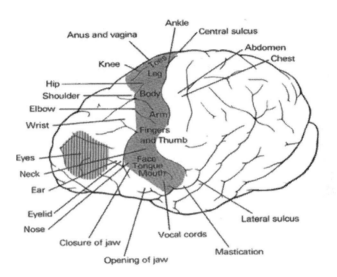

Located in the very back of our brain, the occipital lobes are responsible for our eyesight. They contain the primary visual cortex which helps us interpret the information sent to us by our eyes (more specifically the retinas located in the back of our eyes). Remember that our cerebral cortex is contra-lateralized; well, so are our eyes. The right half of each of our retinas sends information to the left side of the occipital lobe and the left side of each retina sends it to our right occipital lobe.

Temporal Lobes

Located just above our ears on both sides of our head, the temporal lobes contain the auditory cortex and control our hearing. What makes the temporal lobes so unique is that they are NOT lateralized. The left temporal lobe is involved in hearing from both the right and left ear.

One critical structure in the temporal lobe is Wernicke's Area. It is located in the left temporal lobe and is responsible for interpretation of both written and spoken speech. We use Wernicke's area both to read and to listen. Damage to Wernicke's Area (Wernicke's Aphasia) leaves one unable to understand what they are reading or hearing. See Fig. 3, p. 34.

Anterior cingulate cortex (ACC)

Serves to focus attention on "interior events" or internally generated stimuli; e.g., those which hypnosis or meditation help us to focus upon. Paradoxically, as a 2nd home of Von Economo (VE) neurons along with the Frontal Insula, it is also one of the sources of exterior, social behavior. John Allman's research on VE neurons at CalTech has been based on three propositions:

1) That "self-awareness and social awareness are part of the same (brain) functioning";
2) The VE cell system "allows a rapid, intuitive read of emotionally charged, volatile situations...(that) would enable one to quickly adjust to changing social contexts," and that...
3) VE neurons expedite communication from the ACC and FI to the rest of the brain.

Research completed thus far lends support to all three. Recall ACC's location in the brain --"a region on the inside front edge...of the deep chasm that runs from the front of the brain to the back." (p.195). Clearly, given its roles in enabling awareness and meditation, the ACC is another part of the brain facilitating the emergence of spirituality. See Fig. 2 and the article by Chen cited earlier for more.

Parietal, anterior and premotor cortexes: Areas of the brain associated with seeking stimuli. The Premotor Cortex executes movement.

Ventromedial or subgenual cortex [the lower part of the internal surface of the prefrontal cortex] "This is where emotions are experienced and meaning bestowed on our perceptions." (p.182) It is also the brain's emotional control center and:

"the part that best incorporates the whole of our being, making sense of our perceptions and binding them into a meaningful whole." (p.197) [and thus contributing to spirituality]

The latter is due largely to the fact that the connections between this region and the limbic system beneath it are very dense, closely connecting the conscious mind with the unconscious.

- ❖ **Hippocampus:** Stores long-term memories.
- ❖ **Premotor cortex:** This: "...divides the sensing and doing cortex from the area that is given over to man's most impressive achievements – juggling... concepts, planning and predicting the future, selecting thoughts and perceptions for attention...and... endowing these perceptions with meaning."
- ❖ **Brainstem, midbrain, thalamus and wholeness:** These are essential to consciousness and soul. In addition to points provided on this earlier, note that these: "...are part of a system that directs and controls conscious attention by shunting neurotransmitters to various parts of the cortex." (p.183)

Breaking down holistic phenomena such as consciousness and spirituality into parts is problematic at best. One of the mysteries to be plumbed is exemplified by the way the brain breaks up sensations into memory components which get moved back and forth from the hippocampus to and from the frontal cortex. [p.192] This begs a key question: How are the parts integrated into an identifiable whole? Consider:

"A state of mind is an all-encompassing perception of the world that binds sensory perception, thoughts, feelings and memories into a seamless whole." (p.162) Those in a manic state [experiencing "mania"]... "see life as a gloriously ordered, integrated whole. Everything seems to be   connected to everything else and the smallest events seem bathed in meaning. A person...is euphoric, full of energy and flowing with love. They are also in a state of full creativity – the connections they see between things...are often used by them to make new concepts." (p.197)

Clearly, this more holistic view is quite contrary to the approach of neuroscientists that is subject to critical review in the section on "Humanism" in Chapter 23. We shall see that the humanist view is more holistic, though not without some shortcomings.

One important step in the process by which states of mind are generated is revealed by the creation of long-term memory. A memorable event is reflected in the brain by the simultaneous firing of bunches of neurons that one neuroscientist calls "mosaics."[32] Repeated attempts at recollection etch the firings into long-term memory. The simultaneity of the firings is due to the fact that firing by one excites the firing of its neighbors. Thus, even recollection of one element of the overall memory brings others to mind.

This schema can be extended to help explain higher (non-sensory) levels of memory. A repetitive pattern will be assigned a signal in memory akin to a mnemonic. A mosaic of these, for instance, might be a design, a mathematical model of some phenomenon, an opera, or – voila! – even a NSB!

Yet many mysteries of the mind remain for ongoing research to unravel, questions of "meaning" among them. What is most important to note at this point is that research on the brain has finally rejected Cartesian dualism [also called "Descartes Error" by some] – the view that mind and spirit exist in some heavenly sphere separate from the material universe. We have also learned that higher cognitive functions are not necessarily the result of mass-action of neurons not subject to localization. Increasingly precise brain scanning and mapping techniques "are showing just how precisely it is possible to pin down even the most sophisticated and complex machinations of the human brain."[33]

---

[32] Calvin, William H. (1998), "Competing for Consciousness," in Carter, op.cit., p.171.

[33] Carter, op. cit., p.25.

Research on the brain-as-a complex adaptive system (CAS) has identified those parts integral to the genesis and nurture of human spirituality. There are many facets of spirituality, including holiness, sacred(ness), blessedness, awesome, wondrous, godlike, heaven(ly), marvelous and meaningful. These include matters miraculous and sacramental. There are related practices such as focus, attentiveness, reflection, imagining, meditation and prayer. Do they all emanate from one part of the brain?

The primary section is the prefrontal cortex part of the cerebral cortex. The cortical areas focus attention, control impulses and integrate stimuli. These inhibit the limbic system, home of emotional drivers, enabling thought to be substituted for action. The prefrontal lobes are slow to mature. Note the impulsiveness of children. These lobes are not fully working until children grow into their twenties.

Pandya believes that the site of the soul is the brainstem, though soulfulness exists with the aid of memory, pattern recognition, imagination and other powers situated in other parts of the brain located primarily in the right lobe. Woody Allen quipped: "You cannot prove the non-existence of the soul; you just have to take it on faith." Much more seriously, Pandya observed:

> "Neurosurgeons operating within the brainstem are known to tell their postgraduate students: 'I need not emphasize the need for the greatest accuracy and delicacy when operating here – we are now in the abode of the soul...**The soul has often been termed the God within each of us.**'"[34] [my emphasis]

Christopher Pallis (1983), discussing the definition of whole-brain death, implicitly provided a modern concept of the soul consistent with the above:

---

[34] Pandya, Sunil K. (2015?), **"Understanding Brain, Mind and Soul: Contributions from Neurology and Neurosurgery."** Sunil Pandya is a neurosurgeon and a thinker and writer on medical ethics.

"The loss of the capacity for consciousness and of the capacity to breathe (after brain death) relate to functional disturbances at the opposite ends of the brain stem...the former (loss of consciousness) is...a meaningful alternative to...departure of the soul."

Pause here. Pallis' "abode of the soul" seems to contradict the research finding reported earlier, that "the primary section is the prefrontal cortex..." Not really. A strategic pause will enable us to pull things together. The brainstem is conduit for many of the critical biochemical flows that feed the prefrontal cortex and other parts of the brain. This does not make it the situs of the soul. Except for those parts specialized to the motor functions, practically the whole human brain contains the soul. For the soul has many parts. The brain has many levels. The soul is an integrand.

Look back at the Ventromedial or subgenual cortex for example. It is just one part of the brain that controls some of what we call soulfulness. Other parts among those that were described earlier enable brain functions that make the brain:

- ❖ A far more creative and effective search engine than Google could ever hope to be;
- ❖ An integration machine far more brilliant than any mathematical calculus; and
- ❖ A builder of structures and levels far greater than the greatest architects and builders have even imagined.

Each level contains integrands from the levels below. Thus, the brain can search for elements of memory, combine them with perceptions, link them to ideas, bring in elements of imagination and VOILA!, emerge with a spiritual realization that can, at one and the same time, relate to a thing (e.g., an old, favored table or a hanging religious icon) and a concept (e.g., selfhood or everlasting life). All the items cited here may reside in various portions of the brain. No single area of the brain is responsible for conscious, soulful experience.

Return now to Jaynes' perspectives on consciousness, the source of soulfulness. He focuses on the roles of Broca's and Wernicke's areas of the brain. These were identified earlier in Fig. 2, but only Broca's area was then discussed. That of Wernicke's area was postponed until now because of its major role in Jaynes' hypothesis of how auditory signals of speech and hearing -- gathered in that area -- transformed hallucinations in the right temporal lobe into a "god center."

Note first that: Wernicke's area, chiefly the posterior part of the left temporal lobe, along with parts of the parietal area...is the most indispensable to normal speech. It is quite thick with large, widely spaced cells, indicating considerable internal and external connections.

Jaynes writes: "While there is some disagreement as to its (the area's) precise boundaries, there is none regarding its importance to meaningful communication...The language of men was involved with only one hemisphere to leave the other free for the language of gods."[35]

Fig. 5

Anterior Commissure

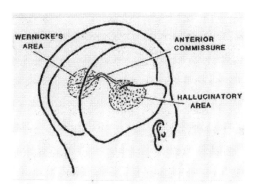

---

[35] Jaynes, op. cit., p. 102; Fig. 4 is drawn from p. 104.

Key to this evolutionary process was a pathway of transmission from Wernicke's area to the "neurological structure necessary for language (that) exists in the right hemisphere as well as the left." The latter overlaps the "hallucinatory area" as shown in Fig. 5, above.

The pathway's name is "Anterior Commissure." Why is this distinguished from the huge inter-lobe communication channels we noted earlier – the "corpus callosum" with over 2 million fibers? – Because the temporal lobes in human beings have their own private pathways. Jaynes continues:

> "This...band of fibers collects from...the middle...of the temporal lobe included in Wernicke's area, and then squeezes into a tract only slightly more than one-eighth of an inch in diameter as it plunges over the amygdala across the top of the hypothalamus toward the other temporal lobe...the tiny bridge across which came the directions that built our civilizations and founded the world's religions..."[36] See Fig. 5.

Language evolved to provide the "code" to enable these transmissions between the two semi-independent sides of the bilateral brain. This, in turn, facilitated the evolution of consciousness that "gradually" (over 3 millennia) arose to enable our species to survive multiple crises as indicated earlier.

In addition to his extensive research using other sources, Jaynes detected the crucial transition from the bicameral brain to conscious mind through careful reading and interpretation of the **ILIAD**, a classic composed in parts over centuries.

Conclusion

We conclude here where we began: We human beings do have a brain containing a conscious mind, and the mind is home to a soul. Mind and soul

---

[36] Jaynes, op. cit., p. 104.

arise out of a physical brain, not from a mythical heaven on high. For more, see **SCIENTIFIC AMERICAN's** 2017 edition of "Mysteries of the Mind." It is subtitled "New insights about the brain…"

Chapter 4

Atheism As Negativity

Introduction: WHAT IS ATHEISM?

Atheism is not an affirmative belief that there is no god nor does it answer any other question about what a person believes. It is simply a rejection of the assertion that there are gods. Atheism is too often defined incorrectly as a belief system. To be clear: Atheism is not a disbelief in gods or a denial of gods; it is a lack of belief in gods.[37] Now that we have defined atheism by what it is not, what is it? Truth is a two-sided coin.

An "Atheist" is "a person who does not believe in the existence of a god or any gods," according to the Merriam-Webster dictionary. Un-surprisingly, more than nine-in-ten self-identified atheists say religion is not too or not at all important in their lives, and nearly all (97%) say they seldom or never pray. A recent poll found that church membership in the US had declined by 20 percentage points.[38] And yet many do not see a contradiction between atheism and pondering their place in the world.

---

[37] Source: **AmericanAtheist.org.**

[38] Crary, David (2019), "Poll: Church membership in US plummets over past 20 years," **Associated Press** (4/20).

In fact, three-in-ten (31%) say they feel a deep sense of spiritual peace and well-being at least weekly. A similar share (35%) often thinks about the meaning and purpose of life. And roughly half of all atheists (54%) frequently feel a deep sense of wonder about the universe, up from 37% in 2007. In fact, atheists are more likely than U.S. Christians to say they often feel a sense of wonder about the universe (54% vs. 45%).[39] These data are quite consistent with our framing of a NSB.

Some adults who describe themselves as atheists also say they believe in God or a universal spirit. At the same time, some people who identify with a religion (e.g., say they are Protestant, Catholic or Jewish) also say they do not believe in God [people like me]. Also. there are many people who fit the dictionary definition of "atheist" but do not call themselves atheists. About three times as many Americans say they do not believe in God or a universal spirit (9%) as say they are atheists (3%).

TRENDS

Along with the rise of religiously unaffiliated Americans (many of whom believe in God), there has been a corresponding increase in the number of atheists. The share of Americans who identify as atheists has roughly doubled in the past several years. Pew Research Center's massive 2014 Religious Landscape Study found that 3.1% of American adults say they are atheists when asked about their religious identity, up from 1.6% in a similarly large survey in 2007. An additional 4.0% of Americans call themselves agnostics, up from 2.4% in 2007.

Religiously un-affiliated people have been growing as a share of all Americans for some time. The Pew Research Center study cited above makes clear just how quickly this is happening. The study also shows that the trend is occurring within a variety of demographic groups – across genders, generations and racial and ethnic groups, to name a few.

---

[39] Pew Research Center's 2014 **Religious Landscape Study**

Religious "nones" – a shorthand we use to refer to people who self-identify as atheists or agnostics, as well as those who say their religion is "nothing in particular" – now make up roughly 23% of the U.S. adult population. This is a stark increase from 2007, the last time a similar Pew Research study was conducted, when 16% of Americans were "nones." (During this same time period, Christians have fallen from 78% to 71%.)

35% of Millennials (those born 1981-1996) are "nones.," and the unaffiliated are getting even younger. The median age of unaffiliated adults is now 36, down from 38 in 2007 and significantly younger than the overall median age of U.S. adults in 2014 (46). Even older generations have grown somewhat more unaffiliated in recent years. For example, 14% of Baby Boomers were unaffiliated in 2007. 17% now identify as "nones."

Nones" have made more gains through religious switching than any other group analyzed in the study." Only about 9% of U.S. adults say they were raised without a religious affiliation, and among this group, roughly half say that they now identify with a religion (most often Christianity). But nearly one-in-five Americans (18%) have moved in the other direction, saying that they were raised as Christians or members of another faith but that they now have no religious affiliation. That means more than four people have become "nones" for every person who has left the ranks of the unaffiliated.

Not only are the "nones" growing, but how they describe themselves is changing. Self-declared atheists or agnostics still make up a minority of all religious "nones." But both atheists and agnostics are growing as a share of all religiously unaffiliated people, and together they now make up 7% of all U.S. adults (up from 4% in 2007)

Conclusion

We have discovered that a precise definition of atheism almost doesn't matter. For both the numbers and the percentages of those religiously unaffiliated have been growing for decades. That this presents a great opportunity for a New System of Belief should be obvious. Building on this historic opening, this book will reveal the needs and desires for a such a genuine NSB.

Chapter 5

LIFE

Introduction

Forewarning to the interested reader: You are about to embark on the longest chapter in this book. Its longest section disproves one of the foundational beliefs of Christianity and other faiths – that there is life after death.

As a treatise to foster a new spirituality grounded in reality, however, this book rests on a fundamental assumption: The beauty and sanctity of life. The apprehension and realization of the full meaning of life arises in the (so far) topmost rung of the evolutionary ladder: human life topped by the human brain. Your individual life; indeed, your brain, offers a unique contribution to the world. In the words of Don Rapp:

> "Life is a fact, life is an art, and your life is your future...Thanks to the myriads of partnerships between our brain and our body, we are capable of planning and executing a purposeful future."[40]

---

[40] Rapp, Don (2007), **ON BALANCE: Mastery of Physical Balance for Life.** Tallahassee, FL: Fulcrum Press, p.47.

Or, as frequently heard from young celebrities: 'I have only one life to live, so it's up to me to make the most of it.'

Let us now turn back the clock to trace life from its beginnings.

The Early Origins of Life

Here, we rely substantially on Stuart A. Kauffman, who addresses this topic in Chapter 5 of his fine book **REINVENTING the SACRED.** He opens with:

> "Almost all scientists are persuaded that life...arose naturally in the universe...and that it almost certainly arose spontaneously on earth some 3.5 billion years ago...If life is natural, then part of the call for a transcendent creator God loses its force...To the devout who require that a Creator God has brought it (life) forth, science says wait: we are coming to see that it all arose naturally, with no Creator's hand."[41]

"Naturally" refers to the synthesis of small, molecular, organic-chemical "building blocks" of life compounded of basic elements created within stars, then discharged into the universe when stars explode as supernovae. It also embraces the possibility that some of the organic compounds may have arrived on earth by way of comets or asteroids. Kaufmann writes:

> "Carbonaceous meteorites have complex, carbon-based molecules and even lipids that can spontaneously form bi-layered, hollow vesicles called liposomes...These...are astonishingly similar in structure to the cell membranes surrounding contemporary cells."[42]

The origin of life has long seemed to be a mystery of a miracle or a miracle of a mystery. Kauffman has brought mystery or miracle down to earth, out of the realm of myth and into the discipline of science. He does so with consummate

---

[41] Kauffman, op.cit., pp.45 and 89.

[42] Ibid., p.48.

intellectual honesty – by objectively reporting the progress of research on the topic and, as well, questions unanswered and work to be done. He also notes that "The science is exciting."

The story starts with organic compounds at the cellular level and within. It relies on a number of cross-cutting, integrative themes, including:

- Self-organization: The emergence of spontaneous ordered behavior in even randomly constructed networks that enable "parallel processing" on the boundary between order and chaos.
- Irreducibility to physics: Featuring processes and behaviors that cannot be ascribed to computations derived from physics.
- Emergence (to be discussed at length in the next chapter): Features modes of organization of wholes from parts that arise from the dynamics of complex adaptive systems in ways irreducible to their parts or to physics.
- Autocatalytic processes: Those that are interactively self-generating, as in A affects B and B affects A.
- Dynamic criticality: A process that reaches a threshold, sometimes called a "tipping point", beyond which the whole is qualitatively different from any parts.
- Complex metabolisms: Metabolic processes are fundamental to the maintenance of life. Complex metabolisms arose early in life's origins.
- Thermodynamic work cycles: Work cycles that are thermodynamically interactive and that fight entropic disorganization [according to the 2nd law of thermodynamics].
- Multiple platforms: Dynamic systems that spring from and modify basic platforms. For example, alpha-helix proteins or peptides are a basis for auto-catalytic sets.
- Open systems far from equilibrium: Systems that input energy from their environment sufficient to drive them to the edge of chaos.
- Propagating organization of linked processes: Effecting linkages between key sectors of systems, including those of our economy and government(s). We live now in a world of loops which is dominated by too many boxes.

Here's the overall punch line for all those who would otherwise leap ahead to find it: "At a minimum … it is scientifically plausible that life arose from nonlife…"

Kauffman: "The first central question about the origin of life is the onset of molecular reproduction." The answer began with Watson and Crick's discovery of the "template structure of DNA," enabling replication of DNA, RNA or some similar molecules. 40 years of research, however, revealed that the template model failed in the absence of a protein enzyme catalyst. Again, an insight of Kauffman:

> "While the symmetry of the double helix is lovely, I have always believed that the basis of life is deeper and that it rests on some way on catalysis, the speeding up of chemical reactions by enzymes."[43]

Another avenue of exploration came to be called the "RNA world view" – that early life could be generated entirely by RNA molecules and "a simple mechanism to support the synthesis of RNA from organic precursors." This was inspired by a discovery that RNA molecules could be catalysts. Research that followed has tried to discover an RNA polymerase that could catalyze the reproduction of any RNA sequence. Thus far, however, it has been only partially successful.

Kauffman had reservations surrounding this line of inquiry. Why? -- Because the probability of the right RNA polymerase appearing…

> "seems to be less than 1 in 10 to the 15th power – a rare molecule indeed!... Current cells use protein enzymes exclusively, not RNA…Proteins are chemically more diverse than RNA molecules…This… does not rule out an RNA world but, if true, it would…support a role for (only) small proteins in early life."[44]

---

[43] Ibid., p.55.

[44] Kauffman., p.53.

More promising than RNA are small peptides. Kauffman bet that these, especially those bound to metallic ions, organometallic molecules, will be more capable of catalyzing a diverse set of reactions, thereby playing "a fundamental role in the origin of life." Why? – Because they are related to catalytic antibodies, those that can catalyze reactions.

Complex organic reactions are also facilitated by containers that place reactive molecules in dense proximity. These have been found to be provided by the bilayered membrane vesicles, liposomes, cited earlier as "almost identical to cell membranes." Other experiments have demonstrated "molecular reproduction of a simple structure…a cell membrane."

Kaufmann continues the story by taking it to another level:

> "My second intuition is that life is based on some collective autocatalysis, in which the molecules of a set catalyze one another's (trans)formation. This stands in contrast to any theory that a single molecular species…is the basis of life."

Discoveries by Gunter von Kiedrowski validated Kauffman's insight. The capstone of these was set when he:

> "constructed two different, single-stranded hexamers…A & B, such that A catalyzed the formation of B from two…fragments of B, while B catalyzed the formation of A from two… fragments of A."

Kauffman comments: "This step is crucial," calling the A&B system "collectively auto-catalytic" and remarking:

> "…no molecule in the system catalyzes its own formation. Rather, the system as a whole, A, B and their…fragments, are jointly autocatalytic. A kind of catalytic closure has been achieved…each molecule's formation catalyzed by some molecule in the system."

Additional research by chemist Reza Ghadiri demonstrated that folding, alpha-helix proteins can also form collective autocatalytic sets. He also succeeded in generating collectively auto-catalytic groups of peptides. Thus, we find that life can arise on multiple platforms, in ways independent of any underlying physics, leading Kauffman to conclude:

> "…it is catalytic closure of a set of molecules that is the backbone of life…the emergence of such collectively autocatalytic polymer systems is to be expected (& so) **molecular reproduction may be an emergent property of complex chemical-reaction networks…**" [45] [emphasis mine]

One more factor is needed to complete the story – "kinetic control." Kauffman introduces this as "something of very general importance," and for good reason. Kinetic control is essential to constrain the behavior of the parts of a system so that it becomes a whole that behaves as an integrated dynamic system. Kauffman writes: With kinetic control…

> "…collectively autocatalytic systems are…examples of the kinetic organization of process, in which…the causal topology of the total system constrains and guides the behavior of its chemical constituents…a case of 'downward causation'…(but) the downward arrows do not point exclusively to the parts; (they) also point upwards to the organization of the whole. (i.e.) **The whole acts on the parts as much as the parts act on the whole.**" [46] [My emphasis]

Evolution

Over the nearly 160 years since Darwin published his revolutionary volume on **THE ORIGIN of SPECIES**, various writers have written how he had eliminated the Creator God from the story of life. Indeed. And yet other authors, Dinesh D'Souza among them, continue to insist that such a God exists as the initiator of human life. Darwin left them time and space to do so

---

[45] Kauffman., p.57.

[46] Kauffman., p.58.

because his theory begged the question of life's origins. Thus, the prior section has addressed the issue.

The validity of the evolutionary process continues to be in evidence, to the extent that any of us can observe evolution in real time. Peter and Rosemary Grant, for example, found this in the evolution of finches on a Galapagos island.[47] Another scientist observed "evolution taking place at an explosive rate" among cichlid fishes.[48] I have observed plant species evolving in my backyard, season after season.

This section will build on the previous by integrating the origin of human life into the evolutionary process. Darwin's theory is completed by taking its already vast time frame even much further back to life's very origins.[49]

Kauffman is a major help here, too, when he writes, proceeding from his prior observations:

> "An evolved cell is an autocatalytic whole, whose organization of processes and closure of causal tasks (in order) to reproduce came into existence via heritable variation and natural (evolutionary) selection."[50] [Parenthetical insertions mine to add a little clarity.]

---

[47] As noted by Chris Irmsher in "Origin of the Specious," **WALL ST. JOURNAL BOOKS** (Dec. 9-10, 2017). Also see Chapter 1, "Conceptual Outline of Current Evolutionary Theory," in Kauffman, Stuart A. (1993), **THE ORIGINS of ORDER: Self-Organization and Selection in Evolution.**" New York: Oxford U.P.

[48] See "The Mystery of Lake Malawi," SMITHSONIAN (March, 2019).

[49] Additional perspectives are provided by Pennisi, Elizabeth (2017), "'Supergenes' drive evolution: Flipped DNA speeds the emergence of new sets of traits," 357 **SCIENCE** 6356 (15 September).

[50] Kauffman (2008), op. cit., Chapter 5, p. 58.

Kauffman's major contribution to our understanding of evolution, however, is to introduce "self-organization" into the process at all stages, as well as bring Darwin's one and only driver, natural selection, into the pre-Darwinian processes of life's beginnings.

Spontaneous self-organization is apparent in even the earliest molecules and cells whose auto-catalytic behavior drove the origins of life.

Kauffman refers to this as "The Origins of Order."[51] A wonderful example is provided by the one-celled organism called a paramecium. It is so frequently studied in classes on basic biology that it has been dubbed biology's white rat." A marvelous geometry pervades its parts. Its well-ordered structure is a prelude to that of a neuron in the human brain. Neurons are single cells, too. The paramecium did not swim naked in primordial seas. Nor does the neuron in the semi-liquidity of our brains. See an image of a neuron below as Fig. 6.

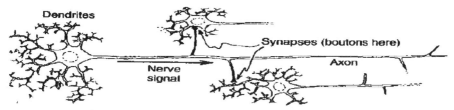

Quantum theory and the brain

Fig. 7.1. A sketch of a neuron, connected to some others via synapses

Fig. 6

Neuron of the Human Brain[52]

---

[51] Title of Kauffman's 1993 book, already cited.

[52] From Penrose (1994), Fig. 7.1, p.352. This is closer to the "Von Economo" neuron than to others.

Both neuron and paramecium are sheathed in a cytoskeleton, the most important parts of which are bundles of tiny, hollow tubes (the "microtubules" mentioned earlier) organized in a structure with a fan-like cross section. Each of the latter is a protein polymer consisting of 13 columns of molecules called "tubulins." Such is the structure of a paramecium's "cilia," the hair-like protrusions from the cell's cytoskeleton used for swimming. See Figures 4 and 5 from Penrose (1994), pp. 358 & 359, copied below as Fig.'s 7 & 8. 13 columns appear to be nearly universal among mammalian creatures' microtubules.[53]

Fig. 7

Cytoskeleton

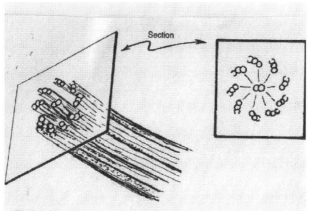

Fig. 7.3. Important parts of the cytoskeleton consist of bundles of tiny tubes (microtubules) organized in a structure with a fan-like cross-section.

---

[53] This and subsequent paragraphs in this section rely heavily on Chapter 7 of Penrose (1994) on "The Quantum Theory of the Brain," pp. 349-392.

Fig. 8

Connectivity of Microtubules

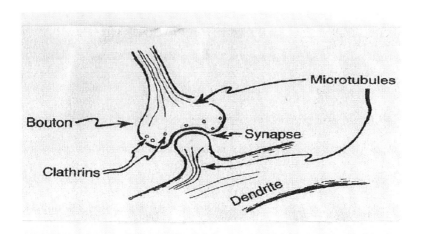

Each tubulin is a dimer" (Latin for 2-fer) because it has two parts – tubulin-alpha and tubulin-beta. Each is composed of about 450 amino acids, long recognized as among the building blocks of life. An electron placed at the alpha/beta border, can shift from one position to another; thus generating the dimer. The alpha and beta parts are called "conformations." They correspond to two different states of a dimer's electric polarization. Penrose (1994) writes:

> "The state of each dimer would be influenced by the polarization states of each of its six neighbors (because of Van der Walls interactions between them), giving rise to certain specific rules governing the conformation of each dimer in terms of the conformations of its neighbors. This would allow all kinds of messages to be propagated and processed along the length of each microtubule…" [Note: The Van der Waals force is a weak attraction between molecules which have electric dipole moments.]

What is the significance of microtubules (MTs) to the brain? MTs in neurons are usually very long, but they can grow or shrink. They transport neurotransmitter molecules and form communicating networks. Each MT communicates with those nearby by means of connecting MAPs [microtubule associated proteins].

MTs are also responsible for maintaining the strengths of synapses and organizing the growth of new nerve cells. They extend from a neuron's nucleus up to presynaptic endings of its axon. In the other direction, they go to other neurons' dendrites and dendritic spines. The spines are subject to growth and decline and so make an important contribution to brain "plasticity." [See Fig. 6, earlier, for illustration of a neuron.]

Clathrins also make such a contribution. These substances are found in the presynaptic endings of neurons. They are built from protein trimers called clathrin triskelions which form 3-pronged polypeptide structures. Those clathrins focused on the release of neurotransmitter chemicals at synapses have the structure of a truncated icosahedron – like that of a soccer ball! More generally, clathrins help to graduate the strength of synaptic connections. See

Fig. 9, below.

Fig. 9:

Figure of a Clathrin

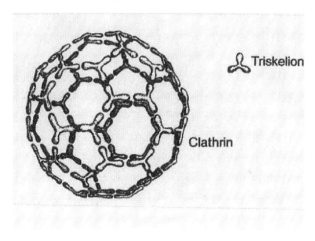

Triskelion

Clathrin

The microtubules organizing center is called the "centriole," consisting of two cylinders of nine triplets of microtubules. These each develop and grow another cylinder that organizes into two segments, separated but forming a "T". The microtubule fibers connect the centriole to separate DNA strands in the cell nucleus. The DNA strands separate, starting the process of cell division known as mitosis. The fact of two different "control" structures – nucleus and centriole – is characteristic of eukaryotic cells found in all animals and nearly all plants in our world.

Eukaryotic cells evolved at an earlier stage from so-called "prokaryotic" versions that possess no cytoskeleton. These still exist as bacteria and blue-green algae. Carl Sagan postulated that early prokaryotes had become infected by "spirochetes" similar to spermatozoa, with tails made of cytoskeletal proteins that evolved into single cells with cytoskeletons. Thus, the beginning of an ongoing evolutionary process leading to – guess who? – US!

Penrose proceeds to reveal the enormous computational power of the human brain [up to 10 to the 24th power, compared to the 10 to the 14th power of advanced computers] but then redounds to the basic thesis of his book, that: "the faculty of human understanding lies beyond any computational scheme." He bases his conclusion on the role of quantum coherence in cytoskeletal activity, writing:

> "If it is microtubules that control the activity of the brain, then there must be something within the(ir) action…that is different from mere computation… quantum coherence…"

Indeed, a wide-raising debate has been going on around the question of how the brain is similar to, or substantially different from, a computer. Neuroscientists and advocates of artificial intelligence (AI) have argued for decades that the brain is a computing machine. Kauffmann and many others, however, have demonstrated that the brain is not because it's operations are "non-algorithmic." Having reviewed the literature from both sides, the judgment of this author is that the latter have won. See further on (Chapters 20 and 22) for more on this crucial issue.

Life After Death

Belief in life after death [hereafter, designated by "LaD"] is indissolubly linked to faith in an external God in heaven. One cannot viably exist without the other. It is hard to imagine LaD without a powerful, external God, just LaD is unimaginable without a heaven. A leading advocate of LaD is Dinesh D'Souza, the author of **LIFE AFTER DEATH: The Evidence**, published by Regnery in 2009. Let us review the pros and cons of D'Souza's views (hereafter designated "D'S"),

In his Chapter 6, "Undeniable Teleology: The Plot of Evolution," D'S primarily relies on an incorrect association of evolution with plot or plan. Though, earlier, he had employed a probabilistic theory (quantum physics) to support his pro-LaD predilections, he then proceeded to ignore the probabilistic nature of Darwinian evolution.

More serious, however, is the fact that his view of evolution begins with life already having been created and only then evolved. Though he cites (and, apparently, has read Kauffman), he ignores Kauffman's model of life's emerging through an evolutionary model that emphasizes "selection" of organisms that exhibit spontaneous self-organization. He also is ignorant of, or has chosen to ignore, other, new, research on the origins of life which reveals, on the basis of 3.5 billion years old empirical evidence, a selective evolutionary process at work throughout the earliest stages of life.[54]

The latter points to a more general problem with D'S' LaD 's "The Evidence" – that so much of it hinges on lack of such, pointing to LaD hinged to an external "God" as the prime source of awe and wonder. He largely glosses over the fact, most recently demonstrated by an article in the August, 2017 **SCIENTIFIC AMERICAN**, that science since the Renaissance has repeatedly pushed back religion as the source of any truth; i.e., displaced religion and pushed back the boundary between religious myth in favor of reality.

---

[54] Reviewed in **SCIENTIFIC AMERICAN** of August 11, 2019, pp. 29-35.

D'S further plays fast and loose with various sources and arguments in order to advance his case for LaD. Like others, for example, he looks to post-modern science for support but overlooks the fundamental difference between micro-micro and macro levels of reality. He always takes care to include counter-arguments but then also overlooks the fact that, in so doing, he is undermining the underlying bases of his own claims.

Though appearing to honor science, D'S tries to discredit it by focusing on a set of scientists that appear to do research driven by a "God avoidance" mentality. For example, he quotes one, Leonard Susskind, as rejecting the false comfort of a creationist myth.

He writes: "Real science requires explanations that do not involve super-natural agents…Here again, the scientists are following the atheists by going into 'god avoidance' mode."[55]

Thus, D'S goes on to claim that modern physics "undermines the premises of materialism" while interpreting Bohr to write: "Reality has shown itself stranger than science fiction." At least the latter is true, even though Bohr does not fit into D'S' world view.

D'S': Three proofs – that life after death exists –

D'S "Proof" #1: That brain and mind are separate. "Soul" exists as part of the mind. It is immaterial and a source of the afterlife. "To reduce mental transactions to physical…is the "essence of reductive materialism…"

Yet this line of thinking ignores emergence [as elsewhere in D'S; see Chapter 5 on this]. D'S' Chapter 7 on "The Spiritual Brain" is based on quite arguable reliance on, and misuse of, reductive materialism, on dualism and a presumed (no evidence supporting) connection of soul with LAD. "Reductive materialism" denotes the ability to trace actions at the macro-level to

---

[55] From D'S' book on LaD, p. 85, quoting Susskind from his 2006 book **THE COSMIC LANDSCAPE.**

causative forces at the lower levels of a system. D'S frequently misuses this concept, as in referring to Dennett's "the mind is the brain" as a "classic case of reductive materialism."[56] In fact, the mind is emergent. Mindfulness becomes a primary quality of the physical brain. "Dualism" originated with Descartes, who claimed that the spiritual realm was separate from the physical or material realm. This view, known as "Descartes' Error," was refuted earlier.

The brain is a "gateway or receiver for the mind." Neuroscience shows brain states [BS] are akin to mental states [MS]. But D'S uses a few poor analogies to 'show' that BS do not "cause" MS. In an essay entitled "Human Immortality", Henry James hypothesized: "the existence of a cosmic immaterial (external) realm that… supplies consciousness through our brains. [parenthetical here is mine] D'S follows James to a 'T', thereby bowing before "Descartes Error."

Other mistaken observations or remarks in D'S' book, noted with page references in brackets [])) are as follows:

- o **Science as "promissory materialism":** that science will one day show that our entire mental world is an illusion." [115] But Bronowski has shown otherwise, writing of science:
- o **"Its values are the human values:** honesty, tolerance, independence and common sense…Science has filled our world because it has been tolerant and flexible and endlessly open to new ideas…science is a democratic method."[57] Are these basic values "illusion"(s)? Answer: Definitely not.

---

[56] D'Sousa (2009), p. 116.

[57] Bronowski, Jacob (1977), **A SENSE of the FUTURE.** Cambridge: MIT Press, and **SCIENCE and HUMAN VALUES**. Here, too, recall earlier remarks as to how science has steadily demoted religion and myth as explanations of reality by grappling with "immaterial" hypotheses.

- o **"Brain states aren't 'about' anything; they just are."**: But my mental states are about something…refer to something external to themselves (though in fact, at first "private" in nature).
- o **"Four things…true of mental…not brain, states…:** privacy, absence of specific location, intentionality and infallibility…" But this rests on a mistaken (as we have seen) assumption --that the mind is separable from the brain.
- o "materialists' last refuge…functionalism…" [118] – But D'S doesn't allow for "qualia."
- o **"Science has shown its "blind spot":** it's operations are confined to a restricted domain…limited to the study of things that are objective and publicly observable …the scientific argument vs. the soul collapses…the soul is not material or objective." [125] But there is no scientific argument vs. the soul as such.
- o **But Q.E.D.: mind & brain are separate:** D'S has already used a mistaken assumption in drawing this conclusion, implying via a leap too far – that "immaterial minds and consciousness might survive the termination of our physical frames." The "Q.E.D." is so circular as to be almost tautological since D'S uses the assumption of separation to make arguments in support of his "proof."

D'S' "Proof" #2: Vindication of Dualism [D'S' Chapter 8]: On "The Immaterial Self: How Consciousness Can Survive Death," D'S ignores brain science with regard to consciousness and how historical memory is the key to its "survival" of death. He opens with a quote from **THE ETHICAL BRAIN** that is mistaken at the outset: "Brains are automatic, rule-governed, determined devices…"[ignoring the probabilistic nature of brain processes]. He then proceeds to devote a whole chapter to reaffirming Descartes' dualism. Why? -- because dualism "enables LaD…and: "It has made a remarkable scientific comeback." [p.127], continuing: If dualism is true, then LaD is…possible (&)…plausible" [109] But we have already found that dualism is untrue.

D'S further claims that Proof #1 will show "aspects of…mind are irreducible to material bodies."[128]. Not so, as indicated earlier. Then D'S writes: "Dualism as a philosophy is supported by everyday experience," but this is followed by two silly examples, not "evidence.".

D'S continues with reference to Leibnitz "Law of Indiscernibles" [p.128]: If mind [M] is independent of brain [B], then one "should be able to say something about M that is not true of B." And yet this is not necessarily true. Independence depends on lack of interactivity rather than categorical differences, but there is no lack of interactivity between B and M.

D'S' conclusion from Descartes proceeds from an assumption made without proof provided -- that mind is separate from the brain. Likewise, D'S drawing of implications from medicine assumes M, B separation. Otherwise, his examples can be read as NOT supporting dualism; rather, the opposite via documented interactivity between M and B.; e.g., neuro-plasticity: "If your mind is independent enough to create changes in both your body and brain, it seems reasonable...to suppose that it can survive the dissolution of your body and brain." [131] Again: This assumes M, B separation and it is a leap too far.

D'S, like others, then turns to quantum (Q) physics to try to buttress his case, but the interventionary "role of observer" does not support dualism. Schwartz and Stapp apply Q-theory to show "how mental states affect physical states." [132] D'S thus says "consciousness [C] operates at the quantum level to create a physical force." And so he identifies "consciousness [C] as the "missing link." D'S therefore concludes that "If there is LaD, it is presumably C that survives..." But C has not been analyzed up to this point. Nor do Schwartz and Stapp or D'S acknowledge the vice-versa in their presumed Q-Theory statement: That physical states can influence mental states.

Nonetheless. D'S moves on to accept the view of Stephen Pinker, that "We have no scientific explanation" of consciousness. Here, as elsewhere, however, there is no recognition of scientists' attempts to model, investigate and explain "emergence" [nor even a cite of the word in the book's index]. His next misstep is to go from our inability to construct "zombies" with conscience, to "the unavoidable implication that human consciousness has no physical explanation... (and that it) so far has eluded scientific investigation." [134]

The latter is false. There is ample evidence, and each of us can testify from our own experience, that physical states affect our mental states. What about orgasm and a host of similar experiences?

The following statements of D'S are also false:

- o **"There are no physical facts or scientific laws** that lead to the prediction or explanation that there should be consciousness [134] Consciousness lies beyond all known scientific laws and explanations. " [136] Again, such statements are false in ignoring the emergence of new states from the dynamics of complex adaptive systems [CAS], as we shall see in the chapter on "Emergence."
- o **"Consciousness has no good evolutionary explanation..."** Not so. See Penrose (1994) SHADOWS of the MIND: A Search for the missing science of consciousness.
- o "Consciousness is not required for any of the activities that humans need for survival and reproduction." This is obviously nonsense.
- o **"Consciousness doesn't even help us with figuring out other people:**, because we have no access to their consciousness...we can collaborate with others in the absence of anyone having inner states...Consciousness is irreducibly immaterial and subjective."[135] Wrong. People are conscious of other's consciousness through their interactivity with them. Collaboration can hardly occur without consciousness [C].
- o We **"have to recognize that there are both physical and mental things as distinct** realities in the world." [136] But this does not imply A, nor D'S' conclusion that "C is not part of the body...C merely comes with the body" [and so returns to James' theory]. Here D'S is contradicted by his own arguments in favor of dualism.
- o **"Two central features of human nature – C and free will...are irreducible to matter** and appear to be independent from it...no natural explanation... human bodies and brains are perishable...C and free will are not...They are defining features of the human soul...(so we can derive the) implication that whatever happens to our bodies and brains, our souls live on." [144] Another leap too far without even a pretense of "evidence." {Parenthetical mine}

My contrary thesis is that: $C = f\{M, B\}$ and that it is the basis of Soul. Apposite D'S' slam of Dennett: D'S is "ideologically compelled" to deny the death of M and C with that of B. His "conclusions" are overstated, oft not justified by prior arguments, and buttressed by too many presumptive judgments. Also, as indicated earlier, they are often circular. Too many lines of argument in D'S' "proofs" turn out to rest on his assumption that his external god exists. Additional examples follow.

D'S' "Proof" # 3: [See Chapter 10]: Locates an eternal realm beyond physical law. – D'S aims to show that "there is an eternal part of this (world) that inhabits this realm now and (we) will rejoin it when we die." He tries to dismiss "empirical realism" and opens with Berkeley's circular idea: "The only things we perceive…are our perceptions." Then he continues with Berkeley's absurd subjectivism, to wit:

- ❖ **"The material world outside our senses does not exist…**a devastating blow to empirical realism." [another leap too far, contradicted by experience].
- ❖ **"the subjective mental realm is largely outside the realm of science**"[contradicted by many findings from neuro- and psychiatric-science].
- ❖ **"the objective physical world is apprehended through subjective mental experiences…the entire experience**…has occurred in your mind." [Entirely false. As science has demonstrated, there are many objective ways and real instruments to "apprehend" the physical world.] [151]

D'S then looks for support from Kant and Schopenhauer. Kant's "noumenon" is "the world as it is…the real world that is independent of our experience;" the "phenomenal is the empirical world." Outside of the latter, "there is no space and no time." [157] D'S proceeds to translate "noumenon" as "a realm not bound by material laws." [a leap too far, p.157] … "a realm to which our reason and experience have no direct access. [obviously mistaken] … the manifestation of another world, a reality hidden behind the veils of human experience" [an assumption with no evidence provided in support]

As for Schopenhauer [via D'S]: "The 'I' cannot be experienced directly because it is not part of the noumenal realm." [not part of the "world as it is?] All of this implies a "remarkable conclusion" – that reality consists of two different entities, mind and material. But this reveals an implicit assumption – that "mind" is immaterial – not part of the brain. Also regarding

Schopenhauer and from him: the self is noumenal/ undifferentiated, "we humans are…one. [clearly untrue from simple observation in the U.S. – the most diverse country in the world].

Schopenhauer acknowledged that the will to live is the driving force of our existence but, according to D'S, he also contends that:

> ➤ **" fear of death is…an illusion** because the real or noumenal part of us cannot die…" [162]
> ➤ "…at death we are fully integrated into the realm of the noumenal…"[Both here and above: "The world as it is"?]
> ➤ **"death (is)…a discovery of our one true oneness with each** other and with infinite reality…When we die, our separate-ness is over…" Discovery after death? Nonsense. Also, we as yet have no proof that reality is infinite.

Thus, D'S concludes that: "Schopenhauer and Kant show the existence and characteristics of the noumenon, the world behind the world…this unseen reality…(and so) there is good reason to believe in the after-life." [Quite strained this, and another leap too far]

It is also important to also note that D'S rests his case for morality on "Cosmic Justice" [CJ]. This is simply a more sophisticated version of dependence on the "old time religion" that calls for eternal punishment for sinners (the dark side of life-after-death). The perpetuation and advancement of human life, emanating from each of us as both individuals and members of groups, somehow doesn't qualify as a sufficient modifier. His line of argument is, again, quite circular, as in: "The foundation of morality is the existence of an external God" that provides CJ. LaD [requiring such a God] is a foundation of morality. No, life before death provides such a foundation.

D'S repeatedly falls back on his "presuppositional" logic to fills gaps in his arguments in favor of LaD. What is his prime presupposition? – the same as that with respect to CJ; i.e. his (external) God. So, his presupposition of God is used to close his argument to favor LaD, which cannot exist without an external God-in-heaven. Along the way to this remarkable "proof", D'S also misuses evolution as due solely to "selfish beings" in the face of scientific evidence that the rise of altruism was also an essential part of evolution.

What is most troubling from the standpoint of a NSB, however, are D'S claims that LaD, along with its god and heaven, both supports and enriches life. One weakness in his line of argument here is his reliance upon a reading of history that, he claims, consistently demonstrates that beliefs in LAD correlate with people's happiness, satisfaction and life goals. Evidence? Such claims ignore the sharp disjuncture between modern and pre-modern times. They also neglect to recognize that correlation is not causation. Nor is real evidence to the contrary covered such as that provided by Hitchens.[58]

A NSB without LaD is likely to be more supportive of the continuation of trends towards more democracy. Why? – Because the NSB as outlined herein represents the fulfillment of two major historical events: (1) the Reformation and (2) the Incarnation. Recall that the Reformation took power out of the hands of priests, prelates and hierarchy by putting the power of the Bible, its reading and guidance directly into the hands of ordinary people. Don't forget Jesus, either: His incarnation [God in Christ] most truly allows the incarnation of us all as spiritual beings, with Christ in our consciousness as a primary role model-- if we choose to make him so.

And so, especially as discussed in the Chapter on "Spiritual Politics," the democratization of incarnation and spirituality provides a foundation for the salvation of our democratic republic, which arose out of the rise of democracy and a concomitant fall in reliance upon ancient, hierarchical, undemocratic values. Unfortunately, the latter persist, especially in China, where they continue to buttress an authoritarian, undemocratic regime.

---

[58] Hitchens, Christopher (2007), **GOD IS NOT GREAT: How Religion Poisons Everything.** New York: Hachette Book Group USA.

D'S thesis: That "...belief in life after death makes your life better..."(216) seems superficially unquestionable. The evidence in support of D'S' thesis?:

- ❖ Harold Koenig, in his 2008 book **MEDICINE, RELIGION & HEALTH**, summarizes a wide body of data... that religious people who affirm the afterlife are healthier than non-believers... with respect to less stress and depression, less suicide, less vulnerable to other ailments & greater life spans.
- ❖ Jonathan Haidt, in his 2006 book, **THE HAPPINESS HYPOTHESIS**: "Religious people are happier than non-religious...(including) more fulfilling sex lives..."[59]
- ❖ Arthur Brooks, in his 2006 book, **WHO REALLY CARES:** "Religious believers (are)...more generous, both with their time & money..."
- ❖ D''S' "prospect of an afterlife provides a motive for morality and generosity because it is linked to cosmic justice." (217)

The latter claim has already been cast aside. Other counter-arguments to D'S' "thesis" are grounded on six (6) points:

1) **The externality of a sexist god** can in truth never be known to us. He (why not 'she') presumably "lives" up high in a heaven that does not exist nor is rooted in the realities of life – This is only a god of our imagination, not one who can recognize us, think for us, and answer our prayers for sustenance and succor. In fact, though prayer is good (as shown in Chapter 9), time spent in praying to such a "God" is misdirected, wasted and disabling in a world where our only realistic hope for help lies in friends, neighbors and democratic government(s).
2) **Foolish adherence to beliefs with no foundation** in fact, such as virgin birth and LaD; one the basis of Christmas and the other, of

---

[59] Strong counterpoints to both Koenig and Haidt are provided in Hitchens (2007), op. cit.

Easter, the two major Christian holidays. Ancient pagans had already found reasons to celebrate the seasons. And so the issue is not such celebrations but their grounding – in fantasy? or in natural and/or historically realistic events?

3) **Lost opportunities for building community.** The value of community has been severely diminished during an age of TV, where even "reality" shows are suspect. The losses from lack of a sense of place and no place of grace are beyond measure. One indication was provided via reporting on the Las Vegas shooter. When a reporter queried his neighbor about him, the response was: "I never talked to him." Lost opportunities are increased by dependence upon cellphones and social media. How often have you seen people staring at cellphones rather than talking to neighbors? These losses are not attributable to denial of LAD.

4) **Declining church attendance and the deadening of spirituality:** Church is a social as well as a religious institution. These declines cannot be remedied by traditional religions. How much of church attendance is not inspired but induced by a need to "go along, get along" and/or a desire to 'give the kids' some spurious basis for moral and ethical standards that may not be demonstrated in the home?

5) **LaD is a false and therefore wrongful incentive for moral behavior.** As indicated at the outset, it is more likely to be an incentive for murder. Why? – Because LaD is supernatural, and such imaginings are more readily associated with the dark sides of human life.

6) **There is no such thing as "Cosmic Justice;"** at least, no such institution to provide it. Justice, if there is to be any whatsoever, is made by way of people and institutions peopled by people, not via fantastic, supernatural imaginings.

D'S' Chapter 5 can be viewed as his key chapter on LaD. Titled "The Physics of Immortality", it partly relies on interpretations of quantum physics found to be fallacious as indicated earlier. Otherwise, too, and surprisingly, this can be deemed the weakest chapter in D'S' book. It is the one where one might suspect the most convincing evidence is to be found, based on thousands of reports of "near death" experiences. D'S' pays no attention, however, to the multitude of U-Tube videos that could help buttress his case for LaD. Many of these are quite inspiring, what with testimonies of "revelations" of "God" and "Heaven" from near-death experiences.

The problem is that these cannot be viewed as scientific evidence proving the existence of LAD. Why? – Primarily because the cases documented do not prove brain death. Thus, the reported near-death visions are attributable to hallucinations arising from points of near-death and/or points of transition to the recovery of life.

Thus, D'Souza's case for Life-after-Death is erroneous on most points and sadly misleading or deficient on others.

"As for the association of "soul" with life-after-death, there's nothing like an outrageous claim given religious imprimatur to deceive mankind."[60]

Choice in the Fight for Life

As argued from the beginning, spirituality is the highest quality of what it means to be human, and yet it does not require the presumption of an External God [EG]. After all, there are major gaps between an EG and Man as well as between Heaven and Earth. What if the only ears listening (or not) are those of other human beings? Suddenly, the locus of responsibility shifts to you and other human beings and your ability to commune and work with them by way of communication, cooperation and collaboration [hereafter referred to as the "3C's"]. The locus (loci) of comfort and commiseration also shifts from the illusion of heavens above to the reality of down to earth life on earth.

Do you despair of mutually satisfactory relationships with others -- involving learning, helping, 3C's and love? Then one might as well despair of oneself. Look at the tenacious force of life all about you – the growth and patterns of life displayed by trees, flowers, shrubs, the ebb and flow of the seasons, the beauty of rivers and seas – in view for all with eyes to see. That force is with

---

[60] Hitchens, op. cit.

you, within you, ready to be expressed in so many ways. That force is evident from your first cry at birth.

All our lives, we spend time searching for matter and meaning in ourselves and ourselves in relation to others. Such understandings take hard work and deep thought right here on earth. They are not sent to us from on high. Our only god is the God of Life.

With a NSB, there are no major gaps; only those relatively minor, partially overcome by the web and woof, cross patterns and interactivities between and among people of all sorts. This observation does not fail to recognize the multi-contrarian nature of inter-group differences, nor how NSB can serve to bridge them. In contrast, belief in an external god (EG) provides a ready-made basis for rationalizing them. Each man, family and community have their version of the EG to worship. EG worship provides ample rationalization of self- and other-group differences, helping to maintain the 'minor" gaps.

After all, comfort and chance are basic motivators. They are also markers – bifurcations -- between deterministic and probabilistic worlds. The former is sustained by way of hierarchical patterns of influence and domination. A key question for any system of belief is how it can enable people to live in an in- or un-deterministic world governed by chance [including the so-called "free" market]. How very much harder it is to live a life rooted in reality than one of illusion!!

The choice between an EG and a NSB raises other difficult questions such as:

- o **A comforting solace of the EG** as a possibly constant factor (or "presence?") vs. the indeterminate presence of other life forms in the lives of human beings. And yet, with a NSB:
  - ➤ The "indeterminate presence" would be supplemented and complemented by the everlasting presence of human life and nature. Unfortunately, these are too often segmented and fragmented into broken patterns. Only the genuine and pervasive spirituality induced by a NSB can convey a sense of unity in the presence of disabling and fragmentation-aggravating disunity.

- ➤ A NSB would prove to be essential to the maintenance and enrichment of the web and woof of human and man/nature interrelationships – Even though there may be a possible catch-22 here: A shared spirituality is key to reducing gaps between people and groups, but overcoming gaps is needed to facilitate a shared spirituality. It's up to us to turn vicious circles into virtuous. Life is full of them.
- o What are the overlaps and juxtapositions of finitude and infinitude?

It is so easy to sense infinity, even in the midst of the distracting finitudes of our lives. For example, when sitting in the office of an optometrist, sitting between two mirrors. Looking from one side to another, I realized that the number of reflected images was uncountable. Uncountability is one concept of infinite. The vastness of our universe is another. Nobel Laureate in Physics, Freeman Dyson, has written how it is "infinite in all directions." Diversity of life forms is a third. We have not yet finished counting these and we never will. The mutability of species is also uncountable.

- o How can we "evangelize" spirituality?: Only by living it among others, as by:
  - ➤ Each of us realizing that we each have a soul and that soulfulness requires attentiveness to the higher consciousness of our spirituality and care for the soul of it.[61]
  - ➤ Transforming expressions of "spirit," such as "team spirit" into deeper forms and displays of spirituality [e.g., holding hands to form prayer circles].
  - ➤ Living the Golden Rule: Love our neighbors as ourselves.
  - ➤ By counting the blessing of love and life in and around us.
  - ➤ By raising our children as spiritual beings; and by…
  - ➤ Throwing out of our homes and lives all the distracting forces and graven images that so plague us; for example, by saying "Just say NO" to TV!

---

[61] As shown in Thomas Moore's book on CARE of the SOUL.

The latter is most difficult of all, for among the "distracting forces and graven images" are those illusions most deeply rooted and supported by our culture. Resting one's system of belief on illusions such as a God-in-heaven means that we are resting our lives on the supernatural. The foundations of Christian belief are noteworthy, with Christmas the key, in 2 ways:

1) Virgin conception & birth; &
2) Incarnation (God-in-Man), though Christ's whole life and work should be seen as the Incarnation. Easter celebrates Christ's resurrection – the opposite pole of his "virgin" birth.

Thus, both birth and death of "our Lord" are relegated from the real to the unreal, from the natural to the supernatural.

Lives surrounded by truth and light lie with our never-ending search for them in the real world of living things; not in insensate probes of the supernatural, where we can easily descend into darkness and alienation from our souls and those of others. An external God-as-listener to individuals, especially to their prayers, is nonsense. The cacophony of billions of voices = noise. The only ears one can hope to hear us are those of other human beings!

Consider more on distractions and offsets therefrom: In the context of an external god, distractions redound to the nearly unlimited noise that distracts. The constant barrage of distracting advertising and programming on TV [and now "social" media] frequently threaten to distract us from our souls and soulfulness. Souls are integrands, but souls and soulfulness [hereafter abbreviated S&S] are only allowed play on Sundays. Then, as elsewhere, worship of an external god helps to rationalize or partially offset the ill effects of irrational life and work patterns.

Contrast again: Meditation within the NSB context enables us to fight or offset the distractions all around us. As shown in Chapter 5, meditation is beneficially open to all, even though the meditation trend and "industry" appears to be graduated by class along with related activities including education and self-help modules. A NSB challenges us to identify and distinguish the true sources of distraction from S&S and develop ways to fight back or at least ameliorate their impact on our lives.

Earlier, the "3C's" were mentioned as a source of offsets. Nevertheless, it is important to attend to the ways that facilitate or discourage authentic communication modes of communication, cooperation and/or collaboration [3 C's]. Avoid "top down" ways and seek to demonstrate "bottom up." Unfortunately, most of us have learned the 3C's from an educational system that does not encourage them.

Traditional ways of teaching and learning are adverse, such as teacher/pupil relationships, as with a teacher at the head of a class seated in a geometric rectangle facing him or her. Change the geometry. Arrange the seats in a circle to foster a better process of learning altogether.

FINALLY, take care what icons you care to honor. There are many, and it's hard to avoid celebrities and graven images. My favorites are two, shown here below:

i. **The Tree of Life**, representing the searching, branching and multiform rootedness of life; and...
ii. **The 8-fold knot**, an ancient and modern image that represents the fact that "everything is related to everything else." See Fig's. 10 and 11, below, for both images.

Fig. 10

The Tree of Life

Fig. 11

The 8-Fold Knot

All that can be said is that "God is God." Similarly, "Life is Life" (and the processes that sustain Life). One could add to God the processes that sustain God, but the latter do not stand up to critical evaluation as do the life-enhancing processes of life. Put the two words together and you get **God is Life & Life is God**. The life-force is within us, not "out there." So don't forget to offer a toast after at least one meal per day: "L'Chaim!" [TO LIFE!].

Chapter 6

EMERGENCE

Introduction

Emergence of varied forms has long elicited wonder and curiosity. How have such beautiful or amazing new things come to be? They range from the near sacred, such as language, writing and music, to the very practical, including tractors and bacteria resistant to antibiotics. Emergence occurs when a dynamic, complex adaptive system [CAS] generates a new set of characteristics that are qualitatively and irreducibly different both from the system's past and its components. The old saying: The system is "greater than the sum of its parts" pertains," but more: The system is not reducible to its parts, nor can the parts leading to the systemic change be fully identified. Consciousness is an emergent quality of the human brain. Spirituality, in turn, is an emergent quality of consciousness. Thus, understanding emergence is of utmost importance, not only to this book but to all aspects of human life. It is also necessary to be able to detect and measure consciousness as an outcome of both physical and mental health.

Peter Corning has observed that:

> "In evolutionary processes, causation is iterative; effects are also causes. And this is equally true of the synergistic effects produced by emergent systems. In other words, emergence itself has been the underlying cause of the evolution of emergent phenomena in biological

evolution. It is the synergies produced by organized systems that are the key."[62]

Emergence creates an entity that is qualitatively different from a system that has become chaotic. A good example of this is creation of the United States of America out of the American Revolution. Failure of the first attempt of the colonies, formation of the Articles of Confederation, led to chaos rather than a stable relationship of collaboration among them. Convening a Constitutional Convention was viewed as a parlous undertaking. Even attendance was open to question. Fortunately, the new nation was blessed by fine leadership, especially in Washington, Madison and Jefferson. They came forward at a juncture when the new nation could have failed to establish a strong national government dedicated to "We the People."

The U.S.A., newly constituted as of 1787, was a system of a far "higher order" than the Confederation, in large part because the new Constitution called for a federal government with a centralized portion. The key components are a strong executive, bicameral federal legislature and Supreme Court. The tripartite structure – Executive, Legislative and Judicial – was replication of a self-similar (fractal) pattern also replicated at state and local levels.

This U.S.A. example reveals that, in order to be (or become) both dynamic and stable, any system needs a balance between dynamism and interactivity at lower levels and more centralized leadership and guidance at higher levels. Lacking these, any complex, dynamic system could return to the "edge of chaos," at which point the system would either move to a more stable, higher-order system, or fail. The key to which outcome will prevail lies in the process of emergence.

---

[62] Corning, Peter [2002], "The Re-Emergence of "Emergence": A Venerable Concept in Search of a Theory", **COMPLEXITY**, 7.

The ups and downs of the debates over the new U.S.A. government and Constitution illustrate just how problematic the process can be. Leadership from a person widely known and beloved was crucial. That person in our history was George Washington. That is why he, rather than the other distinguished members of the Continental Congress – Jefferson, Madison and others – is on our $1 bill.

The U.S.A. is an example of complex adaptive systems [CAS], defined as:

> "Systems (that) are characterized by a high degree of <u>adaptive capacity</u>, giving them resilience in the face of perturbation. Other important properties are adaptation, communication, cooperation, specialization, spatial and temporal organization, and reproduction."[63]

Systems vary by their levels of complexity. The complexity of the human brain rivals that of our galaxy.[64] "At each level of complexity entirely new properties appear"[65] in the process of systems' self-organization and evolution. New properties are subject to selection during an evolutionary process as noted earlier.

Other influential factors in the process of emergence include system complexity numbers of system components, their interactivity, teleological (goal-seeking) behaviors; cybernetic, feedback-driven influences, and the impacts of factors external to the system.

✓ Neuro-anatomical factors favoring complexity include:

---

[63] **WIKIPEDIA** on the Brain.

[64] Vazza, Franco, & A. Feletti (2017), "The Strange Similarity of Neuron and Galaxy Networks," **Monthly Notices of the Royal Astronomical Society,** (465).

[65] **WIKIPEDIA** on Emergence.

- ✓ Dense local connections favoring formation of neuroanatomical groups;
- ✓ Connections among such groups distributed in a "patchy" fashion;
- ✓ Abundance of short reentrant circuits [those enabling reciprocal connections among neurons and neuron groups]; and
- ✓ Functional modulation of neural activity.

According to the great philosopher Karl Popper, many of these factors, separately or altogether, can be labelled "situation-dependent" elements-crucial to emergence with respect to the likelihood that events in the world can be realized.[66] According to Jaynes, the impacts of "situational" factors external to the system of life of our earliest ancestors were crucial to the emergence of consciousness. Until about the start of the 3rd millennium B.C., ancient people who evolved into homo sapiens had lived in relatively stable hierarchical systems in which "voices" provided the rules of living.

Careful scrutiny of multiple sources led Jaynes to conclude that the pre-historical human brain was bicameral – there is no evidence of consciousness arising until early in the 2nd millennium B.C. Why? Apparently because early humans were struggling to deal with a multitude of huge crises besetting them during the second half of the third millennium B.C. -- massive volcanoes, cooling of the earth, exceptionally large migrations, crop failures, et al.

These presented major challenges to bicameral minds. Glimmers of conscious thought began to emerge in response to major disruptions to which the old rule-based "voices" could not provide redress. Those who could cultivate conscious attentiveness, begin to think about problems and become part of larger groups and settlements were more likely to survive. Survival and consciousness were products of both top-down and bottom-up factors. The

---

[66] Eccles, John, and Karl R. Popper (1977), **THE SELF AND ITS BRAIN: An Argument for Interactionism**. Springer.

human brain evolved. Connectivity between the lobes and among other parts increased. See Jaynes excellent book for more.

There are two major classes of emergence, strong and weak. Weak emergence is amenable to computer simulation; not so for the strong variety. Weak emergence typically arises from "bottom up" modes of causation. Strong emergence may involve such factors, but it is more typically driven by a "top down" process -- the direct causal action of a high-level system upon its components. "No simulation of (such a) a system can exist, for such a simulation would itself constitute a reduction of the system to its constituent parts."[67] Weak emergence is readily demonstrated on a computer by way of cellular automaton routines such as "Conway's Automaton, discussed further on. Consciousness arises through a kind of strong emergence that is the focus of this chapter.

Kauffman goes to great lengths to distinguish "weak" from "strong" because of his abiding concern for the maintenance of the biosphere as the fundamental source of life on earth.[68] In this, he departs from his "physicist friends" by emphasizing the impossibility of prestating the "configuration space" [CS] for the emergence and evolution of species. CS refers to a system's space of possibilities.

Theorizing about emergence goes all the way back to Aristotle. He surmised that emergent structures are other than the sum of their parts on the assumption that the emergent order will not arise if the various parts simply interact independently of one another. Some disagree. According to their arguments, the interaction of each part with its immediate surroundings causes a complex chain of processes that can lead to order emergent in some form. Some systems in nature are observed to exhibit weak emergence based

---

[67] Bedau, Mark A. (1997), **"Weak Emergence," PDF online.**

[68] The major reference relied upon here is Kauffmann, Stuart (2000), **INVESTIGATIONS.** New York: Oxford University Press.

upon the interactions of autonomous parts. Some others exhibit strong emergence that cannot be reduced in this way.

Downward causation is attributable to three basic factors:

(1) **Constraints internal to a system that are non-linear consequences of the organization of the system-as-a-whole**. Examples are found in cases of system stability, whether of an energy well or a far-from-equilibrium form.

(2) **Non-linear constraints internal to the constituents of a system:** one level down from the constraints mentioned above: Here, in fact, we find some of the most interesting kinds of emergence. Processes internal to cells are strongly constrained by the overall processes of the organism. Such processes can even enable the generation of complex molecules that would not otherwise exist. An example is the influence of surroundings on the internal processes of a computer chip.

(3) **A 3rd kind of downward causation** involves constraints on the generative processes -- sources of constructive variation -- as well as the activities of lower levels. Obvious examples here are biological. Changes in the organization of an ecosystem, for example, can alter the selection pressures on the constituent organisms. Similarly, but at a much larger scale, alterations in the earth's biosphere can change the selections and variations with respect to species and ecosystems. In such instances, we find a downward causation via selection that is among the strongest kinds of emergence.

And so it is important to try to distinguish parts from wholes. Wholes produce unique combined effects. Many of these, however, may be co-determined by interactions between the whole and its environment. In accordance with his synergism hypothesis, Corning stated:

> "It is the synergistic effects produced by wholes that are the very cause of the evolution of complexity in nature." The ability to reduce everything to simple fundamental laws does not imply the ability to start from those laws and reconstruct the universe. Any constructionist hypothesis breaks down when confronted with the twin difficulties of scale and complexity. At each level of complexity entirely new

properties appear. Psychology is not applied biology, nor is biology applied chemistry. To repeat: The whole becomes not merely more, but very different from the sum of its parts."[69]

As Gantz concluded: "Reciprocity between component and system levels is inherent in the dynamic of emergence."[70] Components enable the system to search, and the system attraction to pointer states drives the selection. Higher levels and lower levels are alike in facilitating the organization of process.

Processes Generating Consciousness in the Human Brain

Edelman writes: "The functioning of the cerebral cortex is largely responsible for the content of consciousness."[71] This is because the activity of specific cortical regions is linked to similarly specific aspects of consciousness. But this still begs the fundamental question: What explains the whole existence of consciousness, notwithstanding whatever we may be conscious of, including consciousness of one's "self"? As we learned earlier, no single area of the brain is solely responsible for conscious experience.[72]

As the previous chapter has shown, the human brain is far more complex than any computer ever built or imagined. The processes of the brain are similarly complex. Nevertheless, complexity proves to be paradoxical. It is both a challenging problem and a promising solution towards understanding the mystery of how higher orders of complexity generate the emergent experience of consciousness. The research of Edelman and his colleagues has been especially helpful.

---

[69] Corning, op. cit.

[70] Gantz, op. cit.

[71] Edelman, op. cit., p. 53.

[72] Ibid., p.51.

The key to understanding how complexity generates consciousness is to realize that nine (9) fundamental processes are at work:

1) Differentiation: Distinguishing those things felt, heard, done or otherwise perceived by human actors;
2) Integration: Organization around common denominators revealed by the interactivity of human actors. Functionally segregated areas are reciprocally connected. These reciprocal pathways are among the main means for the integration of distributed brain functions. They provide a structural basis for reentry (see # 6, below).
3) Linkage: Interactions among organizations, maps and/or groups;
4) Categorization: Identifying similarities or common denominators, and putting similar people and things into categories;
5) Memory: Ability to repeat or repress a mental or physical act. Does this seem strange as a definition of memory? Indeed. It takes us away from memory-as-representation to focus on memory-as-action. Values, emotions and salience place strong constraints on establishment of a conceptual, category-based memory focused on recollection of images.
6) Reentry: This a process of continuing, recursive signaling between separate functional areas [brain maps]. The signaling proceeds along parallel, mostly reciprocal connections. It alters and is altered by its targets. Parallel, reciprocally signaling targets connect separate maps. Interchanges synchronize and coordinate various maps. These help to ensure integration.
7) Value: This designates categories of memory that are associated with value-preferences and constraints – very important to selection of both categories of thought and attendant actions.
8) Development of Concepts: The brain has demonstrated an ability to combine different categories to construct a new, more general category reflecting and representing some common feature. This is registered in higher-order mappings.
9) The Unconscious: This, the largest part of the overall brain, handles the regular, repetitive, minute-by-minute, hour-by-hour thoughts, movements and routines. At first, these need to be registered in other parts of the brain to direct or restrain actions. As time goes by, the actions are learned with repetition. They become habitual, registered in

the unconscious. The major part of the brain controlling the body's regular functions is located in the brainstem.

"Maps" is one of the most important concepts in our brain-science vocabulary. It connotes mapping as a process. What does this mean? Putting people and things into categories is one form of mapping. Computing an algorithm is another: One variable is transformed, or "mapped" into another. The brain is partly a mapping organ.

Processes also need to be distinguished by the nature of their interactivity: One way or two? Parallel or circuitous? Two-way is reciprocal. Reciprocity is a major, powerful feature of interactivity among parts of the brain. We have learned the power of parallelism in computing. So, too, in the case of the brain.

In the process of evolution, reentrant conductivity [RC] arose between the multi-modal cortical areas responsible for categorization and those parts of the brain controlling value-categorical memory. RC came to be implemented by a system of intra-cortical fibers that link one part of the cortex to the rest and, as well, by a large number of reciprocal connections joining cortex and thalamus

Thalamocortical circuits to mediate these reentrant interactions originated in three major divisions of the thalamus: the Specific Thalamic Nuclei, Reticular Nucleus and Intralaminar Nuclei [See Fig.12, below] The Specific Thalamic Nuclei are reentrantly connected with the cerebral cortex. The Reticular Nucleus has inhibitory connections with the latter, and it can select or forbid various combinations of brain activity. The Intralaminar Nuclei send diffuse projections to the cerebral cortex and help to synchronize its overall level of activity. All these lead, acting via reentry, to the creation of a conscious scene [see Fig.12]. The central principle underlying the evolution of consciousness is the emergence of new reentrant systems.

Fig 12

Divisions of the

Thalamu

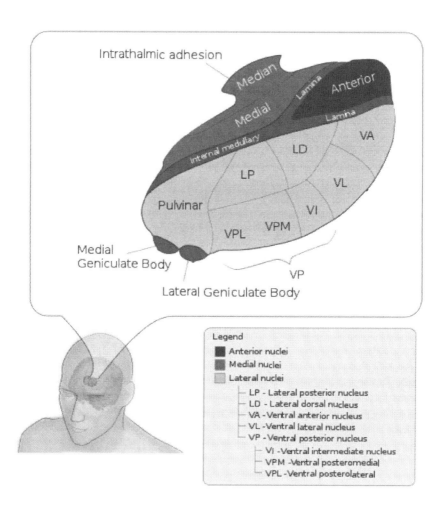

The Mechanisms generating consciousness are shown below in Fig. 13.

Value-level and categorized signals are correlated and lead to memory in conceptual areas. This memory, capable of conceptual categorization, is linked by reentrant paths to current perceptual categorization of external (world) signals. This reentrant linkage results in primary consciousness, which is a scene made up of objects and events. Some of these are causally connected. Primary consciousness can connect them through memory via its previous value-laden experience.

Fig. 13

Mechanisms Generating Consciousness

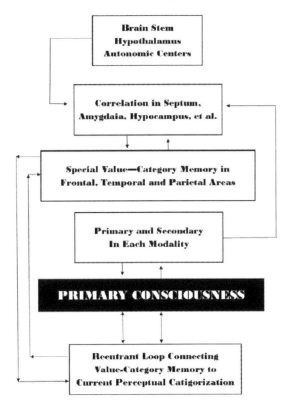

(The black box represents Primary Memory)

Integration is assured if functionally segregated maps in the cerebral cortex operate coherently, together, across many levels of organization. The latter has been described as "the binding problem"[73] whereby linking must be accomplished among neural groups. At higher levels, binding has to be manifest among widely distributed neural maps. Such binding occurs as a result of reentry across brain maps that estimate short-term temporal correlations and synchrony among widely spaced neuronal groups. Coherent, actionable output results when there is a selection of circuits temporarily correlated under the constraint of a value system. Binding thus plays a central role in mechanisms leading to consciousness.

This all brings us back to a basic concern raised at the outset: How to detect and measure the presence of consciousness? The completion of a long program of research provides landmark techniques to provide some answers. Consistent with earlier observations, the detection and measure of consciousness is by way of an index of complexity, called a perturbational complexity index (PCI).[74] Experiments with this index by a set of investigators found a PCI value of 0.31 was able to perfectly distinguish between conscious and unconscious states across a diverse set of those participating in the experiments.[75] (See Fig. 14, below.)

---

[73] .Kauffman (2000), op. cit.

[74] Here we rely on Koch, Christof (2017), "**How to Make a Consciousness Meter," SCIENTIFIC AMERICAN (November), p. 28.**

[75] Casarotto, Silvio (et al., 2016).

Fig. 14

Perturbational Complexity Index

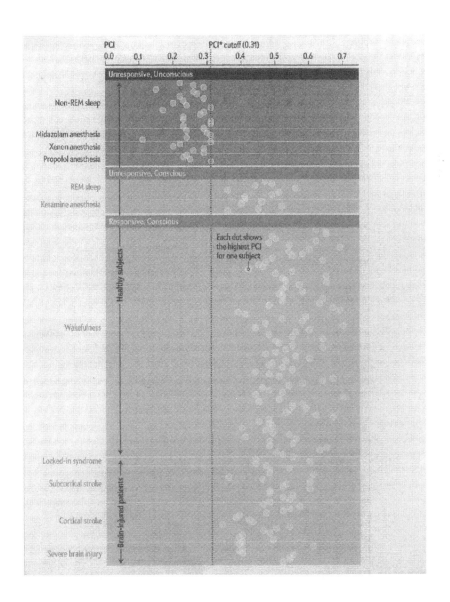

The experiment employed an advanced, high density electro-encephalogram [EEG] method – a skull cap with 256 electrodes producing maps that show the distribution of electrical energy across the brain.

> "The method zaps the brain by sending a sending a single pulse of magnetic energy via an enclosed coil of wire held against the head, a method called transcranial magnetic stimulation [TMS]."[76]

Unfortunately, this landmark study did not include indicators or measures of any higher levels of consciousness such as spirituality, These are readily available from a variety of sources.[77] Thus, the next step in this line of research should be to select and include appropriate, select indicators and/or measures to at least compute correlations between brain activity and the emergence of spirituality, all the time keeping in mind that correlation may suggest but does not prove causality.

Computer Models of Emergence

Generation of emergence has long been recognized as one of the most amazing outputs of complex adaptive systems [hereafter abbreviated CAS]. The most user-friendly CAS model is that of a computer automaton. The most familiar example is that of Conway's automaton.[78] This generates a pattern in

---

[76] Koch, op. cit., p. 32.

[77] See references from the National Institute of Aging's Workgroup on Measurement of Religion and Spirituality. Also see

wwwresearchgate.net/post/What_is_the_best_scale_questionnaire_to_measur e_spirituality, and Daaleman T.P. and Frey, B.B. (2004), "**The Spiritual Index of Well-Being,**" **ANNALS of FAMILY MEDICINE**, pp. 499-503, and the following two chapters.

[78] See pages 138-142 of Holland, John H. (1998), **EMERGENCE**: From Chaos to Order. Reading, MA: Addison-Wesley Publishing.

the form of a "glider" that is emergent -- qualitatively different from the starting pattern. It is, however, an example of weak emergence. Conway's automaton is illustrated by a square pattern of five occupied cells surrounded by empty cells. All cells are interconnected as illustrated by Fig. 15, below.[79] The dynamics of this cellular system are defined by three basic features:

1) **Basic mechanism:** A single cell containing a single particle {cell state = 1}.
2) **Connectivity:** As shown in Fig. 15;
3) **Transition function:** If the state=0 and exactly 3 neighbors are in state 1, then the state of the cell becomes 1; otherwise, it remains zero. If the state =1, and either 2 or 3 neighbors are in state 1, then its state remains 1; otherwise, it becomes zero. [See Fig. 15 for an illustration of the first step of the process.]

---

[79] Courtesy of Holland (1998), op. cit., p. 137.

Fig. 15

Conway's Automaton

Basic Mechanism for Conway's Automaton:

 8 inputs, 2 states {1, 0}

Transition Function:

  If the state is 0 and exactly three neighbors are in state 1,
   then the state becomes 1; otherwise it remains 0.
  If the state is 1, and either 2 or 3 neighbors are in state 1,
   Then the state remains 1; otherwise it becomes 0.

Basic Mechanism connected to its immediate neighbors:

One-step transitions for some simple state patterns:

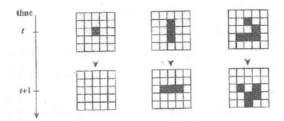

Conway's automaton represents a game called LIFE. It is also a simple model of what Holland calls a "constrained generating process." The emergent pattern moves diagonally across the cell space. The probability of such a moving form emerging is almost impossible to compute. Why? -- Because of non-linear interactions among the cell-particles and because a 5 by 5 array in LIFE has 32 million distinct patterns. As Holland writes: "...no extant analytical technique will predict the existence of a glider pattern." The three basic features cited above characterize other CAS's, notwithstanding many other additions and variations to computer models.

Several other computer models were constructed by Holland. We need not review them here, for what is most noteworthy in Holland's work is his distillation of shared features from the variety of emergent phenomena. Such observations aid future model building. These features are:

- The definition of model building blocks as mechanisms; that is, units that respond to actions or information by processing these inputs into outputs in the form of resulting actions and/or information.
- Translation of system rules into features of mechanisms.
- Linking mechanisms together into networks. Linkages need to incorporate constraints imposed by fixed landscapes as well as situations in which links can be made or broken.
- Identifying "The set of possibilities generated by the constrained actions of the mechanisms." [Recall Kaufman: These cannot be pre-identified in a CAS.]
- Define the "global state" of the system at hand -- condensation of "everything that is known".
- Assignments of brain space: E.g., when we move more, say fingers, we have more space devoted to these in the motor cortex than do parts of us we do not move
- Directionality, up and down: The top of the motor cortex controls the bottom of our body and the bottom of the cortex controls the top of our body. If that is too confusing, just know that every time you voluntarily move your body, you are using the motor cortex in the frontal lobe.
- Provide a specific procedure:"...for defining hierarchies of subassemblies" that would use more complex mechanisms built up

from the basic mechanisms...the resulting organization (would) parallel the hierarchical nature of most systems exhibiting emergence."[80]

Many of the features conducive to consciousness as an emergent quality of the brain as a CAS noted thus far have been tested by Edelman and his colleagues in a model comprising 65,000 neurons with over 5 million connections. [81] As described by Edelman in a footnote, other features of this "Brain Regions Model" are:

> "In register: sectors in a primary and secondary area of the visual cortex ..., two corresponding regions of the dorsal thalamus...and two regions of the dorsal thalamus nucleus...Individual neurons, both excitatory and inhibitory, were modeled as single compartment, integrate-and-fire units using cellular constants from regular-spiking and fast-spiking neurons, respectively. Synaptic interactions occurred through simulated channels that provided voltage-dependent...and voltage-independent excitation, as well as fast...and slow...inhibition...All connections were endowed with conduction delays. In addition, units were endowed with a background level of irregular, spontaneous activity through balanced ...excitation and inhibition."

The model was tested with tasks that require integration of signals generated by the activities of multiple, functionally segregated areas. Successful tests have demonstrated...

❖ How reentry solves the binding problem by coupling the neuronal responses of distributed cortical areas to achieve synchronization and coherence.

---

[80] Holland, work cited, pp. 128 & 129.

[81] Lumer, Edelman & Tononi, "**Neural Dynamics in a Model of the Thalamocortical System,**" 2 CEREBRAL CONTEXT 7 (1997).

- ❖ That reentrant signaling within cortex and between cortex and thalamus, supported by fast changes in synaptic efficiency, can rapidly establish a globally coherent process.
- ❖ The process emerges at a well-defined threshold of activity, quite stable and coherent, dynamic and self-perpetuating.
- ❖ That stability means that, although there is always a large pool of continuously firing neurons, those in the pool change from moment to moment. In other words, change is key to stability.
- ❖ That the process – characterized by the strength and speed of reentrant interactions – originates from the connectivity of the thalamocortical system.
- ❖ That integration and rapid functional clustering occur in the thalamocortical system and that reentry is the major mechanism by which integration is achieved.
- ❖ The system can select from among a large repertoire of coherent states, and Darwinian selectivity is the distinguishing characteristic of the model.

Complexity of neural processes can be influenced, not only by neuro-anatomy but also by neuro-physiology -- levels of arousal. To repeat: A high degree of complexity is a necessary requirement for any neural process to sustain conscious experience.

Has our Universe been "fine-tuned" for Life?

Martin Rees claims that the answer to this question is "Yes". He writes that our Universe has been fine-tuned in terms of the following six dimensionless physical constants.[82]

---

[82] Source: Martin Rees (1999), JUST SIX NUMBERS, HarperCollins Publishers; and Rees, Martin, and J. Gribbin (1989), **COSMIC COINCIDENCES: Dark Matter, Mankind, and Anthropic Cosmology. New York: Bantam**

- ✓ **N,** the ratio of the strength of electromagnetism to the strength of gravity for a pair of protons, is approximately 10^{36}. According to Rees, if it were significantly smaller, only a small and short-lived universe could exist.
- ✓ **Epsilon** (ε), a measure of the nuclear efficiency of fusion from hydrogen to helium, is 0.007: when four nucleons of hydrogen fuse into helium, 0.007 (0.7%) of their mass is converted to energy. The value of ε is in part determined by the strength of the strong nuclear force. If ε were 0.006, only hydrogen could exist, and complex chemistry would be impossible. According to Rees, if it were above 0.008, no hydrogen would exist, as all the hydrogen would have been fused shortly after the big bang. Other physicists disagree, calculating that substantial hydrogen remains as long as the strong force coupling constant increases by less than about 50%.
- ✓ **Omega** (Ω), commonly known as the density parameter, is the relative importance of gravity and expansion energy in the Universe. It is the ratio of the mass density of the Universe to the "critical density" and is approximately 1. If gravity were too strong compared with dark energy and the initial metric expansion, the universe would have collapsed before life could have evolved. On the other side, if gravity were too weak, no stars would have formed.
- ✓ **Lambda** (λ), commonly known as the cosmological constant, describes the ratio of the density of dark energy to the critical energy density of the universe, given certain reasonable assumptions, such as positing that dark energy density is a constant. In terms of Planck units, and as a natural dimensionless value, the cosmological constant, λ, is on the order of 10^{-122}. This is so small that it has no significant effect on cosmic structures that are smaller than a billion light-years across. If the cosmological constant were not extremely small, stars and other astronomical structures would not be able to form.
- ✓ **Q**, the ratio of the gravitational energy required to pull a large galaxy apart to the energy equivalent of its mass, is around 10^{-5}. If it is too small, no stars can form. If it is too large, no stars can survive because the universe is too violent, according to Rees.

✓ **D**, the number of dimensions in space-time, is 3. Rees claims that life could not exist if there were 2 or 4 dimensions of space-time, nor if any other than one (1) time dimension existed in space-time.

There are more than two-dozen other parameters that influence the "fine-tuning" of our universe, though they may be somewhat less determinative than the six above. See: Barrow, John D. (2003), THE CONSTANTS of NATURE, for more.

Some observers have been unable to imagine how this exquisite "fine tuning" could have emerged without the intervention of an all-powerful God. Such views are part and parcel of a deterministic universe. Given the fact that the Universe is probabilistic and indeterminate, however, one can as well imagine a Universe evolving over billions of years and emerging into one that fulfills fine tuning criteria such as those we have just described.

Conclusion

Selectivity sharply distinguishes the Edelman model from those that long have tried to characterize the brain-as-computer. Notwithstanding the ability of Edelman's theory and computer-enabled models to simulate the most essential operations of the human brain, however, there is not nor shall there ever be, a computer model that can completely replicate what the brain is capable of. Nor, contrary to many neuroscientists, can one associate spirituality with one certain part of the brain. Especially to the degree we succeed in bringing it into aspects and things of our daily lives, spirituality is and will be distributed throughout.

The brain not only enables consciousness, it is an unpredictable source of unpredictable, indeterminate, creative imagination. No one appears to have done better at illustrating this point than Kauffman in his discussion of "Mind."[83] With reference to some simple, basic examples – including the screwdriver, engine block and check cashing – he concludes:

---

[83] Kauffman, op. cit., pp. 184-196.

"The human mind, like a ghost ship, keeps slipping free of its computational moorings to sail where it will. It does so because it is non-algorithmic. This freedom is part of the creativity in the universe. It is our own creativity as humans."[84]

Unfortunately, Kaufmann went from here to make a highly questionable leap – from "creativity" to "God as the Universe of Creativity," as noted earlier. Nevertheless, the ongoing model-building and research on the mind/brain systems of Edelman, Kauffman and others have served to take the marvel of emergence from being just a subject of magic and myth into the realm of scientific investigations – with no loss of wonder at the scope, variety and beauty of emergence and life in any of its forms.

---

[84] Kaufmann, op. cit., p. 188.

Chapter 7

A New System of Belief

in the Context of Evolution and Time

Introduction

Why? Why? – Questions I use to ask my mother over and over again, so much so that she figured a stock reply: "Because Y has a long tail." Little did she know just how profound a response that is. For long-tailed probability distributions are fundamental to understanding so much, including distributions of city size, incomes, wealth and knowledge. We will return to their relevance to spirituality in due course.

The answers to "Y" in the case of a NSB are essentially similar to what is said to justify other religions – wondrous awe, depth, infinitude, mystery, holiness and so much that is sacred in nature. "Nature," in fact, is a key word here that helps to distinguish NSB from God-in-Heaven based belief systems.[85] Ongoing research on life forms and life processes, as well as cosmology, serves to enhance rather than reduce our sense of mystery. Marriage vows continue to be sacred, along with celebrations of birth and death. Life, in its infinitude of existing and potential forms, continues to be a source of

---

[85] But not from some other belief systems. See Chapters 19 - 21.

"wondrous awe." Life as God, a God of Life, might even help to advance the cause of world peace. Consider:

> "Awe makes spiritual and religious people feel a greater sense of oneness with others...In an analysis of 56 astronauts' memoirs, interviews and oral histories (they) appeared to experience increases in spirituality and universalism – that is, the belief in an interconnected humanity."[86]

Time

"Infinitude" – the knowledge and sense of infinity -- continues to be germane, certainly not a term to be used carelessly. For the growing knowledge base arising from research generates as many questions as answers. Research relevant to life ranges from the extremely small (nanometric – billionths of a meter) to the vastly large (billions of light years). As for the latter, Nobel Laureate physicist Freeman Dyson claims that "The universe is infinite in all directions." As for the former, micro-microscopic level, there has been a convergence with cosmology as quantum physics is found to be influential in biology as well as in cosmology.

On the side of life rather than physics, infinitude figures as we face the seemingly infinite variety of living things. The already great diversity of human life forms knows no limit, nor that of other life forms more generally. The enormous scope of life has been multiplied by the discovery of micro-biota in the human gut, along with a variety of other microbes and viruses. Any one of us can observe the wondrous variety of living things every day. "Lift up your eyes..." Observe the infinite variety of clouds. Then bring them down to treetops. See how leaves and needles seek the light. Imagine the dendrites of branching growth replicated in the root systems. No wonder that "The Tree of Life," extends both ways, all the way up and all the way down. Recall Fig. 10.

---

[86] Hutson, op. cit.

A NSB, like anything else, is defined not only by what it is but also by what it is not. Here, we recognize the Spiritual Naturalist Society [SNS] as an example of what NSB is not, even though, superficially it may appear to be a substitute. SNS advertises itself as:

> "an organization that **works to spread awareness of spiritual naturalism as a way of life,** develop its thought and practice, and help bring together like-minded practitioners in fellowship. Its motto is "happiness through compassion, reason, and practice." [87]

What's the difference? -- Simply that a NSB focuses on life and the time of our lives.[88] Spiritual naturalism is but one feature of a NSB, not a belief system in its own right. What's our "motto": God in Life.

The common denominator? -- Spiritual belief is properly and firmly rooted in natural rather than supernatural or "heavenly" spectra. Why again? Because life is not only immeasurably rich, deep and various in all dimensions, it is ever real, undeniable, obdurate, powerful and relentless always – in seeking, affirming and generating life in all dimensions. As noted in **SCIENTIFIC AMERICAN:**

> "Our planet contains a variety of extreme environments – from scalding thermal springs to highly pressurized ocean depths to salt deserts and sunless subterranean caves – and all of them harbor life forms."[89]

---

[87] This and more accessible at www.spiritualnaturalistsociety.org.

[88] "Time of our lives" is the title of a great Cole Porter song which continues with: "I never felt this way before." Another all-time classic is "**As Time Goes By** (words & music by Herman Huffeld).

[89] Riesch, Rudiger and M. Plath (2017), "**Pollution At the Limits,**" **SCIENTIFIC AMERICAN** (April), p. 57.

Death has no special meaning in this schema but for its necessity to make room for new life. Otherwise, death is anathema. There should be no death penalty. It amounts to us playing at God and with evil – the deliberate taking of human lives. Abortion should be further limited. Only all that generates, gestates, nurtures and advances the power of life should be honored. Not to do so is to give reign to the "dark side." Why?-- Ponder the downside of reliance upon supernatural or even some of the most heavenly forms [apparitions?].

One case underlines the dangers – the case of the Lundgren Cult. The self-styled prophet leading the Cult, Jeff Lundgren, claimed to hear the voice of God. He whipped his followers into fits expecting the "last days" – Christ's 2nd coming. Jeff displayed no sensitivity whatsoever during his trial for the murder of a whole family of two adults and three children. He coldly spent 5 hours speaking to the jury on his own behalf during his trial. He said: "I am a prophet, not a false prophet" and showed no remorse for the deaths. He claimed that their killing was justified because they did not see the "truth" (according to Jeff).

Spirituality

The Holy Spirit, the main legacy of Christianity, is also a core concept of the NSB. It is the spirit that can arise in anyone. The Christian model of God-in-Man is Christ. Similarly holy and prophetic models are revered by other religions. Incarnation is fundamental, yet devotees of the NSB may have no desire to celebrate Christmas. Why? – Because the Holy Spirit is incarnate in each and every human being to the extent that we recognize and cultivate the spirituality of our souls. Spirituality and soulfulness are immanent qualities emerging from the consciousness of the human brain and mind.[90] There is no reason to believe that they are given to us by a God we cannot know, let alone through a virgin birth.

Christ's birth may well have issued from a truly immaculate conception arising from a loving, sacred union of Joseph with Mary. There is no reason to

---

[90] See Chapters 22 and 25 for more.

call upon the intervention of angels. The incarnation of a holy spirit is accessible to every human being who tries to realize and nurture its incarnation in all aspects of his or her life. It takes conscious effort by each of us to recognize our spirituality and cultivate it with care such that even some of the so-called "secular" activities that occupy most of our lives are transformed and elevated by a holy spirit.[91]

The virgin birth is one of two key events that are fundamental to Christian belief. The other is the resurrection. Both are beliefs of the type cited earlier. To believers, neither can be proven unequivocally true or false even though scientific reasoning and evidence lead to conclusions that both are false. Other misleading inferences arise in similarly unscientific ways. How often do we attribute feelings arising from the holy spirit to the "heart" rather than "mind." The heart is neither a cognitive nor a deliberative organ.

The burgeoning field of research on the brain is revealing where various thoughts and feelings arise, including those which resonate with a spirit felt to be holy. These emanate from a soul immanent in human brains and minds, not the heart, even though some feelings may generate a higher pulse rate. Here again, neither the wish nor ability to live a holy life requires the presence of a personal God who, as Him, would in any event, at most, represent only ½ of humanity. Fortunately, and increasingly, we find the need to know herstory as well as history.

God-in-Man is realized through our innate potential spirituality plus concepts and ideals of what it means to be a good, fully developed human being. We can think of our God as being the summa par excellence of all the goodness and truth that we may strive to attain. We see this seeking after godlike qualities by all sorts of people these days. Hollywood stars are too often viewed as if they are mini-gods. Yet the hankering is misdirected and futile, chasing after false gods and graven images.

---

[91] Note that, from this point forward, we drop capitalization, for use of "Holy Spirit" insinuates that a "holy spirit" is accessible only to Christian believers.

Even in view of Hollywood's Moses and Jesus[92] we need to be reminded of the most fundamental among the ancient lessons from the Judeo-Christian tradition: There is but one God. The precise scope and meanings, specific implications and manifestations of that God under a NSB, however, will differ from person to person, by location and among cultures. Why would anyone be surprised by this variability when existing religions have branched, divided and varied in so many ways? Christianity, for example, has subdivided into 43,000 denominations.[93] The irreducible common denominator?: Life ever after.

The Life Force

As for movies, the one most suggestive of a NSB is Star Wars, in which the Life Force is so central. God is not mentioned. People say: "The Force be with you." Yoda embodies and expresses the importance of meditation and prayer leading to deep-self insights and other understandings. Obi Wan Kenobi is a saint like figure representing true courage and leadership. The scenes take place in the backdrop of an evolving universe. Our faith in a life-force represented by a God-of-Life is reinforced by the remarkable discoveries scientists have made to reveal the remarkable, breadth, variety and tenaciousness of life forms prevailing in the most incredibly adverse and hostile environments imaginable. Everywhere one looks, one is struck by the relentless persistence of the life force. The will to live is universal.

The scope of the life force, in fact, has grown along with documentation of its evolution and durability. Even unto the universe. Some cosmologists conceive of our universe as an incubator of life, as if the universe were a fertile and benign force for the gestation of life. It is, but only in locations that constitute

---

[92] **MOSES: The Lawgiver**: A TV series during 1974 & 1975 starring Burt Lancaster; **JESUS**, subject of many films; the major ones produced were released in 1979 and 1999.

[93] Pritchett, Gary (2017), Sermon given at Seafarers' Chapel, Shell Point Beach, Florida (April 30).

a tiny portion of its vastness. Overall, the universe is a furiously fast moving, ever changing, seething and violent place. Yet its very violence produces the basic elements that, combined and recombined, result in life forms. Explosions of supernovae spew carbon, iron and other elements that formed in their cores. Enormous clouds of gas float in and between galaxies and, under the influence of gravity, coalesce into new stars.

The universe is home to "superclusters" of galaxies, each of which is home to billions of stars.[94] Some of these have planets rotating around them. Astronomers have discovered hundreds of the latter that may host life in some form. As the numbers of such alternative worlds have mounted, the likelihood of finding living things in them has increased, too, until it now seems highly likely that life exists elsewhere in the universe.

When the latter is in fact confirmed, the impact will be as profound as when Copernicus' research revealed that we are not the center of our solar system. The God in heaven above may then be confirmed as the God of Life here on this and other planets. We are not alone in the universe. Not that we'll be able to visit the others to check in person. They're much too far away – at least thousands of light years distant.

Unlike major religions, NSB is consonant and resonant with a proven scientific theory, that of evolution. As a scientific concept, evolution could be falsified; but efforts to prove it wrong have failed while evidence supporting it continues to mount, year after year since the publication of Darwin's **ORIGIN of SPECIES** in 1859[95]. We have already made note of evolution proceeding in real time to generate new species. Whales are another example.[96] So, evolution is not just a concept of grand scope characterizing change-in the-

---

[94] For details, see Libeskind, Noam I. & R. Brent Tully (2016), "**Our Place in the Cosmos**", **SCIENTIFIC AMERICAN** (July)

[95] Darwin, Charles (1859), **ORIGIN of SPECIES**.

[96] Article in **SCIENCE** (April, 2017).

large. It pertains to all levels. As one author stated: "evolution assembled our intuitions to cope with very particular circumstances,"[97] an insight that will prove to be both pregnant and regnant.

National Public Radio (NPR) online observed that "An evolving system creates its own possibilities of becoming." Evolutionary patterns of development have also been observed in the development of institutions. Why not religions? NSB might be one point in evidence here, for one could view it as a late stage of evolution of the spiritual side of mankind or, at least, of the unfolding and democratization of the Christian world view. Here, incarnation is seen as the seminal concept, of God-in-Man.

The realization of goodness and truth is the challenge facing every person – a constant struggle inherent in human life, the resolution of which is up to us, individually and collectively. It is not something to be bequeathed by a higher power, but to be bestirred in each of us by the compelling potential of our spirituality. In these terms, NSB represents a higher level of consciousness, of truth-seeking-in-action-for-living. As in our democratic system, "We the People" are the power, for good or ill. It is we who create heaven or hell and all shades in between. These do not exist somewhere on high or way below. They are creations of our species here on earth, as the brutal history of the last century amply revealed.

Thus, NSB is also a higher evolutionary form in offering new or adapted systems of governance, including those of any religious organizations that may arise under its name. Moreover, as indicated earlier, a NSB induces personal/social responsibility at all levels that finally removes any dependence or deference to vestiges of royalty and other hierarchical, undemocratic forms. So, for example, "Lord of Lord," "King of Kings," high school class's Kings and Queens and other such references would be excised from hymns and schools. Religion would no longer be an anomaly out of sync

---

[97] Chatfield, Tom (2018),"**Everything is Relative,**" **NEWPHILOSOPHER, Issue** 22 (November).

with the spread of democracy and personal responsibility. It makes no sense to empower mankind spiritually while disempowering people otherwise.

A Higher Level of Consciousness

What is the higher level of consciousness to which a NSB can lay claim? It starts with two strong feelings:

1) a sharp, pervasive sense of the value of time overall, especially in light of the expected, limited span of a human lifetime; and of any time incorporated in the "necessity of now;" and
2) A sense of the sacred.

As for (1), most people might be tempted to say: "What else is new? Aren't we all living hurried lives?" Yes, but how often do we stop to step back from the hurried moment to say of it, with Faust: "Steht auf, du bist so schön"{Stop; you are so beautiful}[98] or to ask: "What time is this place?" Most don't get to ask such questions until it is too late and they are taken out of time by death.

(1), above, also raises a tough question from Einstein's theory of relativity respecting a measure of space-time and its context. Its measure, the value of space-time now, in the present, depends on past accomplishments, future expectations and a sense of place. Analysis and discussion of the relevance of relativity for human, social science must wait for another occasion, perhaps another book not yet written. I am convinced that Einstein's relativity will prove to be of great value in helping us to understand human relationships, more than those just physical.

It seems that the creation of space and time is more apparent in the human than in atomic frames. For example, when one loves his or her work, it seems that little time has passed, especially during concentrated, intensive bouts of

---

[98] Goethe, Wolfgang Von (1832), **FAUST**.

it. Of course, much more needs to be written on this. See Chapter 23 on "Work and Spirituality" for a start in the direction of "more."

What is key to both (1) and (2), above, is present awareness. It commands us to try to be both participant and observer. Of course, we are all participants in our own life, but observers, too? The dual stance requires training. No surprise here except that it's an Einsteinian world,[99] and most folks are still living in the space-time frames and coordinates of an earlier era, the Newtonian. One reason is that their religion(s) are still placed in the latter, and they show it even if they don't know it.

Earlier, it was stated that there is no necessary conflict between science and religion. Except that science is continually adapting and discovering while religion (relatively) stands pat. Which provides another reason; in fact, a quite compelling reason for a NSB. If a religion cannot incorporate key features of science into its belief system, then that religion is likely to either die or wallow in its stasis while science glories in its dynamic.

Another way to view incarnation is that it brings a "higher level of consciousness" down to earth. Why seek such a level "up there" via an unknowable God in an unknowable heaven when you can realize it in your everyday life in the context of an infinitely wondrous but increasingly knowable world in a Universe "infinite in all directions"? Every human being can at least sense the presence, depth, history, variety and mutability of life, also infinitely wondrous. The foundational features of human life, cited earlier, are not only well-known to virtually all; they are also readily sharable, as illustrated by conversations of women on family life.

It should not be such a big jump, as in established religions, to realize the sacred – those things that are truly so, and what they mean. What is sacred?

---

[99] The preface to the old song, "As Time Goes By" is seldom sung but can be quoted: "This day and age we're in gives cause for apprehension / with speed and new invention / And things like 4th dimension./ Yet we get a little weary of Mr. Einstein's theory..."

Candidates are whatever gives rise to sensations of wonder, marvel, mystery and awe. And though magnificent mountains and other incredible landscapes may first come to mind as embodiment of these three qualities, the primarily sacred realm overall is that of life among the living, day by day. Isn't it incredible that a sense of the sacred is aroused by physical things? – among us human beings, even the most carnal. The copulation of lower species of animals seems quite mechanistic. We have translated and transformed "carnal" into "sacred union," rightly so.

Part of our amazement unto this deeper sensibility is that so many natural wonders put human life into context of the deep history of our lives and planet, and these within the infinitely greater setting of the Universe. And we sense a paradox: That we, human beings, and our ability to sense and create beauty, have arisen out of the evolution of a physical universe, and our consciousness and understanding of this provide a richer sense of what is truly sacred than any sensations aroused by even the most magnificent religious cathedrals. Why, too? – Because of genomic codes that continue to create, recreate and evolve a great chain of being, at the peak of which is our human species and our multi-variate and multi-faceted minds and (hopefully) increasingly beautiful souls.

Here, our sense of the sacred begins to give rise to reverence. Birth, conception, gestation, the seasons, human love, devotion, rebirth and renewal transmute our sense of the sacred unto reverence (and vice-versa). Again, how much more real, meaningful and mutable for these being rooted in reality than in religious myths, rituals and speculations! And how much more meaningful in also being knowable, especially with a realization that the knowing, our growing knowledge, does not detract from wonder, awe and reverence. Rather, it pushes outward the scope of the latter while pushing forward the borderline between the known and unknown. So, we increasingly realize an overlap between science and religion – more than simply a lack of conflict. We can believe in miracles, too, especially as we see them manifest in our own lives.

Miracles and Surprises

After all, what is a miracle? It is an event full of wonder that we cannot explain. The world is full of them. The scope of the world of miracles may be circumscribed by one's level of education, but it is impossible for any but the most rotten cynic to dismiss the sources of wonder and awe. This is why so many can swear by the old saying "Save a life and you save a world."

One key mark of a miracle is that it's unexpected. A surprise. What would a life be without surprises? Like an "Aha" moment? It could be quickly forgotten and forever thereafter missing, but some live on in memory. How about a song arising and ongoing from a personal miracle – my meeting and falling in love with another senior citizen, Helen Livingston, late in life. The odds of such an encounter have been figured as 1 in 10,000. Nevertheless, Erica Carlson, Prof. of Physics & Astronomy at Purdue, emphasizes teaching by analogies that provide "Aha" moments of insight.[100]

The staying power of an NSB, however, doesn't rely on surprises, any more than does that of any religion. So much in life relies upon repetition, custom and habit. Like the 7th day of each week. This was originally set aside for contemplation, prayer and worship, but the day has been corrupted by the commercialization of our culture. But some time needs to be set aside for sanctity. And yet regularity and repetition of spiritual practices should not be allowed to disallow the element of surprise. How marvelous the moment we can experience each morning, for example, as witnesses to the rising sun! This and other regularities need to be transformed and sanctified as holy. They are moments to pause, stop and realize their life enhancing nature. Let us do our utmost to spiritually elevate the ordinary over life-ever-after.

---

[100] Carlson, Erica W, (2019), "Dive into the fundamental rules that govern physics and chemistry," **THE GREAT COURSES** (April 25), p. 6.

Life Ever After

After rejecting life-after-death at the outset as an aspect of, or basis for, a NSB, what does "life ever after" mean? It does not pertain to any individual, but rather, to the human species and, as well, to other species upon which the sustenance of human life depends. So, we can now return to discuss life-after-death as a collective and holistic concept. What is genealogy, after all, but stories of generation after generation, life "as it has been, is now and shall ever be, world without end"?[101] That is the only sufficient meaning of life ever after – that life continues on and on after those of us who are born to life as "it came to pass, not to stay,"[102] then to pass away. Such a perspective helps to enrich life's meaning, resting as it does on the realization of just how preciously brief and briefly precious is whatever allotment of time on this earth has been provided us.

This species-level perspective by no means denigrates the significance of the human individual. Rather, this significance is greater for all in light of any of our individual strivings to make the most of his or her life.[103] Those who do so to the utmost stand as role models, heroes, inspiring to the rest.[104] The best among us earn recognition to the extent we serve some community larger than

---

[101] For a wonderfully scientific-humanist account of human history emphasizing "generation after generation," see Jacob Bronowski's **ASCENT of MAN**, based on his pre-Discovery Channel TV series.

[102] The phrase in quotes is the title of a little gem of a book by Buckminster Fuller (1976).

[103] A significance denied by an alternative new system labelled "Syntheism." See Chapter 24.

[104] See, for example, Johnson, Paul (2007), **HEROES**: From Alexander the Great and Julius Caesar to Churchill and De Gaulle. New York: Harper Collins Publishers.

"#1". "Giving back" is an increasingly recognized, even popular motivator for people of all types and levels.

Our broader perspective may be expressed by historians who set forth human history in terms of great movements, cultures and happenings. Even so, a focus on the human individual points to the growing importance of family histories – as both contextural for individual development and rich sources of information illuminating whole cultures and changes in human behavior in the context of our times. [105]

History and Time

It is puzzling, therefore, to find that some, so-called "primitive" cultures value family history more than most "moderns." Male members of the pre-historical Akha tribe, for example, pride themselves on being able to recall male leaders and stories of their families going back 50 generations! By contrast, a friend of mine from a choral group in which we both sing the base line, can talk a blue streak telling stories of his family going back 4 generations, none of which have been written down. Myself, I take pleasure in simply saying: "I come from a long line...that my mother fell for."

Notwithstanding any history, a spiritual perspective on time must somehow devolve on the cusp of a moment -- to face "the necessity of now." For at any time, spirituality can be lost or found, maintained or cast aside, affirmed or negated. A cusp in time marks the intersect of past and future. It usually also marks a point at which decisions are made and actions taken. How can one maintain a spiritual frame of mind in the midst of the hurly-burly of life 'til death?

Life and a spirituality rooted in life, are ongoing, continuous. Time is not. Time is discontinuous and discrete. As Muller indicates, the measure and

---

[105] See Olson, Charles (1970), **A SPECIAL VIEW OF HISTORY**, another little gem of a book. It not only points to the importance of individual histories per se but those set in the context of locality and community.

meaning of "now" has long been a conundrum in the physics of time. He concludes:

> "By the flow of time, we mean the continual addition of new moments...in the continual creation of new nows."[106]

Here, "continual" does not mean "continuous." Perhaps a playwright wrote it better: "Though the moments quickly die / Greet them gaily as they fly."[107]

So, "now" is a cusp, a brief break in the fabric of space-time. Stop. Pause. Ask. What have I forgotten? What do I need? What should I do? These questions allow spirituality to insinuate itself if not already in mind; first, via consciousness, of mindfulness. Spirituality then flows with discretion once sparked by the indiscretion of the discrete cusp. Life overflows with such breaks. Spirituality steps in to bless moments with the continuity of a spirituality that can, if we allow the possibility – evoke or invoke our higher consciousness and bless even the most mundane moments with meaning and direction.

---

[106] Muller, Richard A.(2016), op. cit., starting with Chapter 3: "The Leaping of Now," especially p.304.

[107] Chorus of the young maidens from Gilbert & Sullivan's **PIRATES of PENSANZE.**

Chapter 8

Spirituality, Mind, Soul and Spiritual Discipline

Introduction

Where does spirituality reside in such a way that it is continually accessible to us at any time and over the full range of human experience, from the mundane (and presumably superficial) to the critical (life or death moments)? Remember, human life is a trilogy. Each of us has a body, mind and soul. Spirituality belongs to the latter, so it could be equated to soulfulness. And yet, the latter may be aimless without mindfulness. So, spirituality springs from the higher consciousness of mind. Therein lies the soul. Since all of any life that has a chance to endure the ravages of time is the highest and best of that to which we have been devoted, soulfully, we have here discovered the only sign of life in the hereafter with a real chance to live on. It is that which represents our soul.

Soulfulness

Our soulfulness, however, would not exist in the realm of a "heaven" other than that which we help to create here on earth. The memory of what we best represent is only retained over time by our family or other historians, depending on the scope of our life and the extent of our good works. John Steinbeck's character Ethan wonders: "Maybe it is Ellen (his daughter) who will carry and pass on whatever is immortal in me."[108] So do I wonder, too. According to the **OXFORD ENGLISH DICTIONARY**, "soul" is defined as at the outset: "The spiritual or immaterial part of a person, regarded as immortal." Our recasting soul at the center of mortal human life is nonetheless consistent with this definition as long as we keep in mind that immortality is historical, not heavenly.

The upsurge of research on the brain is in the process of discovering[109]] that the placement of the soul is in the mind. This roots spirituality in the body as well; that is, in things incarnate, even unto the glorification of the carnal and all things ordinary. I.e., there is an unbroken connection, via a variety of neural links, among all aspects of human life from the ordinary to the extraordinary. What is the nature of this connection? It's a self-similar pattern visible in nature at all levels and scales from low-to-high – the pattern that Benoit Mandelbrot called "fractal."[110] This essential self-similarity offers the possibility that soulfulness can be associated with any old thing. As it has, in countless households!

There's no limit to those material things to which we attach special meanings of a spiritual nature. Likewise, there's no limit to the applicability of fractals, in either direction, from the very small as seen in powerful microscopes, to the extremely large, as glimpsed through the most powerful telescopes

---

[108] Steinbeck, op. cit., p.192.

[109] For useful references, see Graves, Mark (2016), **MIND, BRAIN and the ELUSIVE GOAL: Human Systems of Cognitive Science and Religion.** New York: Routledge, Ashgate Science and Religion Series, or Moreira-Almeida, Alex, & F. Santana-Santos (eds., 2012), **EXPLORING FRONTIERS of the MIND-BRAIN RELATIONSHIP**, especially Chapter 6: "Neurological Correlates of Meditation & Mindfulness..

[110] See Mandlebrot, Benoit (1986), **THE FRACTAL STRUCTURE OF NATURE**, and Bearse, Peter (1999), "The Fractal Revolution," **THE ETHICAL STANDARD.**

scanning the universe. All the way up and all the way down. Richard Muller reported that the director of one of his research projects "devised an innovative way to transmit data over slow international networks...using the math of fractals to facilitate data compression."[111]

Like other segments of human life, spirituality has been allocated its quantum of space and time, mostly on Sunday according to locations and times that have been set, mostly by others, that have become accepted and habitual. A key point arising from earlier sections, however, is that, for its meaning to be assimilated, people need to be conscious of its continuity so that it can leaven and elevate life at any time. In other words, spirituality itself needs to become a good habit, too, but one in which the "way" brooks no barriers of time, space or occasion. Rather than a barrier, any occasion then becomes an opportunity for the insightful and transformative power of one's spirituality to be brought to bear.

A fractal paradigm can help to enable adults to fulfill the great potential of their spirituality. Its basis lies in any individual's ability to heighten his or her consciousness at the point of any cusp – any break in a routine pattern.[112] The first reaction should be one of heightened awareness, mindfulness, humility, empathy and care, not fast or simple reactions. Again: **Stop. Pause. Think** or meditate. Then ask: What do I need to obtain or do? What have I forgotten? If another is involved, think how to elicit his or her spirituality so to help bring forth "the better angels of our nature."[113]

---

[111] Muller, op. cit., p.154.

[112] My personal version is represented by a formula: $I/X \sim SP * 3\{AIM\}$; where I/X represent the edge of a cusp. I is start; X is end. SP= strategic pause; $A \sim$ alertness, attentiveness and/or awareness; $I \sim$ intermediacy, intensity or intimacy; $M \sim$ mind, mindfulness or mentality. Note that Soule's **DICTIONARY of ENGLISH SYNONYMS** specifies "soul, spirit..." as the first two synonyms of "mind."

[113] From the 2nd Inaugural Address of Abraham Lincoln.

Spiritual discipline begins with physical exercise. Phys-Ed instructors usually recommend that people perform an exercise regimen daily for at least half an hour. One's mind and spirit need exercising, too. So, we should recognize that one can be thinking, praying or wondering while working out. Then, it's easy to extend ½ hour to a whole hour, adding selective reading and spiritual reflection to the "work out." Which hour of any given day will vary from day to day and person to person depending on a number of factors well known. What's most important is that time be so dedicated for at least 5 days of every week.[114]

Steinbeck's Ethan reflects on waking up:

> "Coming out of sleep, I had the advantage of two worlds (as) the layered firmament of dream and the temporal fixtures of the mind awake...First, I referred to my remembered dreams...Then I explored the coming day for events...Next, I followed a practice learned from...Charley Edwards...he opened his mind and his heart to his family. He went over each one in turn...he caressed them and reassured them of his love. It was though he picked precious things one by one..."[115]

This passage reminds me of waking up with Elena, precious to me.

Especially heartening and soul-building are the many amputees among trees whose insistent life force is displayed by new branches and fresh, blowing leaves (fractal life forms – you can see the pattern of a tree in every leaf). The stories of human amputees also reveal great spirits at work; e.g., the story entitled "Standing Tall" in the 4/12/17 number of the **TALLAHASSEE DEMOCRAT**, on Devin Richards.

---

[114] A woman speaking recently on NPR recommended 3 hours of restful meditation each day, but a regular, mindful meditation of 1/2-1 hour per day would be OK for most.

[115] Steinbeck, John (1962), **WINTER of OUR DISCONTENT**, p.190.

Questions

Reflections are often prompted by questions. We all know the old saying: "If you don't ask the right questions, you don't have a snowball's chance in hell of finding the right answers." Questions and answers have an inevitable way of differing among people, sooner or later (as they should). What's a good set of starters? – questions that reflect on our vulnerability and defensiveness, those that probe towards deeper meanings, and some that ask: "Who am I? – the answer to which may provide the deepest and most salient answers of all."

Try these:

- Do I have at least one friend with whom I can talk about the serious questions of life that we share?
- Do I have a spiritual side to my life? If so, what arouses it? If not, why not? What kind of life am I trying to build for myself and significant others? Is there any place or value for spirituality in that picture?
- Who do I love and who loves me? What are the qualities of my close relationships and how can I elevate them? How much love do I bring to my relationships with others?
- How is my love of life expressed in my relationships with others?
- How do I mark my love of life at the beginning and end of each day?

What do such questions have to do with spirituality? Note that the questions have to do with one's self-understanding and realization of the qualities of life among the living, along with remembrances of those whose life and love have been influential in making us who we are. For what is spirituality if not one's ability to reflect and act upon what is most important to living a good life? Spirituality makes us aware of the dangers of letting ourselves get caught up in, sometimes even overwhelmed by, the messy minutia of daily living. It's what enables us to step back and see things from a new angle, using a different set of lenses. Even to speak messages at a higher level.

Spirituality and Everyday Life

Yet, we should not see a once a day meditational moment as sufficient to either the need or challenge of our spiritual natures. Every cusp, break or pause in our day-to-day routines provides, if not a special need, then an opportunity to bring the power and revelation of spirituality potentially to bear; i.e., to invoke our higher and better natures. For example, hunger may signal the need for food at lunch, but we can and should use the opportunity to entertain a higher thirst – for spiritual moments that enable and empower us to recall the higher aims we would like to serve.

Let us put our work into that more spiritual context; like, a blessing before a meal or quiet thoughts while making or serving it. Some moments at work, home or anywhere during any given day may have been stressful. Thus, our spirituality is a call for patience, understanding, grace and forgiveness. Any church worth its salt should realize and provide training to enable folks to engage their spirituality at any moment when the four qualities just cited are called for. Too often, there are conflicts in either home or work. Then spirituality must enter as a call for reflection or meditation, for a moment of peace.[116]

Our spirit should never stand aside from any aspect of life as if it were only accessible by way of a higher-level figure like a priest or bishop. No, the holy spirit is ever alive and near to us – the spiritual version of a public good accessible to all, anytime. It is the spirit of the Reformation, which democratized religion by infusing it with the spirit of "We the People" – the first three words of our Constitution – contrary to the authority of the priesthood. Thus, religion became a driver of democracy.

Democratic movements, in turn, helped to focus and reinforce people's attention on the individuality of conscience informed by the universality of the human holy spirit. The spirit of "We the People" was thereby strengthened. Some may be wont to deprecate the beliefs of our Founders because some of them were 'merely' Deists. They might thereby be considered flabby religious believers. But the spirit of "We the People" cannot be denied, especially if guided by men like Thomas Jefferson.

---

[116] Then an old song may flood into memory, the opening line of which is: "Let there be peace on earth and let it begin with me..."

How do we come to recognize and cultivate the spiritual side of human nature? Traditionally, this starts with the rite of baptism. This is a fine feature of conventional religion in that it informs the guardians of a newborn as to the child's potential human spirituality and engages them to share responsibility for training the child in spirituality-building exercises. Nevertheless, years may pass before a child comes to recognize, appreciate and train his or her own spirituality. This suggests that a joyous event might be a later-in-life re-baptism when a young man or woman, fully conscious of his or her spirituality, joins with family and friends to celebrate the recognition.

In the meantime, a new form of religious education should be publicly recognized as a necessary and important, nonsectarian aspect of public education.[117] After all, spirituality flows from and enables the highest and deepest expressions of human life. A question here remains, however: Do we want a NSB to be institutionalized?-- reified? Probably not, but we need to return to the question sooner or later.

---

[117] Here we need to confront the all-to-frequent misinterpretations of the 1st Amendment to our U.S. Constitution regarding church and state, which opens "Congress shall make no law respecting an establishment of religion". This implies that what is being proposed here should not be declared un-Constitutional. Congress would have no role in its establishment and development.

Chapter 9

A New System of Belief and Servant Leadership

Introduction

The incarnation expressed by God-in-Man is best expressed by servanthood; better yet, the servant leader.[118] The concept is powerful. It shows how spiritual leadership empowers followers and enables them to be leaders, too. First, consider Sims perspective:

> "At its base, servant leadership is an attribute of the soul, a spiritual gift...it is congruent with the relational way things work in the ongoing life of the universe."[119]

---

[118] The discussion on this topic draws greatly from two sources: (1) Sims, Bennett J. (1997), **SERVANTHOOD: Leadership for the Third Millennium**. Boston: Cowley Publications, and (2) Palmer, Parker (1976), "Servant Leadership," unpublished pamphlet, and (1980), **THE PROMISE of PARADOX.**

[119] Sims, op .cit., p.29

Servant Leadership

Servant leadership, moreover, is as important to the NSB as to Christianity and other faiths. The most important figure best representing both its essence and practice is Christ himself. The truth of servanthood is paradoxical. Sims writes: "Jesus reveals a way of life, not simply a way of being religious...Paradox will always need incarnation..."[120] For the whole truth of a paradox lies at two poles, each of which is true but opposite of the other. Here, at one pole is "servant"; at the other, "leader." One low, one high; one on top; one subservient. One cannot be a true leader without knowing how to best serve those who might be led.

Whenever I ran for public office, my motto was: "To Help and to Lead." These go together. I aimed to be a servant leader; however, I hadn't yet realized the power of spirituality. Two other paradoxical poles had to be squared away: Body and Spirit; Perfection and Imperfection. The truth of the 1st pair is resolved by recognizing that spirit and spirituality are incarnate in the human body and represent the possibility of its highest aspiration. The truth of the 2nd is the admission that if Christ represents perfection, we ordinary human beings are imperfect, and that which saves us is the grace of understanding and forgiveness. Parker Palmer wrote:

> "Perhaps contradictions are not impediments to the spiritual life but an integral part of it. Through them, we may learn that the power for life comes from God..." (here, the God of Life)[121].

Servant leaders show self-understanding is more important than self-promotion. They openly acknowledge their own failings. Sims sums up the basic features of servant leadership:

---

[120] Sims, op. cit., p. 9 and 14.

[121] Palmer, Parker (1980), **THE PROMISE of PARADOX.**

"making room for others, truthfulness, empowerment, the exchange (or sharing) of power rather than control, a belief in grace and forgiveness...".[122]

It is also important to view servanthood as an integral feature of an evolving universe that has been the generator and gestator of life. We don't have to invent a "God" and "Heaven" to find something great outside of ourselves to revere. The sources of awe, wonder and reverence are all around us, day and night, with the sun, our nearest star, by day, and hundreds of other stars visible on a clear night. The latter, we learn, are but a miniscule sample of millions of stars in our galaxy, one of countless galaxies throughout the universe. Then we see our planet – a beautiful blue orb, floating in the darkness of outer space.

Scientists predict life elsewhere in the universe. It has not yet been discovered. It will be. These images overwhelm our sensibility. Wow! Life is a precious miracle, and so may be our precious planet earth. The images of life are evocative. It is but a short leap to an aroused spirituality that translates precious to sacred. Yes. Life is sacred at all levels, from the individual to the universe, amplified by the realization that our God is Life.

Sims also helps us to see how science links to spirituality through servanthood. He wrote that servanthood:

"is the most enduring form of power, because it is congruent with the way relational things work in the ongoing life of the universe. We know from the quantum insights of postmodern science that everything in creation interconnects. The totality of the created order is a kind of hidden but immensely real network of interrelation."[123]

---

[122] Sims, op. cit., p.37.

[123] This is the focus of a proposed new religion called "Syntheism," supposedly a competitive NSB, but not really. See Chapter 24.

So, indeed, we are servants of life; first, in ourselves; then to others and to mother earth. Many scientists who have long studied our earth home – its origins, geology, atmosphere, history and life-forms – have come to label it "Gaia". This is a Latin term for an organic, life-generating and self-sustaining world – earth as a living organism. I share this view, so much so that I urge people to chant with me "GAIAM!" – a combination of "Gaia" and "I am." As residents of a vibrant, living world that could become a deserted desert home for human life if we do not care for it, each of us needs to take some responsibility for the caring along with others. This must be; in fact, it would be the greatest undertaking of care in human history. The only version of leadership and servanthood up to the task is servant leadership.

Religion vs. Spirituality

Challenges to existing systems always seem to meet a number of presumably insuperable barriers, even more so in this case since the beliefs in question have prevailed for millennia. Yet, we live in a time when "The only thing that does not change is the will to change."[124] Also, existing religions do not command the same hold and devotion of people seen in past decades. Their hold seems to be slipping towards more lip-service and less devotion. If "devotion" can be measured by regular church attendance, consider the following three indicators:

- For decades, less than half of people polled have claimed to attend church services weekly, but research has indicated that less than 20% actually do so.
- Only 27% of millennials, say they attend religious services weekly.
- Between 2007 & 2014, there was a 3.7% decline in weekly church attendance.[125]

---

[124] Olson, Charles (1960), **MAXIMUS POEMS**, New York: Corinth..

[125] From "3 Important Church Attendance Statistics..." as reported by Stretch Internet [www.stretchinternet.com].

Nevertheless, it appears as if: (1) more people have a greater awareness of their spirituality, and (2) Feel a need for a belief system that will help them better address the challenges facing human life in this century and anon.

One aspect of belief already noted is a common denominator among religions and other spiritual practices since ancient times: If there is a God, there is but one. So, in fact, much of the new system this book is suggesting could be adapted for use by existing religions, thus ameliorating direct conflicts. As indicated earlier, the new system is evolutionary even though it might well be considered revolutionary.

Major existing belief systems also envision a God of life. The challenge that any belief system needs to address in this century; indeed, right NOW, is how the innate spirituality of our species can become a more powerful and pervasive influence in our lives at all levels in the face of growing fears and uncertainties. From now being a weak reed, our spirit needs to become a bulwark and strong guide in all our doings.

Every one of us should be viewed as, and seek to really become, a servant leader. The fears we face in these times – so fraught with violence and uncertainty – call for servant leaders. Recall Sims on Servanthood. He draws on his Christian belief, as have Palmer and others writing on the topic. Nevertheless, servant leadership has not taken off within the Christian community. Here, with a NSB, it is central. Why do we have to continue to try to embellish our spirit by way of a heavenly God made-up on myth, when the higher order life force that our spirit represents needs to be placed at the center of our lives, not at the periphery? The center is our life-in-action here on earth. Every day in the life of is a life in the day of. At age 78, I feel this intensely.

Our belief system needs to raise us up from fear to exaltation. Fear is the major hurdle to be surmounted on the path to servant leadership. Again, Sims: "Fear is the operative emotion in all leadership that fails, chiefly fear to know and be oneself."[126] To which we can add: Fear of openness which is driven by

---

[126] Sims, op. cit., p.32

a dog-eat-dog competitive culture. We fear any openness will give a competitor an edge to defeat us. We are all vulnerable creatures.

Servant leadership, at once open to and empowering of others, takes the edge off the fear that drives closure. We are reminded of one of the sayings of the great political philosopher, Karl Popper, who wrote: "The greatest enemy of an open society is a closed mind." Fear and reactive closure are destructive at all levels of relationships, from the interpersonal to the international.

Beyond, but still bound up with our individual fears, are those infecting society-at-large because of the inability of elected officials and governments to resolve serious public problems. These fears taint our democracy. There are temptations to fall back on: tighter, more rigid control systems, or turns to authoritarian demagogues. We also see countless examples of prayers to a supernatural "God" that are not "answered". Bad things continue to happen. They are rationalized by statements that "God has a plan" and "Whatever will be, will be." These are abdications to fatefulness. The spread of servant leadership will enable us to come to grips with both our fears and most problematic issues by facing them with stronger spirits grounded in the reality and power of life.

If each of us strives, each day, to reach towards servant leadership and infuse our acts with our spirituality, we will do much to dispel fear, build trust, and realize truthfulness. Sims book is slim, but full of useful reminders of how each of us can help build a good society. To wit:

> "The ability to empower (others) is what makes great leadership a servanthood; it awakens the slumbering power in the souls of others...this is always the quiet work of the holy spirit...the function of leadership is to awaken trust in the spirit (&) to open people to (its) presence within themselves and one another...To challenge people to give is to do them a favor – the favor of acting out their highest selves..."

Hear this as if listening to Bach's great Christmas Oratorio: The Christian model is still OK, all the more so if shorn of its unsupportable, supernatural trappings. It is Christ Jesus. The aura is enhanced by his humanity, well short of our presumption of super-natural godliness. Christ is the original Christian servant leader. Servant: washing the feet of incredulous disciples. Leader: the Sermon on the Mount. This neither says nor implies anything that would diminish the stature of servant leaders in other faiths, such as Buddha, Lao Tzu or Gandhi.

To the contrary, at some point in the evolution of our higher consciousness and practice of our spirituality – our enhanced human nature – we can well imagine a global synthesis of servant leader qualities. Then we might see how some shortcomings of Christianity can be recognized and surmounted. Recall, for example, Christ's final words from the Cross: "Father, forgive them for they know not what they do." But what if evildoers do know what they do and keep on doing it, anyway?

Many say Christ was a radical fellow. Yes, unequivocally, for Truth and against all forms of falsehood. He overturned the tables of Philistines trading money in the Temple. He opposed the conventional wisdom of his time, offering a New Testament. Above all, he spoke and acted for the least among us, infuriating the nabobs and powers that be of his time. His most radical warning? – "The last shall be first, and the first, last." Not only in his person but in his words and acts were the spiritual depths of humanity made real – God-in-Man -- with grace, forgiveness, and an abiding sense of the sacred.

Subtracting the supernatural from the life of Christ in no way detracts from the profound value of his spiritual servant leadership. "The world is also richer when it declines to abide by comforting formulas."[127] Christ's significance as a real person embodying God-in-Man has been acknowledged many ways -- in popular culture, too, especially as "Jesus Christ: Superstar" in the 1973 movie of the same name.

---

[127] Remark of Michael Kimmelman (2005) in his commentary on the work of the artist Pierre Bonnard, in **THE ACCIDENTAL MASTERPIECE: On the Art of Life and Vice Versa.** New York: Penguin Books.

The Supernatural: Source of the Dark-Side

After all, the incarnation is what fundamentally distinguishes the New Testament from the old. What NSB calls for, however, is a new New Testament. The old New Testament needs editing and pruning. Why? Because there is far too much use of two types of language that:

> (1) Draws from old, undemocratic regimes, like "King of Kings"; and

> (2) Treats the supernatural – virgin birth and resurrection of the body – as real.

There is also the strange supernaturalism of the Book of Revelation, which many commentators feel does not even belong in the New Testament. Our spirituality is not grounded on, nor need it rely upon, outrageously unbelievable and unsupportable supernatural claims. The latter include beliefs that are foreign to God-in-Man, such as those that promote witchcraft and other cults of darkness and death. Are we to be judged by the company we keep, or do we distance ourselves from such company?

The fundamental problem with the supernatural is that it is contrary to the God-of-Life. Many supernatural brands love to consort with death. Is it possible that one reason Christianity is grounded on the resurrection is that people have been unable to confront "corruption" after death? One cannot mix the healthy with the sickly and expect to come out well or whole. In the opera, Wozzeck exclaims: "Man ist ein Abgrund." The latter, almost untranslatable, connotes a complex of depths, all unfathomable, as is the human soul.[128] But human spiritual depth plies the infinities of heights as well. We do not need to invoke supernatural events or spirits to rise to the heights. Let us "lift up our eyes" to the heavens, yes, but quickly bring them down to treetops and the ground to see, revere and nurture the beautiful plenitude of life all around us.

---

[128] See, for example, Marilynne Robinson's "**Humanism, Science, and the Radical Expansion of the Possible: Why we shouldn't let neuroscience banish mystery from human life**," in THE NATION (Oct. 22, 2007)

An essential question to be addressed here is how our behaviors serve to create either virtuous or vicious circles. Both reveal some kind of addiction, the former, good; the latter, evil. Human spirituality, devoted to light and life, once recognized and infused in our lives with a gentle discipline, is a source of virtuous cycles. Devotion to supernatural myths, false gods and graven images is a source of vicious circles that embrace darkness over light and death over life. One set is constructively procreative of life, light (and love); the other, destructive of these. Vicious circles are named so because they represent races to the bottom -- addictive behavior that is self- and other-destructive because self-amplifying in negative directions. Virtuous circles are just the opposite, amplifying positivity. As the old union song asks: "Which side are you on; which side are you on...?" Our spirituality, our souls, have the potential of becoming a virtuous addiction, both raising and deepening our soulfulness and human goodness.

Sacred Places and Practices

There is a raison d'etre for churches, temples and the like. They provide time and space for us to realize and exercise our spirituality. For many, especially those who are struggling with two or three jobs plus families – just to get along – they may be the only such sites. They are important. Trinity Episcopal Church in Apalachicola Florida is one such, where "Holiness resides in this place forever." Where many churches fall short, however, is in two areas: outreach and crosstalk.

"Outreach" means ability to reach outside of the institution and the community it serves. "Crosstalk" means the cultivation of conversations with those who do not share our views. Clearly, the two go together. There is no crosstalk without outreach, and vice-versa. The shortcomings in these are not limited to religious institutions; they infect our society and its other institutions at-large. Thus, here is an area where sharing of our soulfulness can help to transform organizations of all types.

System-wide transformations are the challenge of our age. It is imperative that we adopt a NSB that girds and supports us for the battles that must be fought. Outreach and crosstalk will both broaden the base of struggle and bring us to the battles' edge, but they do not suffice to win victories. Victories worthy of the name are first won within, starting with individual souls that join together into groups. While the latter are building new organization and institutions, individuals are working within workplaces and other organizations of affinity or membership.

The major guidelines of organizational transformation are two: Openness and Learning. Organizations from new to old need to be transformed into learning organizations guided by openness, democratic self-governance, and servant leadership. See the work of Peter Senge for more.[129] At the national level, cross-cutting demands for reforms of all types need to be faced in the context of a new Constitutional Convention [CC] convened with a broad mandate for transformation of our political and federal systems. Though objections to such a broad-based, broad purposed CC are legion, it is time to face the fact that those opposed to such a gathering are primarily afraid of "We the People."

Though "spirit" may be appreciated in most spheres of human activity, there are both needs and opportunities to broaden and deepen its quality. Already familiar, for example, is the spirit of democracy, of work, of sports teams, of gatherings, et al. Practices to invoke and/or strengthen such spirits include blessings, incantations, inspiring passages of music, silent prayers, personal testimonies and symbolic displays. All too often, however, these become proforma expressions led by the SO/SO [same old/ same old] folks.

One example, especially troubling, lies in the singing of our national anthem. We have come to rely on soloists, thus denying both the responsibility and power of our own voices. Why blame Fergie for slipping up with her version of the anthem when most of us hardly sing it at all, can't remember the words,

---

[129] Senge, Peter (1994), **THE FIFTH DISCIPLINE FIELDBOOK: Strategies and Tools for Building a LEARNING ORGANIZATION**. New York: Doubleday.

and are all to willing to pass the buck to somebody else?[130] It is OUR voice! Sing it with heart and soul!

Broadening participation in the our "spirit" offerings may serve to help deepen them as well. Broadening helps to share the supposed "burden" of a self-governing system. In Shell Point, Florida, for example, some folks complained about the need to clean up after July 4th fireworks. An online response to the complainers remarked: "If you don't want to clean up, perhaps you'd better build your house in Russia."

The latter paragraph especially applies to the spirit of American democracy. This has been undermined, corrupted and soiled by hyper partisanship and big-money politics. The spirit, as represented by "Vox populi" has been both distorted and little heard, as revealed by the 2015 Princeton study cited earlier. Here, too, a broader, more spiritual rendering is needed, one grounded upon the prime idea that animated the foundation of our democratic republic. This is ever a work-in-progress: The notion that we can create a society in which every individual has an equal opportunity to develop and fulfill his or her unique capability and contribution to that society. This is the real meaning of the only nation based on an idea, one that honors individuality – the identity and integrity of individual souls.[131] The American Dream – the great American experiment -- is a spiritual ethos with world-wide implications.

Openness and Opportunity

This touches on what may be the most important aspect of equality – of opportunity. This cannot be taken for granted, but there are two others that should be recognized as indisputably equal – souls and citizens. The latter, in a just society, are all equal before the law. Spirituality of souls and

---

[130] Reference here is to the "Fergie" incident as reported by national news outlets on February 18-20, 2018.

[131] Which, again, an alternative new "religion", Syntheism, does not. See Chapter 24.

soulfulness should be regarded as prime markers of equality in any system. We come to realize this to the extent that we interact with loved ones with whom we can share intimate thoughts openly.

Openness is unequally distributed and too often unrealizable, but we can and should assume that each person we encounter has a soul that can be touched and brought forth. In other words, the holy spirit and spirituality should be viewed as a public good. My sharing of soulful thoughts with you in no way detracts from the value of your sharing such with me or others. Rather the opposite, my soulfulness may be enriched by yours, and vice-versa. We are better together. Do not look for equality of mind and body. Such a search is fruitless. That of soul and matters of the spirit are fundamental and attainable.

Once aware of one's own soulfulness, we start to see it all around us among unexpected people and places. The Seniors' Center in Apalachicola where I work, for example, has struck me with soulful folks and images. Joe, Sharon and John, for example; and the art of amateur painters adorning the walls of the dining hall. Another example was revealed by watching an auto repairman go about his work with verve and care even though the task at hand was ordinary in the scope of car service – changing a vehicle's [my old truck's] oil. He further took the time to carefully explain to me what the truck needed in response to possible problems that he had noticed. His interactions with a friend and supplier also revealed a spirit more than superficial. He loved his work, and the love showed. See Chapter 22 for more on "Spirituality and Work."

A more personal example came to me through the medium of popular music via a monthly magazine; that of Leonard Cohen, a soulful example of a popular performer and composer. He was featured in "How the Light Gets In," taking off from one of his anthems.[132] It's like his whole life was spent in search of a life fully soulful. A Jew, he became an ordained monk in a Buddhist monastery. His soul-brother, Bob Dylan, spoke of his melodies,

---

[132] See the article on Cohen by Remnick, David (2016) in **THE NEW YORKER** (October 17).

"which...are his greatest genius."[133] On one of his last tours, "the audience started singing to Cohen as if to inspire him..." One of his qualities was to:

> "Dig in deeper, whatever it was...Cohen has been a spiritual seeker...(he) reads deeply in...the Zohar, the principal text of Jewish mysticism; the Hebrew Bible; and the Buddhist texts...the Gnostic Gospels, Lurianic Kabbalah, books of Hindu philosophy, Carl Jung's "Answer to Job," and Gershom Scholem's biography of Sabbati Sevi...a self-proclaimed Messiah...Anything, Roman Catholicism, Buddhism, LSD; I'm for anything that works."[134]

Spiritual hunger, searching and candor: That works as we search for a NSB that really works for us as any faith in life-after-death does not. As we move forward with our search, recall the chorus from one of Cohen's songs, "Anthem:

> "Ring the bells that still can ring
> Forget your perfect offering
> There is a crack in everything
> That's how the light gets in."

And as Georges Bataille wrote: "Everything is profoundly cracked." Yet, Cohen's life, recently over at 82, also shows how spirituality enriches and bridges gaps to and from life-individual and life-communal. He loved both, deeply.

Organizations and Institutions

OK; so spirituality inspires and enriches the lives of individuals and small communities. What about organizations and institutions? No less so. Because organizations and institutions embrace and represent larger numbers of

---

[133] Remnick, op.cit., p.51.

[134] Remnick, p.53.

people, spirituality becomes even more important to generate and cultivate. There are many who already celebrate their "spirit". These include scouting troops and Masonic, fraternal, veterans' and Rotary clubs as well as patently religious organizations. We hear of the spirit of Rotary, for example, grounded on brotherhood and their motto "Service Above Self." Boy Scouts pledge to be "reverent" among other qualities.

And yet, explicit cultivation of spirituality seems quite limited, primarily to religious groups, and hardly enough, even among them. It should be much more widespread, in recognition of the higher-level capacities of the human mind, and the demonstrated depth of the human spirit. Most organizations are shy of such cultivation. Promotion of spirituality may seem to be relegated to "holy rollers" or "hare krishnas." Building up spirit may seem limited to cheer leaders with pom-poms, commercial boosterism or snake-oil salesmen. But the depth and richness of the human spirit is not to be underestimated or stereotyped. It has been too long in evidence – for millennia, across all regions and cultures of the world. For us as a species, the matter at issue, our greatest challenge, is no less than moving humanity to the higher levels of consciousness, spirituality, inspiration and creativity of which we know that we are capable.

It's not as if we do not have enough trials, initiatives and experiments in this area whose experience provides ample fodder upon which we can spiritually feed and grow. There is a long history of American utopia, including many failures from which we can and should learn. There are many experiments, especially well documented from the '60's, by those who have been seeking the roads to higher levels of consciousness.[135] We have gobs of experience

---

[135] See, for example, Kaplan, Geoff (2013), **POWER TO THE PEOPLE: The Graphic Design of the Radical Press and the Rise of the Counterculture**, 1964-1974. Chicago: University of Chicago Press.

with modes of meditation, studies of dreams, exhibits of the human spirit in action, Yoga, Zen and other spiritual quests.[136]

The American spiritual quest, therefore, is unlimited in both its variety and yet unrealized potential. Yet, for the latter to be realized, the bottom must be recognized, as it has been in **STAR WARS** "dark-side" and countless writings on human nature. All of us should repeat, with Wozzeck, "Man is ein Abgrund." The horror of the negative side of the human race was fully demonstrated in the last century. Nevertheless, our nature as a species is upward of zero, not progressively downward.

The science of cosmology continues to generate incredible revelations of awe, truth, beauty and wonder. We do not need to return to supernatural myths or imaginings. Reality is far richer than fantasy. The higher reaches of the human mind and spirit are limitless, and each of us can add at least some iota to their realization and fulfillment.

Raise Each Other Up

Though the spiritual search is limitless, we each and all need to deal with the facts of our temporal, situational and contextual limits daily. So, what is to be done? Are we to be always trapped in a quandary between our limitless hopes and the limits that we ever seem to be "inside of"?[137] We need to raise each other up. This is the true work of the spirit. This is what sustains our hopes, individually and collectively.

There are ways. First, we each need to be increasingly aware of our mutuality – the interdependence of personal destinies and collective progress. But we each need to start with little steps. First, look in the mirror. Assess the state of

---

[136] For many of these, see Anderson, Marianne, & Louis M. Savary (1972), **PASSAGES: A Guide for Pilgrims of the Mind**. New York: Harper and Row Publishers.

[137] Here again recalling the line of Charles Olson quoted earlier.

one's own spirit. Seek positivity. You can't begin to raise another up if your mood is mostly down -- moody or negative -- and your mind closed. Moods and attitudes are addictive. We infect and affect each other psychologically as well as physically.

Almost every morning, for example, I am struck by the effervescent ebullience of Carrabelle, Florida's United States Postal Service's postmistress Connie when I go to pick up my mail. She is unfailingly upbeat, cheerful and helpful to all. As I said to her one morning, "you light our lives." Another friend, June, is just the opposite. She has let herself be dragged down by alienation from her children and the fact that she has not been able to see her grandchildren. This situation is so troubling that I deigned to offer some advice: "Write them a letter that opens with: "I forgive you; please forgive me. Let us have a new beginning." I have also tried to raise her up by never failing to recognize and compliment her on her strengths and accomplishments. She is a Christian servant-leader. May she act in the spirit of Christ, represented by the crosses she wears around her neck. Myself, I will pray for her rather than pray to Jesus that he intervene to help her. For the spirit of Jesus is real to the extent that it lives on. It does not rest on his resurrection or any childish presumption that he is in "heaven" to save us from ourselves or others.

Look at the relationships that you already have or you would like to have. Starting with friends, ask: How can I raise them up, spiritually and positively, with depth and substance, not superficially? Ask them. Don't act like a Jesus-freak who may say: 'Let me introduce you to Jesus so we can pray to him together.' Nor should we accept the usual cheerful exchange of greetings if someone looks troubled. Ask: "How are you really? Can I help? Talk to me." Self-help might also make a difference.

The do-it-yourself mood enhancement market has been booming for at least two generations since Norman Vincent Peale's **THE POWER OF POSITIVE THINKING** was published. The latest version was recently announced on NPR: "Ways to generate optimism." But the facile nostrums, hype and superficiality of much of the self-help approach have often been apparent. Nevertheless, don't be cynical about simple ways. As the song "Simplicity" says: "Tis a gift to be simple; 'tis a gift to be free; 'tis a gift to come 'round where we want to be..." So, again and again, let us start with simple steps, keeping in mind that each human being we encounter has a soul to be awakened and raised up.

Distractions and Discontinuities

Our souls seek some meaningful continuity in our lives and yet, we are living in an age of continuous discontinuity, marked by dozens of disparate "cusps" calling for our attention each day. The Wall St. market model threatens to overcome us all. It is the market trader's model, facing hundreds of stocks and executing millions of transactions each day. The Fractal Paradigm must be brought into play: Stop, Pause; think, meditate or pray, if only for a moment before proceeding with any transaction of any day. The spirit can enter and should be brought to bear, else much of potential meaning of the moment may be lost.

Frequent distraction is not only disconcerting, it is destructive of any sense of value or meaning. We need to recall the fundamental roots of a life of matter and meaning – that we pause at least a few times each day to provide moments of space for our spirituality to enter in, at least, and possibly to inform and enlighten us and others. See Chapter 23 for more.

Mindful meditation is an activity open to all. It offers seven scientifically proven benefits:[138]

- Reduction of anxiety;
- Feeling younger;
- Less deeply rooted biases [otherwise called "sunk costs"] or less closure towards others and more openness;
- Less likelihood of depression;
- Less dissatisfaction with oneself and one's body;
- Improved cognition; and last but by no means least...

---

[138] Source: Langer, Ellen (1989), **MINDFULNESS. Reading**, MA: Addison-Wesley Publishers.

- Reduced distractions.

We have been meditating on our God – the God-of-Life, not the God of Life-after-death. For life is a binary (0,1) proposition – We are either alive (1) or dead (0). Life is time; time is Life. So, every morning let us celebrate the fact that we can awaken to a new day, feeling the life force still coursing within us. We should also awaken with a sense of delight that we are among other living things – the earth, the sea, trees and grasses, other human beings and other living things. The NSB "can affect the way we heal."[139] Nevertheless, let us realize that our life force is also two-sided. It can serve to honor, embellish, nurture and enrich life, or honor the forces of death and destruction. Recall the old song: "Let there be peace on earth and let it begin with me."

Let us not overestimate the power of the forces of life over death. Nor underestimate the power of the forces of death over life. The number of the latter may exceed those of the former. They are pervasive. Too often, they lie within us, as we harbor hates left over from past adversarial encounters, et al. Love and forgiveness are the only antidotes to destructive and warlike behavior. They begin with love of self and love of life. Feeling this deeply, we can fully and rightly honor and exhibit love of self, each of us, as unique carriers of the life force with soul. Only then can we truly love others as also unique contributors to life on earth. Finally, our love extends to our precious planet, the Gaia of mother earth. GAIAM!

Life in the Universe

We are all life forms living with others on a precious blue orb floating in the vast space of a universe that, overall, appears to be quite unfriendly to life. The universe exhibits all the most violent, fundamentally, death-dealing

---

[139] Vance, Erik (2017), Mind Over Matter," **NATIONAL GEOGRAPHIC** (December, p.30).

forces. The universe also seems to be entropic[140] while life is anti-entropic. Why? Because entropy represents randomness, confusion, disorder and disarray. And yet, anti-entropic life-giving forces are not universal; they are localized. "Life represents a local decrease in entropy. Such local decreases are the source of expanded life and civilization."[141]

From the vast, cosmological viewpoint of "multiverse" theorists, our universe appears as a localized incubator of life. We have seen how scientists point to the fine precision of parameters essential for the generation and maintenance of life that prevail in our universe. Lee Smolin estimates crudely that "the constants must be tuned to within 1 divided by 10 to the 27th power to be within range of creating a life-friendly universe."[142] Under the heading of "God plays dice," some theorists state that our universe, relative to innumerable possible others at the beginning of time, got the luck of the roll with respect to the life-supporting parameter settings.

But the multiverse perspective is like a double-edged sword. It can also be used to deny that our Universe can or should be treated as a "god."[143] The mathematical brilliance of string theory once seemed to promise an explanation of why our universe is the way it is – until "a mind-numbing"

---

[140] Sims "Servanthood" rests on an assumption of the nature of the universe that he attributes to Christ: "the universe is neither indifferent nor unfriendly." Au contraire. Sims' belief seems to treat the Universe like a person and equate it with a personal God, inferences we rejected earlier. As for entropy, as Muller (op.cit.) states: "The universe is constantly creating more." – a mistaken view, as we shall see.

[141] Muller, op .cit., p.115.

[142] Reported in Kauffman (2008), op. cit., p. 28; drawn from Smolin, Lee, **THE LIFE of the COSMOS.**

[143] For more on this theme, see: Bernard Carr, ed. (2007), **UNIVERSE OR MULTIVERSE?**: Cambridge University Press.

number of alternative string theories appeared, each of which could pertain to an alternative universe. Indeterministic (probabilistic) processes of selection among these over eons could, in theory, have led to the universe we life-forms inhabit. Like the evolutionary process we have already set forth, this scenario denies any God-as-Creator. Yet, as Kauffman has pointed out, the theory of multiverses "seems to stand on shaky evidentiary grounds." We have not yet been able to discover alternative universes directly or indirectly.

Indeed; so back to our precious, so far one-of-a-kind Universe (perhaps at least deserving of a capital "U" for the sake of Us). Chapter 4 has already revealed that it has somehow been "fine-tuned" for life. Many scientists see this view as being far too "anthropocentric." Maybe, but multiverse science will have to be more careful, lest their theories are seen as scarcely distinguishable from religion. As in Vedic Culture (highlighted in Chapter 20), wherein countless universes emanate from the body of Maha Vishnu.[144] Can you imagine anything more fantastically unbelievable or empirically untestable?

What is the likelihood of other, localized centers of life in the context of our own vast, expanding universe? From this standpoint, life cannot be seen as "normal." Here, we must turn to the statistics of extremes, because the probabilities are in the tails of highly skew distributions. Life is very chancy, highly abnormal, and so must be seen as extremely precious at all levels. The fight for life is continuous in a discontinuous world fraught with forces of disorder and destruction. As astronomers widen their search for life elsewhere, the precariousness of life on our planet is heightened.

We live in a fractal universe. Our world is unique even as we are, individually. We have come close to destroying our world in the recent past through nuclear war. The danger still exists and can be expected to persist as long as there are sociopaths and megalomaniacs among us and so long as we

---

[144] Swami Prabhupana and A.C. Bhaktivevedanta (2007), **SRI ISOPANISAD**. Los Angeles: Bhaktivevedanta Book Trust (p.89).

insist in treating GAIA as our dump.[145] Perhaps that is why we persist in singing "Let there be peace on earth" every Christmas.

We must raise ourselves up individually and altogether spiritually and otherwise. As ever, the individual is primal. The only group that is primal is the human species. As we raise ourselves up, individually and group-wise, the entire human race is bettered and elevated. The same is true of any subgroup of which we are members. There will always be subgroups at all levels, from nationalities to extended families. Altogether, these represent the marvelous variety of our species and of our nation, the most diverse on earth. The variety in turn demonstrates our incredible adaptability to all kinds of environments and challenges – essential to our survival.

Groups and a NSB

Any group or subgroup contributes to the advancement of human life to the extent that:

> ➢ It sees itself as part of the human race, dedicated to its advancement in whatever line of activity, locale and spirit to which it is devoted; and also...
> ➢ Understands that it should also serve to aid, help and raise up the life of each of its individual members.

The latter is as important as any group-wise goal, primarily because, otherwise, group behavior can be devoted to false gods and graven images deleterious to nurturing and raising up human life. Such were demonstrated by the horror of Nazism and its false-god, Hitler. The Hitler legions included a Death's Head Brigade, symbolic of the Nazi regime's overall death-centered

---

[145] Yale University, et al. (2016), **"The Earth Itself is Now Accelerating the Demise of the Human Species," NATURE** (December 7). As demonstrated daily at all levels, from trash along roads to poisoning our atmosphere, we continue individually, as groups and as a species to treat the rest of the world as our dump.

ideology. In America today, the false gods are those of consumerism and America as #1 among nations.

The graven images of American corporate advertisements are too many to count. Unfortunately, "National triumph goes hand in hand with individual impotence."[146] The fabled American Dream has diminished for nearly half of American citizens, while a majority of U.S. residents believe the American middle class is just a vestige of the past.[147] An ironic saving grace for us is that the Dream remains alive among immigrants, legal or not.

We not only need a rise in the American spirit; we need to cultivate spirituality overall. Raising ourselves up spiritually takes work. We can't expect it to be renewed by a glow from on high. Spirituality overall, and all of its major features, are a discipline. It can be learned like any good habit and will become so as it is practiced daily. A Ted Talk on NPR, for example, described how to learn "compassion," one of the major components of spirituality.[148] We noted the discipline of meditation earlier. Nothing less than a full course of training in spirituality is required. Design of such may follow publication of this book. Nothing less than a raft of input from readers will suffice if the course is to come out right. Your feedback is invaluable.

We opened by questioning life-after-death. That is not for any of us individually. The true meaning and existence of life-after-death, however, is realized when we broaden the scope of our vision – from the individual to community, culture, country and world – and from personal fantasies to

---

[146] Quote from Unger, Roberto Mangabeira, & Cornel West (1998), **THE FUTURE of AMERICAN PROGRESSIVISM:** An Initiative for Political and Economic Reform. Boston: Beacon Press.

[147] According to Exclusive Point-Taken Marist Polls of April, 2016.

[148] See www.npr.tedtalk.org, where Ms. Tipple presents her method, as on NPR on 12/12/16.

factual life histories. Then we see that, YES, there is life-after-death, as in "Life everlasting...world without end."

This shift in vision is essential. For it changes how we view ourselves in relation to others and to the rest of the world. Myself, each day I gaze with wonder at the beauty and vibrancy of life all around me – other human beings, and the relentless fecundity, variety and force of life revealed by nature. Then I realize that, at this stage of our evolution as a species, we have come to play god with respect to all these other forms of life. Our generation of global warming, for example, is already driving the extinction of other species en-mass.

Conclusion

Now that I am in the final chapter of my own life, I can't imagine my physical being living beyond my death. Belief in LaD is a gross conceit and contradiction, as indicated earlier. Such conceit derives from each as Narcissus – so taken with his image in the mirror that he cannot imagine dying. I pray only that the life I love all about me will live on, and that my remains will help feed that life. That is truly life everlasting, world without end.

How can we raise ourselves up, spiritually? There are many tales of spiritual epiphanies. These may be sparked by unexpected, tragic events such as the death of a dear friend or loved one. And yet it is day-to-day life that needs to be uplifted. As in other aspects of day-to-day living, we need to develop good habits, as our parents tried to instill. Those related to religious training may have also been encouraged in Sunday schools. These are easily adapted for use in a NSB with only minor adjustments in language and practice. For example: Blessings before meals, prayers before starting work, classes, bedtime ["Now I lay me down to sleep..."] or other undertakings.

Prayer is fundamental, but it needs to be directed outward, not upward. It needs to be renewed where it has fallen into disuse and spread to moments where it has seldom if ever been applied. Prayer serves to ground us as well as raise us up. From the standpoint of developing spirituality and preparing fertile ground for the "better angels of our nature" to land upon, the banishing of prayer in the schools should be seen as tragic. Moments of silence are another good practice not to be denied or considered superficial or routine. A future NSB manual of best practices would guide us in generating good habits. The practice(s) of spirituality, especially if enabled altogether, would serve to help raise up and otherwise transform our everyday lives. As a Green Beret named Dave was heard to say: "A lot of what we learn, we learn from each other."[149] Indeed.

---

[149] Quoted in Martinez, Amy (2016), "College for Commandos," **FLORIDA TREND** (June), p.78.

Chapter 10

Self-Actualization & Transcendence

Contexts and Examples

Introduction

Although, along with Emily Dickenson I think "Nature is heaven," the first question of "context" to consider is: Are we growing up in a spiritual environment? Maslow groups contextual influences under the headings of "Education" and "Society," to which we will turn in due course. First, the obvious: Most American families, even in the secularism of now, feel the need for church and Sunday school for their kids. Why? – Even many non-believers, to avoid conflict or troublesome conversations, say "I believe in God," if asked. It's often a part of the old, go-along/get along game of keeping peace with one's neighbors.

Like another old saying says: "There's two things to avoid talking about: religion and politics," arguably the two most important aspects of human life. Such views, however, seem a bit too cynical. I prefer the assumption that a least a significant portion of the human race are seekers and discoverers – if not themselves then cheering on those who are. This assumption has been validated through history and evolution.[150]

We are an inimitably curious species. We wonder about what's to be found in the great beyond. We want our kids to grow up to be good people. Also, any neighborhood church also serves as a local social and services center. So, don't press co-parishioners as to the purity, depth and detail of their belief; honor their soulful presence and help them to raise it up. One way is to open up to those who seem to be open to conversations about spirituality, faith and belief. Confess what challenges these pose to you. You might be pleasantly surprised by the responses you receive.

Education and Spirituality

Most voters understand that our primary through secondary educational systems need wholesale revamp or reform, but there's very little shared understanding of how. From the standpoint of spirituality, it may suffice to quote Maslow:

> "Our conventional education looks mighty sick...we could rescue...the school curriculum from the value-free, value-neutral, goal-less meaninglessness into which it has fallen."[151]

So, this is the place to address another fundamental issue: The place of spirituality in education. It should have a place and most often does not. A quick rejoinder from those involved in religious education might be: 'Well, what about religious schools and Sunday schools? Ironically, the main problem here is one they share with their secular schools' brethren: teaching "by the book." This is a version of what some have labeled "extrinsic" education, which relies almost exclusively on external sources, not only books but teachers, school board rules, etc.; in short, sources outside learners

---

[150] See, for example, Daniel Boorstin's **THE DISCOVERERS**.

[151] Maslow, op. cit., pp.170 & 179, respectively.

themselves. "Intrinsic" means helping learners to find themselves, discover their strengths, plumb their depths, learn how to learn, and begin to feel what is in their souls after first learning that:

1) Each of them is a unique individual – living here and now in the finitude of time and never to be seen again after passing on; and

2) Each has a soul that they are here to recognize, nurture and express so each can give something of him- or her- self to others, their families, their communities, their countries and even to the rest of the world.

Self-Actualization

In keeping with (2), above, Maslow's work has pioneered and elaborated the idea of each individual's "self-actualization", followed by his or her "transcendence." So, first, let us highlight what Maslow means by the former:

➤ "Self-actualizing people are...involved in a cause outside their own skin...motivated in other, higher ways... called "meta-motivations." [The latter are detailed in 28 "theses...presented as testable propositions" in Chapter 23]

➤ They are devoted, working at something that is very precious to them...a vocation... (or "calling") and...

➤ They devote themselves to "the search for...the values of being and becoming..."[B-values], ultimate values that are intrinsic...There are about 14 of these..., including the truth, beauty and goodness of the ancients, plus perfection, simplicity, comprehensiveness, kindness, and several more.

➤ They make the growth choice instead of the fear choice a dozen times a day..."to move ... toward self-actualization "[152]

To complete the definition of anything, however, one must not only express what is it but what it **is not**. Self-Actualizing people:

---

[152] Maslow, op. cit., pp.43-45 & 299. See Table 1, pp. 308-9 for a complete listing of "Motivations and Gratifications of Self-Actualizing People..."

"do not...feel anxiety-ridden, insecure, unsafe...alone, ostracized, rootless, or isolated...unlovable, rejected, or unwanted...despised and looked down upon, and do not feel unworthy, nor do they have crippling feelings of inferiority or worthlessness."[153]

Two qualifiers, however, point to economic status as being important influences on one's ability to so "feel." For self-actualizing peoples are "expressing" rather than:

"coping...(& so) gratification of the basic needs...may be a necessary precondition...(in order to move from) living under bad environmental conditions to living under good conditions."[154]

This observation points to a grave danger facing a NSB: That it might serve to strengthen rather than diminish the tendencies that threaten to transform our nation into a class society. We will return to face this.

Motivations

Meta-motivations are set forth in detail in Maslow's Chapter 23 subtitled "The Biological Rooting of the Value Life." The primary among these include:

"...achieving work hardly distinguishable from play, work tasks as "embodiments...of intrinsic values...peak experiences, intrinsic pleasures, worthwhile achievements...inner requiredness (that) coincides with   external... I want to with...; I must...(&) intrinsic values overlap greatly with B-Values...therefore the distinction between self and not-self (outside, others) has been transcended."

In their new book, **THE POWER OF MOMENTS**, the Heath brothers show how "inventive thinking" can help generate "defining moments" during both milestones and everyday events. They further reveal that the same creative

---

[153] Maslow, pp.299-300.

[154] No. 5 of 6 of Maslow's "basic hierarchy of needs" presented on p.282.

skills can be applied to create more peak moments in other contexts. How to start? – "Disrupt normal routines!"

Per the term "biological" noted earlier, it is very important to note that Maslow is not writing as some popular psychiatric therapeutic journalist but as a scientist. He insists that the motivations and value system he sets forth are "instinctoid in nature" and that all that he writes are and have been, as demonstrated by his lifetime of work, "proper subjects for scientific study and research."

Now for transcendence [as if it were easy; it's not, but here's an introduction to start with]. Maslow's chapter on this opens by listing nearly three dozen types. Let's begin at the end with his summary statement:

> "Transcendence refers to the highest...or holistic levels of human consciousness – behaving and relating – as ends rather than means – to oneself, to significant others, to human beings in general, to other species, nature, and to the cosmos."[155]

Among the 35 on his list, the following seven seem most salient:

1) "transcendence of: the ego or one's conscious self...
2) time...;
3) the opinions of others...;
4) one's past -- and transcendence through:
5) love,
6) acceptance of the natural world, and
7) living in the realm of Being [B] – honoring B-values and speaking the language of Being, noted earlier.

To quote another, however, does not connote unqualified acceptance or agreement of the quoted remarks, nor where Maslow's views stand in relation to others on the same topic. First, a point that we will return to and elaborate

---

[155] Maslow, op.cit.,p.279.

throughout – a focus on the individual does not suffice. This is a major qualifier that Maslow also elaborates elsewhere in his book, as in:

"Jesus...taught that our spiritual work does not proceed in isolation. We move forward on the Path only   with the help of others. How we relate along the Way to other beings—animal and vegetable as well as human—becomes a critical element in our search."[156]

One problem with the above is that, perhaps inadvertently, Maslow has misused the term "beings" – very important in his emphasis on human "B-values" – to refer to "animal and vegetable" as well. We should rather substitute "human beings." Another is the inclusion of "perfection." The latter can be dangerous, as indicated by the old saying: "The perfect is the enemy of the good."

But let us not be distracted from Jesus' quotation above, for indeed: "our spiritual work does not proceed in isolation." One example of this was provided by a BBC weekend special event: A public meeting with the Somali community in Minnesota. The interactivity among and between panelists and attendants showed promise of a transformative influence via the promotion of broader understandings between the Somali's and others. By nurturing the faith and hopes of diverse participants in a better world grounded in understanding, such events might also prove to be transcendent.

As for NOW – transcendence of time, even at this moment? – Needleman states: "If we have come into being only from the matrix of time and space, we cannot transcend time and space."[157] But this seeming denial is mistaken on two counts. On the one hand, he is assuming that we come into this world through divine grace, where "divine" means a God on high. On the other, he

---

[156] **PARABOLA** (2016-17), **Myth, Tradition and the Search for Meaning,** Volume 41, No. 4, Winter.

[157] Needleman, Jacob (2004), "All Those Shining Worlds", **PARABOLA** (Summer: Special Issue on the Web of Life), p.26.

believes that a mortal being so conceived cannot transcend time and space. Not only are these beliefs inconsistent, they are belied by evidence from others.

Almost daily, astronomers and cosmologists are extending our understanding of time and space. According to the latest estimates, the extent of our universe is 90 billion light years across (and expanding). Some of them posit models of "multiverses" – a universe of universes. Discoveries and imaginings both "boggle our minds" with majesty and awe that transcends what we know of time and space from ordinary experience. The Atomic Clock, invented in 1955, enabled mankind to take over the control of time from the heavens, making it a creature of Man and his science. The clock relies on a cesium atom resonating under the influence of an electromagnetic field. Recent research promises to increase its accuracy 100 times – to 1.4 / 10 to the 28th power!

Transcendence in Everyday Life

Other examples of such transcendence are found in everyday life in two ways (among others):

> (1) Through what Maslow calls "peak experiences" and

> (2) From work that seems more like play by many who, so enmeshed are they in the work, lose all sense of time and space.

Scientific evidence supporting the latter sensation is that brain chemicals cause our internal clock to tick more slowly. Questions to address are: What are the minimum non-drug features of peak experiences [PEs]?, and are the latter prerequisites to the feeling that one has achieved spirituality?

We have already recognized that PEs can be realized in almost any activity, in athletics, music, science, art and other forms of creativity. Physicist Werner Schrodinger for example:

> "in what his mathematician friend Hermann Weyl called a "late erotic outburst,"...took...his latest mistress up to a villa in the Swiss Alps...to construct a new theory of matter."

Popular song lyrics are evocative of PEs, too, as in "I like to go surfing in a hurricane and make love in the driving rain"[158] Such experiences, however, are small, minor pieces relative to everyday life. Spirituality should both inspire and arise from an entire universe of activities that occupy us day to day. And what about the in-betweens? Also: Is an alert participant/observer stance required to realize the spirituality of any moment of activity? The answer is probably 'yes,' unless there is another involved who would likely be distracting; otherwise, another who might be a soulmate or spirituality trainer.

Maslow's thinking - on self-actualization, transcendence, &c – is seminal, but most of his examples are rather exclusive. They are drawn from the upper levels of educational attainments and professions and thus recognized and realized by only a small subsections of society. This is sad, for clearly, he sees them as applicable to everybody (as indeed they are). We need to propagate and democratize his teachings.

How can we democratize soul and soulfulness? Major venues have already been recognized, including education (starting in pre-school or kindergarten), parenting, churches and avant-garde think-tanks.[159] Each of these, however, will require major changes in their practices. Some were cited earlier, but those and others require explanations and adaptations suitable to a variety of circumstances.

One is heartened by the decades-long rise of what seems to be practically a whole new "industry" promoting self-help (actualization?) in the conjoint

---

[158] Song lyrics heard on Oyster Radio, 12/30/16.

[159] One example of the latter is the Garrison Institute, which "applies the transformative power of contemplation to today's pressing social and environmental concerns, helping build a more compassionate, resilient future. We envision and work to build a future in which contemplative ideas and methods are increasingly mainstream and are applied at scale to create the conditions for positive, systemic social and environmental change."

areas of raising up our bodies, minds and souls of both adults and children.[160] Modest additions and modifications in light of Maslow's ideas might amount to a small and beneficial revolution in terms of a far more widespread training in spirituality. In the final analysis, however, implementation of "The Farther Reaches of Human Nature" comes down to each of us. Here, the possibilities are manifold, and there are correspondingly many good examples. Also, they are of a different nature and quality than the dime-store religious panegyrics of folks who have "found Jesus."

One that I have found to be especially inspiring is that of the late Dag Hammarskjöld, former Secretary General of the United Nations. He said:

> "Our purpose is nothing but peace...Blood, sweat, grime, earth...Where are those in your world of will?...Everywhere – the ground from which the flame ascends."[161]

He was a spiritual seeker who also wrote:

> "We cannot mend the world as masters of material things...But we can influence the development of the world from within as a spiritual thing."

The word "within" here is key, for it has meaning at all levels of human activity. It begins within us, as an essential part of our self-actualization and realization of our "calling" in the world. Curiously, this old idea of "calling"

---

[160] The "father" of the industry was Norman Vincent Peale, whose popular book was cited earlier. In it, "Faith in self and faith in God became...intermixed...," but Peale's creed amounted to superficial self-help advisories to help people along the road to success – not a paean to spirituality. See Lane, Christopher (2016), **"The Gospel of Positivity," WALL ST. JOURNAL** (Dec.). Also see Lehmann, Chris (2018), **"The Cult in the White House," IN THESE TIMES** (January).

[161] Hammarskjold, Dag (1966), MARKINGS

was popularized by Whoopi Goldberg while posing as a nun in the movie SISTER ACT. Our fundamental calling is to recognize ourselves, then make ourselves known, to be recognized as sacred souls acting in the world – to be with and act with others to make our world a better place for future generations. Then "within" applies in a growing circle of our lives' engagements – in work, clubs, churches, institutions and the world-at-large.

Prime Examples

Hammarskjold's "religion" was a Way that imposed a personal discipline that opened inner landscapes of mind, body and soul while commanding a certain relationship with others. In his words:

> "To speak of this interrelated movement of awareness and kinship (of self and other) as "mindfulness"…is to miss its singularity…(&) conscious self-scrutiny."[162]

"He did not live without self-knowledge…It opened him to himself and… therefore to others …and…to forgive others." As a member of the Church of Sweden, he heard Albert Schweitzer deliver his principle of "Reverence for Life," which conveyed much, including a very important message on prayer:

> "To know how to pray is not a small thing: That opening upward, that willingness to be nothing … endowed Hammarskjold with a great breadth of understanding and inner peace…"[163]

Dag lived in relation to…'Someone or Something' that had called him…:

---

[162] Quote here and most of this on Hammarskjold owes to Lipsey, Roger (2016), "Desiring Peace: A Meditation on Dag Hammarskjold," **PARABOLA** (October).

[163] Schweitzer, Albert (1988), **A PLACE FOR REVELATION: Sermons on Reverence** for Life. New York: Macmillan Publishers.

"To be pure in heart means, among other things, to have freed yourself from...half-measures: from a tone of voice which places you in the limelight, a furtive acceptance of some desire of the flesh which ignores the desire of the spirit, a self-righteous reaction to others in their moments of weakness. Look at yourself in that mirror when you wish to be praised—or to judge."

He also said:

> "I cannot belong to or join those who believe in our movement toward catastrophe. I believe in growth, a growth to which we have a responsibility to add our few fractions of an inch. [This] is not the facile faith of generations before us, who thought that everything was arranged for the best in the best of worlds.... It is in a sense a much harder belief—the belief and faith that the future will be all right because there will always be enough people to fight for a decent future...Each day the first day: each day a life...And it engages directly when the time comes: Every hour eye to eye."

[Nice resonance here with my "life in the day of" and, indeed, with my own philosophy.]]

Hammarskjold was exceptional, but there are innumerable similar examples that provide fascinating fodder – not just for spiritual mentors but for teachers and learners of all types.

Another truly exceptional example is Mahatma Ghandi, most remarkable because, emerging from an Eastern culture worlds removed from that of Hammarskjöld, he nonetheless revealed lessons consonant with those conveyed by Dag.

He offered many messages, some ignored, some misunderstood, some as relevant today as when first expressed. Ben Kingsley's Academy Award-winning screen portrayal of Gandhi was a mesmerizing performance, but the script barely hinted at the bewildering complexity of the real man. He was at the same time an earnest pilgrim and a wily politician, an advocate of celibacy and the architect of satyagraha (truth force), a revivalist, a revolutionary and a social reformer.[164] "I believe that all men are born equal," Gandhi once wrote in the midst of one of his campaigns against untouchability. "I have fought this doctrine of superiority in South Africa inch by inch." It took a long time for the Mahatma to turn that implicit belief into explicit action.

Mohandas K. Gandhi arrived in South Africa in 1893 as a young British-trained lawyer. Initially, he was simply affronted that discriminatory laws and bigoted custom lumped educated well-to-do Indians like him with "coolies," the impoverished mine, plantation and railroad workers who made up the bulk of the region's immigrant Indian population. The nonviolent campaigns he waged to bring about equality between Indians and whites over the next 20 years would lead him — slowly and unsteadily but inexorably — to advocate equality between Indian and Indian, first across caste and religious lines and then between rich and poor. Gandhi's campaigns in South Africa taught him how to move the masses — not only middle-class Hindu and Muslim immigrants but the poorest of the poor as well. He had, as he himself said, found his "vocation in life."

Soon after returning to India in 1915, Gandhi set forth what he called the "four pillars on which the structure of India's "Swaraj" — self-rule — "would ever rest":

1) Unshakable alliance between Hindus and Muslims;
2) Universal acceptance of the doctrine of nonviolence, as tenet, not tactic;
3) The transformation of India's approximately 650,000 villages by spinning and other self-sustaining handicrafts;
4) and an end to the evil concept of untouchability.

---

[164] Quotes are from Lelyveld, Joseph (2011), **GREAT SOUL: Mahatma Gandhi and His Struggle With India,** New York: Alfred A. Knopf.

Gandhi had hoped to bring about India's freedom as the moral achievement of millions of individual Indians – the result of a social revolution in which the collapse of an alien, colonial rule would be little more than a byproduct of a struggle for self-reliance and economic equality. Foreign rule did collapse, in the end, "but strife and inequality among Indians worsened."

Gandhi saw most of this coming and sometimes despaired. The real tragedy of his life, Lelyveld argues, was:

> "not because he was assassinated, nor because his noblest qualities inflamed the hatred in his killer's heart. The tragic element is that he was ultimately forced, like Lear, to see the limits of his ambition to remake his world."

Nonetheless, while he may have "struggled with doubt and self until his last days," Gandhi "made the predicament of the millions his own, whatever the tensions among them, as no other leader of modern times has." And, for all his inconsistencies, his dream for India remained constant throughout his life. "Today," Gandhi wrote less than three weeks before he was murdered by a member of his own faith, "we must forget that we are Hindus or Sikhs or Muslims or Parsis...It is of no consequence by what name we call God in our homes."

Chapter 11

Desacralization

If we are to formulate a fully believable NSB that is influential in human lives, we need to be bouncing back and forth among and between levels of discourse, primarily from individuals to communities or from micro to macroscopic viewpoints. So, in the previous section, we saw how the life force and spirituality of two great men were exemplified. We now return to a broader perspective in order to examine negative factors of the context that any attempt to establish a NSB must face.

Earlier, we began to recognize "barriers" to the realization and practice of our innate (biologically "instinctoid") spirituality. Forces adverse to spirituality are rife throughout our society. It's time to face those that are most powerfully undermining all that is sacred, generating what **PARABOLA** magazine calls "desacrilization". The more popular term is "secularization"-- the trend of turning away from things spiritual to those ordinarily secular [**OED** definition: "not religious, sacred or spiritual."] The most familiar example is the rampant commercialization of Christmas. This is but one. The capitalist marketplace is the major force. The imperialism of the market has overtaken most aspects of our world.

The market has become a massive distraction from matters spiritual. Start with the simple fact now multiplied over and over again in our market-dominated life: That life is almost overwhelmingly transactional. Transactions are quick exchanges: No time for reflection, spiritual or otherwise. The pace of exchanges is increasingly fast. Wall St. trading is a metaphor. The traditional trading pit still looks like a transactional madhouse. Electronic "fast trading" is approaching nanosecond speed.

The market also both attracts and distracts our attention. The marketplace of things presents us with an almost uncountable variety and number of choices. Supermarkets provide a rich cornucopia of delicious, attractive edible and non-edible choices. The discipline of the market is salutary and even ethical -- within the constrained rationality of a competitive marketplace. But it is no way transcendental, even via advertising exaggerated to associate products with "spirit."

From the standpoint of our spirituality we should glance at marketplace choices with increasingly skeptical eyes, like looking the proverbial "gift horse in the mouth." Too often, we are burdened with false choices. For too many, the "free" market has become a false god. Its falsity was revealed by the 2008 financial crisis and Great Recession. Its glistening attractions too often amount to graven images. Its advertising pitches, increasingly amplified and broadcast to excite our most primitive (limbic) desires, should remind us of the line "Lead me not into temptation...Deliver me from evil..." in the Lord's Prayer.

Advertising, in turn, supports major media, another huge force of desacrilization [hereafter, abbreviated "desac"]. Here, however, we must take care to set apart what, by contrast, can be labeled "minor" media such as daily commercial and noncommercial classifieds and "informational" pieces in religious media. What's most heavily implicated toward desac is nationwide, expensive, continually rebroadcast media advertising. Very expensive (and annoying) are the 6-7 TV advertisements interrupting programs we are trying to enjoy. The most expensive, costing millions, may be those during the Superbowl; however, content is the matter at issue. The influence of cost here is indirect. Costly advertising [augmented by shills in the print and non-print media] supports a market system that has already been identified as "desac" – adverse to matters sacred and spiritual.

Advertising content, along with the content of the programs it supports, provides impressions of being overwhelmingly pro-desac (implicitly or explicitly). Increasingly violent content has led many parents to try to reduce their kids' exposure to TV. Such TV influences are reinforced by warlike toys grounded in a false patriotism, such as GI Joe, further augmented by even more violent heroes such as the Hulk and the Avengers. [I write this with increasing sadness, a week from Christmas Eve, already missing Christmas hymns that parlay "peace on earth, good will to men."].

When confronted with something as so subhuman like the Hulk, one is tempted to call for controlling the bad influence(s). But this would be contrary to the 1st Amendment. There is a better way: Promote the realization that we are sacred beings seeking to enrich our souls. Public purpose advertising could help but that, too, would not suffice. Let's recognize that TV has become an addiction. So, "Just Say No!", especially to our children. Turn it off or throw it out. I don't own a TV, nor do I want one. That's been my personal anti-desac advisory for many years. Funny here: "anti-desac" brings to mind a childhood spelling challenge: How do you spell "antidisestablishmentarianism"? Perhaps the latter will come back into reuse by those who would oppose NSB, which is definitely dis-establishment.

Think the last paragraph vs. TV has gone too far? Consider an example recently reported by Fox News on Nov. 12, 2017: A saloon in NJ decided to shut off all its TVs to honor Veterans Day. The word went viral. Veterans descended on the joint from miles all 'round. Many talked to each other. A pre-arranged soloist didn't show to sing the National Anthem. So they all sang, as indeed we all should, even if a soloist appears, as is too often the case.

One would think, and can well imagine, that at least the "bully pulpit" provided to purveyors of politics and public life would enable those populating this sector of our society to promote spirituality and/or fight vs. desac. Think again. Their offerings amount to a spirituality that is denatured, lowest common-denominator religion, or people-disempowering. Occasional references to "God" deflect people's concerns from their life on earth and the here and now -- another distraction without real inspiration.

What about evangelicals in public life? The raising of their religious voices may add transient dollops of inspiration, and yet, they also amount to another disempowering distraction from working and worshiping with fellow human beings to raise up our lives on earth together. My proselytizing evangelical friends beg to differ. See Chapter 18 on a "Spiritual Politics" for more.

TV comes into play here again for it has served to "dumb down" public talk, conversations, and understanding on public issues as well as failed to convey the true meaning of incarnation: God in Man. Nearly all we get is infotainment. Note that broadcasting on "public issues" also fails to include some features of religious feeling and spirituality. Prayer in public schools has long been an issue. It has also steadily diminished. Why not bring it back? There are no prizes to be awarded to post-MLK Jr. public speakers here.

And so we now turn to the quality of private life in terms of its spirituality. "Desac" too often prevails here, too. In what proportion of American households do children say prayers such as "Now I lay me down to sleep, I pray...my soul to keep"? Notice that "the Lord" has been omitted. A revised NSB prayer would substitute 'my friends, family, teachers and others'. Perhaps the first and more important question, however, is: What's the share of kids who even recognize that they have souls and soulfulness to be nurtured and raised up? What percent of parents offer blessings before meals and/or ask their children to do so?

A 2018 Washington Post/Pew Family Trust poll revealed that 51% of a random sample of over 1600 Americans say grace before meals at least a few times per week. Tim Keller, the founding pastor of Redeemer Presbyterian Church in New York City, told the Post:

> "It's a powerful way of reminding yourself that you are not self-sufficient, that you are living by somebody's grace, that plenty of other people who work just as hard as you don't have anything to eat,"

International polls show, especially in contrast to our presumably more "enlightened" European friends, that Americans are a more religious people and more likely to attend church regularly. Well, if you think that the latter amounts to greater spirituality, there's a bridge I can sell you. There's a disconnect between organized religion and spirituality. Spiritual talk has been abandoned in all but religious schools. Even nondescript "moments of silence" are bones of contention. In these lacks thereof, public and private reflect each other.

And yet; and yet...More heartening is that the report of a Pew Research Center survey of 35,071 Americans conducted during June 4 – Sept. 30, 2014 found that:

- ✓ 55% pray daily; and...
- ✓ 59% "feel a deep sense of spiritual peace and well-being.

Moreover, Americans' feeling of the latter have undergone a significant increase since 2007 – from 52% to 59% over the seven-year interval between surveys. It is of great interest to notice that this increase has risen in tandem with a 7-point rise in the percentage who report "a deep sense of wonder about the universe" – from 39% to 46%. – in keeping with scientific advances probing the depths of the universe. The conclusion of an article based on the Pew surveys concluded that "Americans may be getting less religious, but feelings of spirituality are on the rise"[165] – in keeping with one of this book's major thrusts.

Meanwhile, arising from the "Swamp" in ways similar to presumed legal constraints on the participation of 501(c)(3) charitable organizations in politics, the separation of "church" and "state" has been and continues to be over-hyped and over-regulated.[166] Might these provide sub-rosa rationalizations for people's lack of commitment and genuine participation, both spiritually and politically? What thinkest thou? It seems that, for too many of us, any exhibition of spiritual faith has come down to cheer leading

---

[165] Masci, David, and M. Lipka (2016), "Americans may be getting less religious, but feelings of spirituality are on the rise," **FACTTANK: News in the Numbers**

(January 21).

[166] A label for our nation's capital according to President Donald Trump.

[like expressions of team spirit at football games] and/or going to church at Christmas, Easter, Hanukkah, Kwanza or the like, mostly for the sake of social appearances and acceptance.

We can and must do better for the sake of one and all. DeSac is not good. Fight it every day in every way by recalling the lodestone of faith-in-life that provides our true, indomitable inner spirit, both individually and altogether. Our bodies, minds and souls are each and all at stake to the extent that we fail to integrate the three – another reason for a NSB.

Even though most of secular "pop" music has also been a major aspect of "desac," the next chapter chooses to emphasize how so much of music heightens and brightens our spirituality.

Chapter 12

Music and Spirituality

Introduction

I was recently at a "Big Daddy & Hot Java" jazz concert that, in my view, was as much a spiritual as a musical event.[167] Lyrics included the words: "We all bleed the same and want the same for our children (and) It don't make sense if you can't have peace." There was love and joy in the faces of the members of their seven-man band.

Similar evocations can be heard weekly on NPR's Sunday evening "Pipe Dreams" program featuring organ music with rising crescendos and spiritual content. One is suffused with the sonority, grandeur and deep beauty of organ music while sitting quietly with eyes closed. E.g., "Music From a Higher Sphere," including Mahler's "Resurrection Symphony." All you sense and feel is the depth of yourself quietly resonating with sonorous rhythms. As I said to the rockin' base player in the Big Daddy band: "We resonate with you." To which he replied, jokingly: "You say that to all band players." I don't.

---

[167] At Rio Carrabelle in Carrabelle, FL,, December 20, 2016, organized by Jack "Bo" Way.

Resonance is a keyword, "soaring" another. For good music, especially if shared, raises up its listeners' spirits higher and higher, soaring as it rises with rhythms. Besides those just cited, the examples are legion – the final movement of Beethoven's 9th as the chorus sings "Freude schone gotefuncken; tochter aus Elysium" – Joy, plaything of the gods, daughter of paradise. Or Les McCann's Swiss Movement concert in 1978: "Let's Make it Real, Compared to What!, accompanied by his own piano strokes, rockin' and risin', with Buddy Harris on sax. Or the throbbing, rising chords of an organ playing Widor's "Carillon du Westminster" in the soaring sanctuary of a magnificent cathedral. We can feel the depth of our spirits plumbed and emergent, then soulfully rising and soaring to the peaks. Soulful, and yet the rising of one's spirit is so downright physical in both the playing and hearing of great music. A paradox?

Opportunities for Music to Raise Spirits

It is no wonder that music is an integral part of every religious service. Coltrane's a **SOULTRANE**. His soulful sax sonorities reach to **A LOVE SUPREME.**[168] The "King of Instruments" is central in most churches. The readings can also raise spirits and elicit soulfulness if they are read well --- with attention to both rhythm and sonority. Reading biblical passages is akin to reading poetry. Reading must be evocative if the full matter and meaning of the texts are to be realized. Unfortunately, most of those to whom readings are assigned for church services are not up to the challenge. Then there are the sermons where, usually, there's also much to be desired. Only a few ministers can sing. Sometimes they appear confused: Are they trying to present a lesson?, or raise the spirits and inflame the souls of parishioners? Lessons are more likely to be learned and spread abroad to the extent that souls are on fire.

Popular music called "soul" was born out of black work cries and field hollers in the Mississippi Delta. It came into its own commercially in Memphis in the

---

[168] Album titles, 1958 and 1964, respectively. New York: Ghislain Quiroz and Falsario Chicote, respectively.

late 1960s. It is concerned with what Faulkner called "the basic truth and verities." Stanley Booth wrote:

> "The biggest thing in pop music today is a blend of folk, rock and... music known as soul. Its spiritual home is Memphis, back where the blues really began...the sounds of deep emotion... audiences cannot help but "feel the spirit" and become clapping, shouting participants... "It's just the way the cats play...It comes from their soulful way of life."[169]

Dissonance?

Clearly, the opportunities for music to enhance spirituality are legion. Unfortunately, awareness of these – as instruments of spirituality – is not, but for the obvious sources in churches and classical choral societies. I've gotten to the point where even a few words suggest or remind me of a song. Then there are "the songs our fathers loved" – as in old hymns, the Great American Songbook, and the Sound of Music: "The hills are alive with the sound of music – the songs they have sung for a thousand years." Centuries ago, human ears were tuned to "the music of the spheres." Now? Cacophony seems to reign more often than not. What has changed, music or ears? Both. Even Bach used some dissonant chords and frequent key changes. Yet spirituality was honored and advanced, not betrayed. Spirits were raised:

> "Several pieces from his years as an organ virtuoso practice a kind of sonic terrorism. The Fantasia and Fugue in G Minor feasts on dissonance... perpetrating one of the most violent harmonies...resulting in a full-throated acoustical scream...Bach believed in God...but the

---

[169] Booth, Stanley (1969), "The Rebirth of the Blues: Soul," **SATURDAY EVENING POST** (Feb. 8), p. 27. Booth quoted Atlantic Records V.P. Jerry Wexler in the last sentence.

mix of his compositions leaves much about his belief system open to question."[170]

Physically, ears are the same now as yesteryear, but hearing has been desensitized. Bing, Bang, Boom! -- whether the music is punk rock or heavy metal, the body moves; the spirit is left hanging or left behind, unraised. One exception is Bernstein's MASS. The very mention of a mass conjures ranks of choristers. How remarkable then, the stark simplicity of Bernstein's opening: One man onstage, strumming a guitar and singing: "Sing me a simple song, lauda loude..." Bernstein's songs with Stephen Sondheim are also evocative. The aching song "Somewhere" from **WEST SIDE STORY** resonates with lines from Saroyan's **TIME of OUR LIVES**, as does the classic old song "**As Time Goes By:** It's still the same old story, a song of love and glory, a tale of do or die..."

What is most to be noted – the common denominators of song and play – is their grounding in real life – its deep longings, tragedies, hard rhythms, triumphs, joys and endurance. Not that some of these are not reflected in hard rock, but where's the meaning if you can't hear the words? One of the best exceptions is the song written and sung by Cat Stevens, "Morning has broken." Two others are John Denver's "Annie's Song," and Pink Floyd's "On the Turning Away." Denver's was written to and for his wife. It opens with the line: "You fill my senses..."

Pink Floyd's opens with "No more turning away, from the pale and downtrodden...," and ends with a question challenging for all of us: "Is it only a dream that there'll be no more turning away?"

Be wary, however, of the growing presence of background music that started as "muzak" composed by real people but is now generated by computer

---

[170] Ross, Alex (2017), "Holy Dread: Bach has long been seen as a symbol of the divine order. But his music has an unruly obsession with God.," **THE NEW YORKER** (Jan. 2, p.66).

programs based on Artificial Intelligence (AI). Trouble is, this trend will put many composers out of work, and for what! As one analyst has stated:

> " AI tools can't understand context or purpose. It's like having a composer who has no other experience of life except reading 1,000 pieces of music and then trying to come up with something similar...AI has no idea what's culturally...or politically relevant... „[171]

This is tantamount to the physicality of music – with a vengeance! Read on for the good side.

The Physicality of Music

The Duke's counterpoint is quite OK: "It don't mean a thing if you don't got that swing" – the rhythms of life. The latter also pulsate, sensually and beautifully, in the (mis-named) movie, **DIRTY DANCING**, especially throughout the song and dance duet of the star couple during the movie's final scenes – "(I've had) The Time of My Life." Lyrics include: "No, I've never felt this way before. I swear. It's the truth. And I owe it all to you."[172] Another great love duet line is: "That's all I ask of you." Who can fail to realize the transcendence of those moments? Or the fact that transcendence is rooted in the physical actions of both playing music and listening or dancing to it?

Perhaps the only popular piece of music that never fails to raise the spirits of both singers and listeners is "Amazing Grace." Yet few know of its origin. It was written by the captain of a slave ship transporting enslaved blacks from Africa to the U.S. Somehow, the captain experienced an epiphany and then wrote the song, which opens with: "Amazing Grace!, how sweet the sound!, that saved a wretch like me..."

---

[171] Thompson, Clive (2019), **"We will Bot You,"** MOTHER JONES (March/April), p. 54.

[172] Lyrics@Sony/ATV Music Publishing LLC, Worldsong, Inc.

A hard-headed critic would likely label the foregoing as romantic musings rather than hard evidence of direct connections between music and the human body or spirituality via the brain. And yet such evidence has arisen from the burgeoning field of research on the human brain. Here, spirituality is equated with euphoric feelings. An article in **WIRED** magazine highlighted much of the research.[173] Music tickles some "universal nerves." The symptoms are those of "emotional arousal." These include the dilation of pupils, increases in pulse rates and blood pressure, lowering of electrical conductance of the skin, a "strangely active" cerebellum, and blood redirected to leg muscles.

The technologies employed in the research were fMRI [functional Magnetic Resonance Imaging) and PET (Positron Emission Tomography). The sample was small: 10 winnowed from 217 who reported emotional responses to music. Altogether, these methods enabled a "precise portrait of music in the brain." What listening to music does is effect the release of dopamine in the dorsal and ventral striatum – "regions long associated with responses to pleasurable stimuli." The same stimuli also arise from sexual activity, doping cocaine, or "listening to Kanye." These observations resonate with some of those made in Chapter 3.

Researchers have also discovered a distinctive pattern of timing in participants' emotional responses detected in the brain. "Favorite moments" in music are preceded by a prolonged increase in the caudate sub-region of the brain's striatum. These brain segments are also implicated in learning and associated regions of the brain important to learning, and those mediating reinforcement of rewarding stimuli such as good food.

Here, researchers distinguish "anticipatory" from "consummatory" responses. Both involve dopamine release, but to different subcircuits of the striatum – those with "different connectivity and functional roles." The timing difference is an advance of 15 seconds before "acoustic climax." Note that music per se

---

[173] Lehrer, Jonah (2011), **"The Neuroscience of Music," WIRED** (Jan.)

is not necessarily a source of euphoric or exciting responses. Music that is repetitively boring fails to excite; e.g., "muzak" in stores. But how about the physicality of the rising, throbbing rhythms of Ravel's Bolero? Couples make love to them.

Leonard Meyer concludes that "...it is the suspenseful tension of music...that is the source of...music's feeling...what triggers a surge of dopamine..." His conclusion with regard to the importance of timing rests on his close examination of 50 measures of the 5th movement of Beethoven's String Quartet in C-sharp minor, Opus 131. He remarks how:

> "...music is defined by its flirtation with – but not submission to – our expectations of order...Beethoven begins with a clear statement of a rhythmic and harmonic pattern, then avoids repeating it in an intricate and tonal dance," saving the E major chord until the end."[174]

B-Flat Major

Another scientific discovery relating to music is also worth mentioning. It is that the key of B Flat Major is one of the basic tonal keys of our Universe. Dr. Andrew Fabian of Cambridge University, dubbed it "the lowest note" in the Universe. Indeed. At 57 octaves below middle C and with a period of oscillation of its notes of about 10 million years, even the double base section of the Cambridge chorus cannot be expected to play it.

Nevertheless, the discovery enables a legitimate entry to tables recording the emotional character of musical keys over the centuries.[175] It has been

---

[174] Meyer, Leonard (1956), **EMOTION and MEANING IN MUSIC**.

[175] See Steblin, Rita (2002), **A HISTORY of KEY CHARACTERISTICS in the 18th and Early 19th Centuries, 2nd Edition.**

characterized in salubrious terms by an international set of commentators; as, for example, the following:

- o Labeled: A "happy key" by an Englishman;
- o French: "Magnificent and joyful, noble, too;"
- o Germans: "Cheerful love, clear conscience, hope…";
- o Italians: "Tender, soft, sweet, charm and grace."

Major, well-known compositions in the key of B Flat Major include:

- o Beethoven's Piano Sonata, and his Symphony #4;
- o Brahms's Piano Concerto #2;
- o Haydn's Symphony #'3, 98 and 102;
- o Prokofiev's Symphony # 5;
- o Schubert's Symphony #5; and
- o Schumann's Symphony #1.

The discovery has had implications for the study of black holes and the structure of the universe. The origin of the basal key vibrato was found to be outbursts from a supermassive black hole in the Perseus Galaxy Cluster, 250 million light years away.

And so, who says that musical art and science are worlds apart? The art of music is recognized by the human brain. Music itself is mathematical. Here, we have found a modern version of the ancient "Music of the Spheres."[176]

---

[176] For more, see Rockwell, John (2004), "REVERBERATIONS: Move Over, Middle C: The Speculative Case for the Cosmic B Flat." **NEW YORK TIMES** (Jan.).

Chapter 13

Spirituality Localized

On the Brain, Person, Place, Family & Community

Introduction

We have found that the brain is the center for both music and spirituality; i.e., the locus of higher-level powers of both perception and action such as prayer, creativity, art, mindfulness and, above all, the soul and soulfulness. The basis of these is consciousness – the conscious, self- and other-aware mind. The dynamic process through which these qualities are realized is that of emergence from a complex adaptive system at the edge of chaos. No one would deny that virtually any brain, especially the human, is a truly complex adaptive system [CAS]. It contains about 100 billion neurons and up to 1,000 trillion neural connections.

Most of the features and practices noted earlier are realized through consciousness. I agree with Nobel Laureate Francis Crick that the soul is "not a thing but a process." Recall that emergence is also a process. Crick.wrote that:

> "In the past the mind (or soul, as in Cartesian Dualism) was regarded as something separate from the brain ...But most neuroscientists now believe that all aspects of the mind, including its most puzzling attribute, consciousness, are likely to be explainable in a more

materialistic way as the behavior of large sets of interacting neurons."[177]

Recall that Chapter 3 focused on the structure of the brain, beginning our explorations of brain segments that figure in spirituality. Another view questions the materialistic focus of neurologists. This question is discussed further on in Chapter 22.

Localization

It is hard to imagine spirituality taking root in a person without that human being having a strong sense of place. On this, I cannot help but reflect on my growing up in Gloucester, Massachusetts. Part of that experience involved St. John's Episcopal Church but, for myself, religion was influential only so far as it related to the historical community that was Gloucester. Gloucester is a city built on the fishing industry. The beautiful church windows represented Christ as a fisher of men. My spirit rose with the singing of church hymns, most of which I remember to this day, often with my father by my side.

My spirituality grew with additional perceptions and memories – a gathering sense of place. The West Gloucester woods and city beaches were my homes for exploration and discovery. I became fascinated with caves, trees and tidal pools. A growing love of nature and living things fed my spirit. A historical community is at least as much a sacred place as a church. As a church acolyte, I felt clumsy. As a child and student of nature, I felt very much at home. How can one's spirit be firmly rooted, and expressed, without a sense of place? My favorite poet is Charles Olson. Why? – Because his **MAXIMUS POEMS,** rooted in Gloucester, offer a sense of being and becoming in that place.

I can't imagine being a traveling salesman. How alienating that must be relative to being rooted in a historical community, where one comes to feel part of the history! I recall Tim Dobson, Pastor at St. Johns, to whom I expressed my sentiment that St. John's (and Gloucester, too) should be "a

---

[177] As quoted by Carter, op cit., p.204.

community of faith" (and, as well, of hope and shared striving for a shared past, present and future). Spirituality well grounded. So strongly did the spirit of Gloucester live within me that I left a 16 year residence in Princeton, NJ after my father died in order to return to my childhood home. After returning, I was elected, served as a Councilor-at-Large and also ran for Mayor of my beloved hometown.

Localization is critical to the nurture of spirituality. Distance detracts; closeness reinforces. A strong sense of self does not grow in isolation. Selfhood only grows to maturity away from narcissism, through life with others. The broadening and deepening of self with and in service to others grows out of living in a family and community of deep history and shared values. Rootedness and grounding, in a place of shared history and values are also crucial catalysts and nurturers of spirituality. Here, we should recall a thought shared earlier:

"Jesus, like Buddha, Muhammad, Moses, and other great spiritual teachers, taught that our spiritual work does not proceed in isolation. We move forward on the Path only with the help of others. How we relate along the Way to other beings—animal and vegetable as well as human—becomes a critical element in our search."[178]

In the frame of our NSB, localization goes along with entanglement and space-filling patterns to foster emergence.[179] Not so with the "Syntheist" alternative. Its authors make a heroic leap like too many others have made in mistaking the implications of quantum entanglement for our all-to-real, macro-level world. Quantum entanglement "at a distance" cannot be construed to deny the import of localization. See Chapter 24 for more.

---

[178] Quotes here and hereafter in this chapter are from B. B. King's autobiography **BLUES ALL AROUND US. New York: Avon Books.** .

[179] But I disagree with insinuations that quantum entanglement at a distance diminishes the significance of human localization close-up in community.

An Exemplary Spirit

The story of B.B. King's growing up provides an example that helps us to see how localization crystallizes, interweaves and amplifies the factors that nurture spirituality – even in a setting, family and childhood that superficial observers would deem to dampen anyone's spirit. B.B. King became a great blues/jazz guitarist and singer. He started life as a stutterer in a poor, single-parent family located in the Mississippi Delta – still recognized even today as a desperately poor section of a relatively poor state. His growing up was like a virtuous circle in which spirituality was both cause and effect. He wrote: "The blues are a mystery, and mysteries are never as simple as they look."

Spirit as a factor in growing up began with his mother, "beautiful, wise and kindhearted." Her spirit was integral to her courage, love, hard work, resourcefulness, and singing in the church choir. Another woman, his grandmother, exhibited spirit through her singing, too, but not just on Sundays – everyday provided multiple excuses to sing out. "Singing helped the day go by" She also talked about the blues, "musical codes" to enable survival through the throes of hard lives. The "warnings to stay out of trouble (were)...passed down to her daughter and her daughter's daughter." B.B. also reported that Great Grandma "made me feel like I matter."

The significant man in King's life was a teacher, Luther Henson – "a wise and wonderful human being," an indestructible optimist with a future-perfect sense of history. He "gave me hope," B.B. wrote. Henson taught that "No matter how bad things seem, change is on the way." He also introduced B.B. to the achievements of great blacks, including Booker T. Washington, Frederick Douglas, Mary McCloud Bethune and Joe Louis. B.B. wrote: "I was touched by people with love in their hearts." This spirit of love was amplified by "Heavenly Music"[180] in church that "got all over my body and made me wanna jump." The Pastor was another fine influence:

---

[180] Title of B.B. King's Chapter 3.

"His sermon is like music and his music...thrills me until I wanna get up and dance...right in the middle of a universe of music filled with nothing but pure spirit...a celebration of love...Reverend is a holy man...He hears what your heart is saying...He knows your soul."

The Reverend, Archie Fair, also introduced B.B. to the guitar, a "precious instrument." B.B. wanted to be Reverend, for he was "filled with the spirit." And so he went on to become a great jazz guitarist who conveyed "spirit" with every performance.

Conclusion

The two key words of this chapter have been "exemplary" and "localization." Because examples have served us throughout – in the cases of B. B. King, this author's "sense of place, localization within the networks of the human brain, and Jesus' non-isolation. So let us now turn our attention to the importance of evolutionary processes.

Chapter 14

The Evolution of Life, Art and Spirituality

Introduction

Not God-at-a-distance, but evolution without any god but a close-up God of Life is key to this book and the development of a New System of Belief (NSB). A recent review of a new book on Darwin's revolutionary text **ON THE ORIGIN of SPECIES** led off with the question "Did Charles Darwin kill God?" Along with Richard Dawkins, my answer is "Yes!" Dawkins's chapter on "Only a Theory" comes down definitively: "I shall show the irrefragable power of the inference that evolution is a fact."[181]T

The affirmation of a "kill God" negative, however, necessitates that of a positive, for it is also true that we human beings yearn for a higher, more spiritual order. It may be ironic if our eons long process of evolution ends with spirituality without a "God" to exemplify man as the best example of the spiritual heights any of us can achieve in our lifetimes.[182]

---

[181] Dawkins, op .cit., p.16.

[182] This section relies upon Dawkins, Richard (2009), **THE GREATEST SHOW ON EARTH: The Evidence for Evolution.** New York, N.Y.: Free Press.

There are two problems in the above paragraph. One is to define what is meant by "higher." The other is that it is by no means clear that achievement of widespread spirituality would mark the apex of evolution. The meaning of "higher" must be understood before the latter statement can even be discussed.[183] "Consciousness" is generally considered to be the highest faculty of our minds. Spirituality is both a feature and extension of consciousness. Yet, there are many other words in the vocabulary of the conscious mind and spirit. Let us recall. The list includes imagination, creativity, holiness, sacred, blessed, awe, wondrous, godlike, heaven(ly), infinitude, marvelous, miraculous, sacramental, incarnation, resurrection, monastic, transcendent, prayerful, mystical, grace, and mystery. "Higher" means "more broadly "embracing," and so "imagination," "transcendence" and "infinitude" are higher-level terms. See Appendix 1 for a "Vocabulary of Spirituality."

One definition of spirituality is: "The instrumentality of the sovereign self as it grows in scope and wisdom." And yet, this definition does not seem "spiritual" enough. What about "spirit" and "depth"? Or saintliness, soulfulness, all-encompassing, visionary, wisdom, reflecting, realization, mythical? Somehow, all the words more or less synonymous with spirituality seem more or less undefined to the extent that they are disconnected with action.

---

[183] The same concern applies to intelligence, especially as the "artificial" version (AI) amplifies native intelligence and the amplification, especially via "deep learning," shows no limit as yet. See Bohannon, John (2017), "The Cyberscientist: Artificial Intelligence isn't just a tool...", **SCIENCE** (July 7) , p.18. A much stronger warning is that of Christopher Koch in his article "We'll Need Bigger Brains" **(WALL St. JOURNAL REVIEW,** Oct. 28-29, 2017) where he writes: "To avoid a dystopian future fueled by the rise of artificial intelligence, we must move quickly to create technologies that enhance the human brain." I agree.

It should be no surprise to note: That which arouses spiritual feelings are actions and instruments, not merely those which seem ethereal by definition. We have already seen how music incites spirituality through organ and choral music, including hymns, masses and requiems (as discussed in Chapter 12). The spiritual resonance of organ music emanates from actions on diapason pipes. Instruments and voices also exemplify how spirit is expressed collectively. Spirits are raised to the rafters by the masses of Bernstein, Haydn, Mozart, Bach and Beethoven; requiems by Faure, Lloyd Webber and Mozart.

The ways and means of spirituality through things and actions are legion. There are random but memorable acts of kindness, prayer books, Bibles, cathedrals with their soaring vaults, psalms, holidays [originally holy days] and celebrations. Even movies -- What about **Ben Hur, Star Wars, The Ten Commandments, The Passion and Last Temptation of Christ, and Exodus**? Plus the more usual religious occasions, including baptisms, marriages, Christmas, Easter, the Lunar New Year and Kwanza, not to mention the rites and rituals of other faiths?

Friedman says **THE WORLD IS FLAT.**[184] He doesn't mention spirituality, though he should have. For there is one sense in which it, too, could be considered "flat," even though it may seem odd to think so of something so resonant with surging waves of inspiration or other peak experiences. Nevertheless, there is equality of opportunity in spirituality. The potential of reaching spiritual heights and depths exists in the souls of the minds of any and every man and woman. According to ABC's "Morning in America" News, Tom Brady's "secret" is spiritual; focusing on depth of quietude"(so his spirit is as "quiet as a glass lake"). But we need not all be Tom Bradys; the same quality of spirituality is open to us all. A democratic, participatory world is "flat

---

[184] The complete citation is: Friedman, Thomas (2005), **THE WORLD IS FLAT.** New York: Picador.

An earlier reference quoted Maslow on "peak experiences." Also recall hearing "My life shall be exalted" in Handel's **CORONATION MASS**. For years, though, my ears deceived me. I thought that I was hearing the same message in the opening stanzas of Handel's **MESSIAH** when a tenor sings "Every valley shall be exalted." I heard "every valley" as "everybody." Since over three centuries have passed since the Messiah was written, perhaps a change in wording is called for. To title a book "The World is Flat" conflates changes over space and time. Spirituality has evolved even though the Messiah and many of the tribes of mankind have not.

Perhaps the best way to trace the evolution of spirituality would be to look at the development of those arts that evoke, celebrate and enrich both the breadth and depth of spiritual feelings -- especially, the arts of architecture, painting, writing, music and sculpture. Thomas Moore wrote: "Stories of artists' intensive pursuit of their vision and craft are a kind of mythology revealing the archetypal dimensions of soulful work."[185] Moore seems to equate soulfulness with spirituality, and he associates many qualities with each. These include passion, grace, curiosity and involvement. But wait just a minute here! Are we here to ignore science? No; only temporarily. We will find that the explanatory power of science is incomplete in face of the richness of spiritual expression, And so, let us now turn to the arts.

The Arts

Architecture: Note the incredible change in size, beauty and complexity of structures, from reliance upon simple geometric shapes such as rectangles (e.g., sarcophagi) and triangles (e.g. pyramids) to the flying buttresses, soaring transepts, grandiose naves, and complex structures of major cathedrals (e.g., Mont Saint Michel and Chartres). A very recent example is "The Vessel" in New York, explicitly designed to "lift people up".[186] An

---

[185] Moore, Thomas (1992), **CARE of the SOUL: A Guide for Cultivating Depth and Sacredness in Everyday Life.** New York: Harper Collins.

[186] "New York City's next monument," featured in TIME (October 3, 2016).

intricate "interactive" and inter-weaving piece of architecture, it opened in 2018 as "the centerpiece of New York City's Hudson Yard development..."

Music: Even though we have already addressed the relationship of music with spirituality in Chapter 12, it is important to note here ways the relationship has been exemplified. Music has exhibited lines of development from the simple to the complex, along the way also gradually increasing its spiritually evocative powers. Simple tonalities appeared first as, for example, in the form of medieval plain songs or Gregorian Chants. More recent examples of greater scope and complexity include extensive repertories of choral music and symphonies; e.g., the spiritual epiphany of Beethoven's 9th.

The latter's reliance upon Shiller's "Ode to Joy", translates to:

> "Joy, plaything of the gods, daughter of paradise; your magic binds us together...All men become brothers..."

These made happiness, spirituality and brotherhood altogether incarnate. The evolution from simplicity to more complex tonal patterns of human/spiritual scope is evident even in some individual compositions, such as Bernstein's **MASS**. The piece is inaugurated by one man on stage with a guitar, singing:

> "Sing me a simple song, lauda, laude...Sing with me as we go along...lauda, laude...For God is the simplest of all..."

It then grows into a full-blown requiem mass with full orchestra and chorus. Return to Chapter 12 to recall more on "Music and Spirituality."

Art: The evolution of art was strongly influenced by developments in science that provided revolutionary perspectives on the nature of the physical universe at all levels, from the subatomic to the cosmic. Human figures in medieval art showed no signs of personality or human dimension. They were devotional, signifying human focus on an external, divine, all-powerful God. The prime advance of art in the Renaissance was its ability to reveal individuality and personality. In this respect, art was a reflection and expression of society-wide forces, primarily the growth of a market economy [recognized and promoted by Adam Smith] and the insinuation of science into natural philosophy [advanced by Francis Bacon]. Painting to capture subjects' personality and character is reflected, for example, in American artists' portraits of Washington, Franklin and Lincoln.

The evolution of art from the Civil War forward can be described as a fairly steady move away from the pictorial to the increasingly abstract. This movement began with Impressionism. Even though Impressionist artists painted natural and/or peopled scenes beautifully, the painted impressions were far from photographic.

Two artistic threads led away from Impressionism. One was led by Vincent van Gogh and Paul Gauguin; another, nearly concurrent, by Georges Seurat and Paul Cezanne. The first developed in paintings influenced by experimental science and its new data. The latter was evident in the work of Georges Seurat and Paul Cezanne's rational and conceptual structural style. His goal was to give Impressionism more universal meaning by stressing formal design. The art of van Gogh and Gaugin led to Expressionist and Symbolist works. Observers could still discern figures and natural scenes but they were increasingly abstract and less pictorial. Cezanne's geometric structures, for example, anticipated more intellectual/rational styles such as Cubism.

Traditional artistic expression in the late 19th century had been grounded upon a Renaissance concept of art. This was an art of realistic expression of both the natural world and human forms. With the Impressionists, a vast change took place in artists' perception and representation of material reality. A series of scientific discoveries revolutionized our conception of the universe. Atomic physics revealed that previously accepted assumptions about real objects and the universe were quite insubstantial. For example, Kandinsky's reading of the new discoveries led him to exclaim: "All things become flimsy, with no strength or certainty." He felt his sense of reality slipping. Even so, there were further revelations in experimental psychology with regard to man's subconscious mind. Motion pictures and domination of the economy by the machine also had great impacts.

Even as artists struggled to understand the advances of science in order to somehow introduce scientific concepts and meanings into their art, science and art began to suffer an unfortunate antipathy between them. Public-culture had come to view science as the study of things yielding cold facts; art as devoted to fanciful splashes of color and imaginative shapes. It took a humanist scientist to bridge the gap. In a small but seminal book, Jacob Bronowski revealed how great science and fine art share common ground in their creative searching for unity in variety. In this, he followed the intuition of a great poet, Coleridge, in his definition of beauty, writing:

> "Science is nothing more than the search to discover unity in the wild variety of nature – or more exactly, in the variety of our experience...the arts are the same search...The discoveries of science, the works of art are explorations more, are explosions of a hidden likeness...This is the act of creation...the same act in original science and original art."[187]

The gradual evolution of art to unprecedented nonobjective renderings was the most radical change effected by post-Impressionism. In the 20th century, with Cubism and the sequence of abstract works that it inspired, art was no longer deemed to be descriptive, nor even an illusionary rendering recognizable by sight. It became an autonomous world viewed in terms of artists' subjective visions and their own internal styles. "Art for art's sake!" – The observer be damned! This was a revolution in terms of form and content – but not of governance. The field of art had always been the province of an elite, a province that narrowed and congealed into an international avant-garde. This increasingly self-regarding set generated an increasing flow of political polemics, manifestos and attacks on middle-class ideology.

The evolution of art from the depiction of natural to completely abstract forms has been described and characterized by the great Spanish philosopher Ortega y Gasset as the "dehumanization of art."[188] He referred to complete reliance

[187] Bronowski, Jacob (1956), **SCIENCE and HUMAN VALUES.** New York: Harper and Row, pp. 16 & 17.

[188] Gasset, Ortega Y (1948), **THE DEHUMANIZATION of ART and other writings on art and culture** [Translated by Helene Weyl]. Princeton, New Jersey: Princeton University Press. 103 p.

upon abstract patterns without any recognizable sign of human life, calling this "the urge to elude reality." Indeed, but Ortega then went a step too far when he degraded metaphor as "the most radical instrument of dehumanization" because of its "surrealism."[189] He also confused metaphor with the supernatural. But 'T'aint necessarily so.'

The uses of metaphor demonstrate some of the most creative powers of the human mind. Kepler, for example, felt for his laws by way of metaphors.[190] Sure; there are abstract metaphors, just as there are inhuman allusions to the dark-side of human life. And yet metaphor also helps us to express the deep beauty and inherent spirituality of human life – through its living-in-action as well as its representations. Nevertheless, Gasset's thesis should be well taken. Increasingly abstract flights of fancy represent increased distances of both artist and observer from human life.[191]

The problem with this evolutionary view of art in relationship to spirituality is that it posits a sharp contrast to what we observed in the fields of architecture and music. Art appears to have gone from spiritual to completely secular, rationalistic abstraction. It's possible, however, to perceive here one possible common denominator with the earlier observations on individuality. This, however, is the individuality of elite sensibilities that appear difficult to link with any broader, more widespread or democratic concepts. Authors of one major source commented:

> "In the 20th century, the neglected artist learned to view his art as a potential esthetic...a weapon of subversion directed at middle-class

---

[189] Gasset, op .cit.. pp.32-33.

[190] Bronowski (1956), op, cit., p. 12.

[191] A fine example of abstraction that powerfully conveys the meaning of a human event is Picasso's GUERNICA. An opposite example, a beautiful, complete abstraction, is that of Gerhard Richter's **ABSTRACT PAINTING** (946-3).

philistinism...One dramatic result has been to compel the avant garde to develop its own community with a set of social ideals based on protest and (their own,) internal standards..."[192]

Art for art's sake?; sometimes, but note that major contrasts have here been somewhat overdrawn by omission. This is the case for both music and architecture. In music, no mention has been made of modern and post-modern adoption of abstract and atonal forms for musical compositions. One justification is that such pieces have been paid little attention but for relatively small, elite audiences and few conductors. Recent far-out architectural designs have fared better. The Guggenheim museum in New York City has become quite beloved. Frank Gehry designs are at least accorded respectful, if quizzical, glances. The difference here is that buildings, no matter how outrageous some architects' proclivities might be, must be ineluctably useful and adaptable. Occupants must have them so and will adapt them to their own tastes, anyway. But they don't have to listen to music that jars their ears.

One example of how occupants invariably work to adapt their dwellings to suit is from post-Stalinist Poland. There, inhuman, stolid, grey, homely Stalinist designs for high-rise apartment buildings in Warsaw have been transformed into human habitation by their occupants. For example, they place lovely flower pots along the edges of concrete porches.

Another example is provided by Levittown. Not long after the development was built, Pete Seeger derided it in song as "ticky-tacky." The inhabitants proved him wrong. Their adaptations and beautifications of the basic designs of their then-affordable housing lent human variety and vitality to the dwellings. The human spirit cannot be contained by bureaucrats, unimaginative layouts or bad designs! Thus, some of the observations in this chapter reinforce those made in Chapter 11 reflecting the importance of locality to fostering spirituality.

---

[192] Hunter, Sam, & J. Jacobs (1976), **MODERN ART**. Italy: Helvetic Press, p.9

A keyword of this chapter; indeed, of this book, has been "evolution." We have seen how the concept applies to consciousness and spirituality as represented by works of art, music and architecture. The challenge: How high is "higher"? For it remains to be seen how evolution may or may not continue to apply as man increasingly proceeds to make himself, not only through culture but, increasingly, through manipulation of the human genome.

The Role of Stories and Myths in Nurturing Spirituality: Traditional tales and myths satisfy a deep yearning of the human soul for companionship in the world.

> "When you cut human beings off from that cosmic world of consciousness – when it is no longer considered relevant – myth then becomes something unreal instead of a sacred reality. In its place arise all sorts of pseudo-myths. [e.g., about aliens & UFOs]."

Contributing to the desacrilization discussed earlier, "the ensuing alienation has also made a sham of the metaphysical and philosophical basis of ethics."[193]

The prevalence and power of myths were evident in President Trump's inaugural at two levels, God-in-heaven and "We the People." God and heaven are at the top of a hierarchical system. The religious labels refer to a medieval hierarchy, as in "God the King" and "Lord God." Far less elitist, populist calls start with the French and American revolutions. Even without reference to our Constitution, Trump invoked "We the People", the low end of the political system, as being now in control with his election. On the one hand, political leaders, like the kings of old, like to have their positions blessed by a hypothetical almighty. On the other, they are blessed by "We the People." Those who invoke both may be twice blessed?

From a scientific point of view, both are mythical. Neither the priests of religion nor of politics cite evidence to support their invocations. The lack of

---

[193] Source of both quotes: **PARABOLA** (Summer, 2004).

any back up for Trump's populist phrases except for himself being on stage is troubling. Trump's mouthing "God Bless America" seemed quite proforma, for he seems to believe that he is God's blessing to America. For nothing was heard to encourage people's ongoing political involvement, or the need for folks to talk with people who disagree with them. The disconnections here may prove the undoing of the latest edition of American populism. "In God We Trust" won't cut it in the face of distrust both within the body politic and between people, their government and what should be but is not yet, **their** politics. A free, self-governing people cannot govern themselves on the basis of myths.

Myths are maps leading to the treasures of man's deepest spiritual potential. In their searching for greater meaning, human beings have discovered ways in which we are all characters in the mythic play. Unfortunately, contending mythologies have become part of an outworn game with little relevance to addressing the real, most pressing problem of post-modern human life. This is the failure of most to recognize that we're all passengers on "spaceship earth," as Buckminster Fuller called it. In-group/out-group attitudes favor admiration and respect only for one's own group while projecting disdain and aggression outward towards others. These attitudes sustained by archaic myths are destructive of the broader social fabric needed to sustain the cooperation and collaboration that is essential to nurture and sustain human life on planet earth. The in-group attitudes serve only to sustain the world as an archipelago of echo chambers.

The four main functions of myth are the:

1) **Mystical**...of opening the mystical dimension in minds.
2) **Cosmological**...of relating us to the cosmos as now known – in such a way that its mystery can be experienced. Living myth has to do with attitudes.
3) **Sociological**...of validating and maintaining the moral or ethical system of the specific social group to which one belongs; and
4) **Identification**...of the group which accepts one as a member – an act of a mythological nature.

Go to any church or synagogue and you'll find the clergy there trying to support an archaic concept of the universe against the findings of science.[194] Religion has been kicking against the findings of science ever since Hellenistic times. Just think: The first chapter of Genesis was composed at a time when the Greeks had already measured the circumference of the earth to within a couple of hundred miles. Religious views present an archaic notion of the shape of the cosmos and the way in which the cosmos came into being. The religious system is also wedded to mythology in terms of the social unit-as-organism.

These views were synchronized with the cycles of the seasons, as our ritual festivals still are:

- o Christmas and the Festival of Lights at the time of the dawning of new light in the winter solstice;
- o Spring festivals celebrating the resurrection of life, and
- o Fall festivals focused on the meaning of harvest time.

All of the basic mythology revolved around that which put the society in accord with the world of nature. Then the individual, who was also a product of nature, was put in accord with nature, too – his own nature – through participation in those rites.

Well, now that's all fallen apart. We now have the idea of micro-macro-cosm, the problem of modern man. All the old, basic, historically grounded traditions were rendered effective through rituals. Rites are the enactments of myths. By participating in rites, one is participating in the myth. Consequently, one activates the accordant structures and principles within one's own psyche. Without some kind of ritual enactment, the whole thing fails to get inside the active aspirations of one's consciousness – unless one

---

[194] A major reason why "humanists" have broken off from organized religion to establish their own venue for celebration of their life together and their spirituality.

happens to be working through actual life problems (again) in terms suggested by mythological considerations."[195]

The challenge this puts to those favoring a NSB is fundamental. It is not a matter of discarding myths or rituals. It is: What set of new rites or rituals can be developed to practice a NSB that would also resonate with the core, life-enhancing features of ancient but still "living" myths?

---

[195] Much of this section has been based on Joseph Campbell's "Living Myths: A Conversation with Joseph Campbell", December 7, 2016, by Parabola editors.

Chapter 15

Spirituality, Soulfulness and Soul

Introduction

Even though we tried to find a definition of "soul," both at the outset of this book and in Chapter 2 on "Belief..." the only part of the dictionary definition that made sense was: "the spiritual principle embodied in human beings, all rational and spiritual beings." And yet, even this is unsatisfactory. For example, why include "rational"? Any one of the species homo sapiens is an odd mix of the rational, irrational and spiritual, but one can be spiritual without passing some test of rationality.[196] We'll see in this section how hard it is to define "soul" without any reference to "rational", so why compound the difficulty of trying to define "soul" by including the challenge of defining "rational"?

---

[196] One might also want to forgive here a seemingly arbitrary separation of "rational" from "spiritual." Various ways of attaining or practicing spirituality, e.g., deep meditation, have been found to yield significant benefits in terms of healthfulness and other aspects of human well-being. What could be more "rational" than these?

Thomas Moore says without hesitation: Don't bother – "It is impossible to define precisely what the soul is;"[197]however, doesn't this seem a bit cavalier? Another soulful thinker seems think so – Albert Schweitzer. He wrote: When I say reason, I refer to the understanding that penetrates to the depths of things…that embraces the wholeness of reality…" Read on to pick up more of this profound thread.

Refining Soulfulness

Recall the synonyms of soulfulness cited earlier. Most, plus some others, are cited by Moore as nearly definitional "qualities" of soul. These include: depth, value, relatedness, reflection, reverence, and mystery. Moore also writes that soul is "revealed in attachment, love and community..."[198] The variety of qualities is part and parcel of a soul's individuality. These qualities arise, develop and are expressed through life experience, which also varies from person to person. There is no basis or reason to claim soul as a gift from a God-on-high. Moore writes: "Soul doesn't pour into life automatically. It requires our skill and attention."[199] We also need not make adherence to any "religion" a prerequisite for soulfulness, even though one writer equates a "religious attitude" with soulfulness and spirituality.[200]

After all, soulfulness is the highest and best quality of the human mind – an emergent phenomenon as discussed earlier. Soul arises from soulfulness

---

[197] Moore, Thomas (1992), **CARE of the SOUL:** A Guide for Cultivating Depth and Sacredness in Everyday Life. New York: HarperCollins Publishers,

[198] Moore, op.cit. (p. xi)

[199] Ibid., (p. xvii).

[200] Johnson, Robert (1998), **BALANCING HEAVEN and EARTH.**

San Francisco: Harper.

which is a product of the human spirit that, in turn, has arisen through human consciousness – a gift of the human brain. All arise from complex interactions within the brain, partly but not entirely in response to the demands of everyday life. There is also an unconscious and a "dark side" of our brain that affects our being and becoming. The battle between the "light" and "dark" sides of our being is the classic struggle between good and evil.

We paid some attention to the darkside earlier with reference to Star Wars. Note that a focus on the God of Life averts the temptations revealed by Star Wars. Recall our recognition of the downside of reliance upon super-natural myths in our discussion of Complex Adaptive Systems (CAS) as discussed by Holland. All this implies the need to refine our understanding of spirituality.

The Demands for and of Spirit

Focus first on what is a very familiar demand – the need and desire for "spirit" to energize and elevate so many human undertakings. It appears whenever we are trying to accomplish something that none of us can accomplish solo, by oneself without the cooperation and collaboration of others. The examples are legion. They include "team spirit", "company spirit," "spirit of a congregation," "orchestral spirit," and "The spirit of America" [last invoked by President Trump in his address to Congress on 2/28/17].

Here, spirit is recognizable, too, as a special feature of the brain's ability to perceive or hypothesize commonalities among different people, things or features. Moore, for example, recognizes "several common issues in everyday life that provide opportunities for soul making...",[201] not simply as problems to be solved. Note the import of "making." Soul is not to be viewed as a preexisting, pre-made something to be used in helping us to face either common or uncommon issues.

---

[201] Moore, p. xix).

Also recall that: "soul" is not a product but a process – "a quality or dimension of experiencing life..."[202] in which ends and means are interchangeable. Neither one "justifies" the other. Recall that life is both an end and a means. "...every ending is a beginning...it is the soul that makes us human."[203] The process is fueled by spirituality – an emergent, higher order, all-purpose "spirit." Spirituality has the quality of light, which transforms all that it touches. The most important transformation is of the mindfulness from which spirituality originates. This is a powerful, mutually reinforcing, virtuous cycle whereby the potential influence and power of spirituality knows no limit.

One very important implication to note here is no less far reaching: That we stop thinking of "spirituality" as stuffed in some box, whether that "box" is a church, a private prayer moment, or any other kind of enclosure. The box has burst its bounds. Our spirit is unbounded. So, in keeping with earlier words, we have all the more reason to recognize and call upon OUR "holy" spirit!

Human life is a process, too, a process of creating matter, meaning, and values thereof and therefrom. Viewed this way, it is everlasting, as matter and meaning are passed from generation to generation as well as documented in human history. The seed of soul is consciousness. Spirituality grows out of consciousness as we come to attach higher and higher concepts and values to the objects, creations and relationships of life. The instrumental behaviors of soul building are attachment, intimacy, caring, sharing, community building, and above all, love. At higher, more conceptual levels, integration and synthesis are key.

"Soul" is not an abstraction. It starts to build from the things and experiences of everyday life. Think on these. What do you value most? These are likely to be relationships above all. There are also precious objects, including creations of our own craft. The skein of relationships grows from homes to teams,

---

[202] Ibid., p.5.

[203] Moore, pp.9 & 13.

schools, workplaces and communities. To greater or lesser degrees, each is imbued with attachments and values. These increasingly come to focus on what is good and better for ourselves in relationship to others. Earlier, we learned that many of the places in which memories are stored in the brain are discrete and separate, but fast-advancing research on the brain also reveals that many neurons important to memory and meaning congregate or are linked throughout.

Thus, soul, viewed as a repository of precious memories as well as other highly valued associations, might be viewed as a place in the brain which enables the recovery of matter and meaning from other parts of the brain, however disparate they might be. This means that the soul is not a generic instrument; it varies from individual to individual. It is the source of our individualities and identities. With powers of synthesis and integration brought to bear on pieces and parts, it is important to the development and identification of personality and character.

The structure of soul-as-process is hierarchically and fractally self-similar to that of life and the brain overall. Perhaps the best model is mathematical, not just via equations but in the qualities of a mathematical mind at work like that of Penrose. We begin with the concept and operations of numbers. Then we conceive of sets, groups, sets of groups and groups of sets, etc. Each level represents a level of integration of lower-level elements. So, with respect to "soul," we conceive of "spirit", then imagination, spirituality, soul and soulfulness.

As we move to higher levels of seeming abstraction, however, it is important to never lose sight of their rootedness in real things. For, notwithstanding the fact that souls are individual, some of the most important meanings derive from relationships and groupings. If our valuations of meaning become too abstract – too far removed from people's lives – then irresolvable conflicts may arise. Some of these could be imagined in abstract art, but what about the real world?

Examples

Consider, for example, the case of the European Union {EU}. It began as a concept to keep the peace after two world wars that began in Europe. So, it came to have value. A European spirit arose; however, the keepers of the spirit's keys were bureaucrats centralized in Brussels. The EU also lacked any fiscal policy or powers. And so now the future of the EU is questionable. As of this writing, many of the conflicts in the EU are coming to the fore – between nation-members as well as between the parts and the whole. It remains to be seen whether and how these may be resolved. Abstractions won't help.

Nevertheless, there are others who now conceive of world government, a still higher level of integration. In order for this to be anything other than a pipe dream, however, globalization will need to involve peaceful, creative and working together interactivity among many more of the globe's disparate groups than just those of scientists and/or members of other elite classes.

One can hardly hope to elevate "spirit" to soul and soulfulness without a reverence for life. The **tree of life** has long been a powerful and spiritual metaphor of growing systems, both root and branch. In winter, it reveals the dendritic branching of fractal forms. I raise my eyes to the firmament, hoping to sing "Oh my Soul", and I see the tops of trees. Every branch seeks the light. No matter how contorted, amputated or convoluted branchings may be, they twist and lead upward towards the light. Every one of us also seeks the light. And so every walk or run turns into a potential realization of spirituality.

It is no accident that Albert Schweitzer's most inspiring sermons were variations on the theme of "Reverence for Life."[204] The English title of a volume of these was mistranslated from the original German, which was "Was Sollen Wir Tun?" -- "What Should We Do?" Actually, the two titles go

---

[204] Schweitzer, Albert (1988), **A PLACE for REVELATION: Sermons on Reverence for Life.** New York: Macmillan.

together, in keeping with Schweitzer's philosophy, so deeply rooted in everyday life, so much a search for the common good...

> "basically a matter of ...small acts...why we must think together concerning the intrinsic good."[205]

That is what he wrote, in keeping with his definition of life continuing:

> "God is everlasting life...Life means strength...feeling, sensitivity, suffering. And if you are absorbed in life, if you see with perceptive eyes into this enormous animated chaos of creation, it...seizes you with vertigo...Wherever you see life -- that is you!"[206]

Vertigo has two definitions, each very pertinent to our feeling for life. One is that we are in stable surroundings but nevertheless feel that we are tilting or spinning. The other is that the surroundings are "tilting or spinning." Either way, life is disequilibrium-dynamic. Life is vertiginous. It's also togetherness. None of us are alone in feeling life's force and grandeur. Schweitzer continues:

> "It is reverence for life...for the impenetrable mystery that meets us in our universe, an existence different from ourselves...yet...terribly similar...The dissimilarity, the strangeness between us and other creatures is here removed...(via) the restoration of shared experiences and of compassion and sympathy."[207]

Schweitzer's fundamental concern has been to set forth the pre-requisites of a good, ethical life. In exploring the "basic nature" of goodness, he insisted that:

---

[205] Schweitzer, op.cit., pp. xiii & 6.

[206] Ibid., pp. 8 &10. This and that following are drawn from Schweitzer's 1st Sermon on Reverence for Life.

[207] Ibid., pp. 10 (at bottom) & 11. The italics are Schweitzer's.

"reason and the heart must work together," spiritually, so that "the moral will is connected to reason,"

He focused on love. This meant to him "harmony of being, community of being." On the other hand, reason "is the desire for knowledge...and happiness," attainable only by plumbing to the "depths of things" in oneself and communities of others, for "All knowledge is finally knowledge of life."[208] [Quotes from Sermon One on "Reverence for Life."]

A good example is the reappearance via Google of a galactic cloud of stars enveloping the landscape of a small town -- a wide-angle, long time photographic exposure-- a scene of soulful wonderment. The scene served as an introduction to an even greater source of wonder, a photographic tour of major galaxies starting from our own -- a galaxy with 400 billion stars centered on a massive black hole. Some say our universe has a soul. Doubtful in reality but a wonderful dream. We'll see.

Development of soul and soulfulness calls for daily care. This is why Moore wrote the book that we have already had reason to reference. The main lesson to emerge from it is the prime importance of tending to the things around us that can give ordinary, day-to-day living the:

> "depth and value that come from soulfulness...(by) cultivating a richly expressive and meaningful life at home and in society.,.(which calls for) mindfulness, awareness and attentiveness...to items of life all about us...(and) observance of how the soul manifests itself."[209]

Let me attest to these from personal experience. My own soul has been seeded by love -- of family, gardening, the sea, tidal pools, trees of life, sea life from seaweeds on up, woods and wood craft, women and other people, and music (no order of priority here). Mindfulness and soulfulness have grown with the

---

[208] Schweitzer, op. Cit., pp.6-7.

[209] Moore, op.cit., p.4.

experience of a life living among these other living things, working with them while being and becoming with them.

Chapter 16

Spirituality and Space-Time

[Including thoughts in response to Gruden][210]

Introduction

Many of those (very many) who have tried to wrap spirituality into their worldview and way of life believe that its realization requires time and space specially devoted to the practice. One of the basic messages of this book is, following an old song, that "taint necessarily so." Most people lack and can't afford the time and space to be so devoted. Spirituality needs to be promoted and practiced at points of action that frequent everyday life. These are many and varied – points at which chores are undertaken, things are made, items are written, words are spoken (&c). Spirituality realized at such points enriches each experience. The points are better spoken; the words better written; things better made.

---

[210] This section draws a great deal, including quotes, from Gruden, Robert (1982), **TIME and the Art of Living**, New York: Harper & Row.

Spacetime

The possibility of spirituality realized through work is recognized later in Chapter 23 and also at the end of Psalm 90: "The work of our hands, blesseth thou it." Here, a focus on the space-time correlates of human activity requires us to recognize both the independence and inter-dependence of time and space. Consider a workplace. Obviously, both time and space are needed for good work. The time it takes to produce something depends on both the quantity and quality of space available for the work, as well as availability of tools and materials. In other words, time depends on space. Vice-versa, space is somewhat dependent on the time required for things to be done.

For instance, more space spells less clutter and less time. Some of the qualities of spirituality are like those of good work: attention, awareness, perception and thoughtfulness. Thus, spirituality transforms space-time – both by augmenting the matter and meaning of tasks to be accomplished -- the ultimate value(s) of what tasks produce -- and by increasing the possibility that these values are realized through the influence of good work(s) over time.

Responsibility in Spacetime

Primary responsibility for the realization and fruits of spirituality falls to each of us as individuals who recognize that we have souls and that only conscious cultivation of our souls will enable us to become the best that we can be. And yet context is also key, for as individuals we work, play and otherwise live in contexts that facilitate, discourage or are indifferent to souls and their spiritual needs, as noted in earlier chapters. Work settings, for example, usually inhibit spirituality. Assembly line work is totally adverse. It has been reduced by substituting robots and other machines for human beings rather than by humanizing work. The great importance of context in each of our lives was tersely stated by Ortega y Gasset when he wrote: "I am I and my circumstances."

Schools are also contexts where we spend a great deal of the space-time of our lives. Yet, to spend is not to invest. How well is our space-time invested?

For too many, too poorly.[211] Recall the human development triad: Body, Mind, Spirit. Body? – only if you play sports. Mind? – Fuh'get about it unless you're in an excel track. Spirit? – the highest quality of what it is to be human – Exorcised. Spirituality has no place in the schools except for that rare, tiny minority who study to be pastors or priests so they can be vendors of institutionalized religion to the rest of us less inspired souls. The most obvious sign of this neglect is the ban on prayers in most schools. Even so, required prayer would not translate to recognition of souls in classrooms and the great importance of their spiritual development. The latter need to be recognized and incorporated into schools' curricula.

With rare exceptions, neither employers nor teachers recognize, and so cannot help employees or students confront, what Gruden calls the "...tragic duality between inner and outer worlds...tragic divorces between our lonely humanity and the pulse of nature..." As one way of overcoming the latter division, Gruden recommends what I have already found through my own experience: "...the runner('s) route...a kind of space-time..."[212] -- the perception and creation thereof. While running, I recall the Biblical invocation "Lift thine eyes..."

> As I start my morning run. I see the light from a rising sun radiating through the trees. Above all, as reported earlier, I see the tops and shapes of the trees of life. No matter how contorted their branches, every one of them, and every one of their leaves, seeks to absorb the new light as their roots suck nutrients from the soil. These images exude and promote spirituality even while I work to keep up the pace. The God-of-Life is at work. Mind and body are winding their way together, interweaving like the dense bracken at the base of the trees, generating a synthesis of light, soul, soil and nature. Gruden's characterization of this, however, is far too intellectual to be real:

---

[211] For more on this point, see Holt, John (1969), "School is bad for children," **THE SATURDAY EVENING POST** (Feb. 8).

[212] Gruden, op.cit, p.1.

"discovering a unified phenomenology...(a more) valid and dignified level of reality."[213]

My experience as a duffer-runner seems roughly similar to that of athletes whose training and focus manages to generate a more voluminous sense of time, a depth perception whereby time constitutes not only the medium of thought and feeling but their very substance. Our total ability to think and feel is proportional to the volume of thought or feeling we can hold in our minds in a given moment. The perception of likeness and difference are best performed by trained minds. The good mind can think more within a given instant, as it is alert to broad and implicit relationships.

Nevertheless, as discussed at length in Chapter 23, one way that spirituality is realized is through work and the awareness, perception and thoughtfulness of its doing. If "mind" fails to resonate with "humanity" and "body" with "nature," then they'll fail to find their way to a unified "level" of "reality." Spirituality is emergent from the mind but energized by the body. The key to learning and making is "Mens et Manus" [Mind and Hands], the motto of M.I.T. The "connectedness of things" is realized both within and without. The common denominator is life-in-time and the awareness thereof. What "divorces" come between man and nature? How else are they to be overcome? -- by gardening?, conceiving and raising a family?, understanding the ecology of life?...All of these and more.

Gruden also writes:

> "The extent to which we live from day to day...intent on details and oblivious to larger (spiritual?) presences, is a gauge of our impoverishment in time...Deprived of the continuum, we lose...the nourishing context..."

This statement, though largely true, fails to recognize what we have already noted -- that the lack of a suitable (let alone "nourishing") context is a

---

[213] Gruden, op.cit., p.2.

common disabler of any spiritual "continuum." Gruden also discounts the possibility that some "details" may spark spirituality; for example, the sight of buds emerging from seemingly dead branches during early springtime. To fail to see the spiritual potential of everyday life is tantamount to throwing us ordinary humans back to pre-Martin Luther days, when only priests were permitted to see the word of God. There is a troubling disconnect here between the large and the small, between "details" and "larger."

The "nourishing context" is not a continuum of time, even given awareness thereof. It is tools and freedom utilized over space-time that enable us to exercise our human powers. "The gauge of our impoverishment in time" is our inability to make creative and productive use of it. Mind and spirit can be invested in any detail, however small. They need not be left to the "larger."

"But if we roof and wall time into chambers of expectation, plan and commitment, our days become memorable. Time takes on significance when we frame it on a human scale."[214]

Equilibrium or Disequilibrium?

Here and elsewhere, however, we need to distinguish and draw out the implications of disequilibrium v. equilibrium states. We can plan and elicit firm commitments only if we're living in the context of a reasonably stable (equilibrium) system. For better or worse, however, we're living in disequilibrium dynamic worlds. In such contexts, when spirituality is brought in, the "chambers of expectation" may be richer, deeper and even limitless. To the extent that we can "wall and roof" time, spirituality may suffer from the constraints of both space and unnecessarily limited time. Thus, Gruden's mixing "wall and roof" with "Chambers of expectation" generates tension, even contradiction.

---

[214] Gruden, Ibid., p.4.

He then ventures into a potentially more perilous space when he writes:

> "In time as well as space, the surrender of the specific…turns out to be no loss at all but rather the…way of expanding into a grander and more general form…a heroic being…" [215]

Perhaps, but this can also be dangerously misleading. The "surrender" is seldom without loss, especially when the "specific" is dissolved into a larger whole. It can also mean that the "more general form" is grandiosity puffed up rather than truly "heroic." Abdication of the ordinary for the heroic ignores the tragic lessons of the 20th century. Hitler was elected in 1933 on the basis of "grandiosity puffed up." As the wise longshoreman, McCarthy, in Saroyan's play, **Time of Your Life,** recognized:

> "…McCarthys are too great and strong to be heroes. Only the weak and unsure can perform the heroic. They've got to! The more heroes we have, the worse the history of the world becomes." [216]

Gruden continues:

> "We seldom think of…specific phenomena as parts of a coherent whole…And in missing… the temporal coherence…we miss the truth about ourselves…Free men and women…can think across time…To approach freedom of this sort, we must begin with a single simple thought… particularly pertinent to moral choices…" [217]

This "single simple" is spirituality which, like light, can transform any of our daily images and actions. Single simples may be ordinary things that hold

---

[215] Gruden, Ibid.

[216] A role played by the author in the Feb.10-12, 2017 production of the great Saroyan play put on by The Panhandle Players at the Chapman Auditorium in Apalachicola, FL.

[217] Gruden, work cited., p.5.

special meaning for us. What is most "pertinent" here, along with relevance to "moral choices," is the sensation and realization of our spirituality. Otherwise, Gruden's thought here borders on incoherence. "Specific phenomena" can seldom be conceived in the moment.

Time's passage, clocked or not, often helps to reveal the reality of change and the value of specific moments. On this, Gruden remarks on:

the "furniture" of the past and "how...we...look for it (change) in the wrong places...and find too late that it has occurred within us."

Furniture represents stability more than change and so, like other valued artifacts of our lives and memories, may give rise to feelings akin to spirituality. Change may mean disruption, giving rise to feelings of anxiety or stress. Other, more positive and profound kinds of change are likely to emerge from reflections or meditations on past changes that are more spiritual than those changes we "look for" in our expectations.

We cannot help but see, as Gruden observes:

> "...the remarkable brevity of our lives in the cosmic scale of time...each day is a minor eternity of 86,000 seconds...a few seconds are long enough for a revolutionary idea...Great drama, like the energy in every atom, is eternally around...and within us... liberated only by coincidence, ceremony, creativity ...periods...pressures...and the simple but painful cultivation of awareness."[218]

Such awareness is key to the emergence of a spirituality that would amplify our lives in time, matter and meaning as well as heighten the care we bring to bear in doing most anything. Our spirituality would not only be "liberated" but also celebrated "by coincidence, ceremony, creativity... periods...pressures..." Gruden goes on to say with regard to awareness:

---

[218] Gruden, ibid., p.7.

> "Perceptions of...phenomena constantly excite our temporal faculties...Our goal should be to make these processes more conscious..."

Indeed; such consciousness is even more salient for realization and expression of our spirituality.

Dimensionality

Four dimensionality suggests new forms of symmetry and asymmetry. Gruden thinks:

> "a mean may exist: a class of phenomena that are symmetrical in space-time...objects which seem to be in time exactly what they are in space...cognate with our sense of beauty."[219]

This passage is very suggestive, but it only makes sense in the case of fixed objects that are durable over both space and time such as sculptures in stone.

Yes, indeed, our goal is to make spirituality more conscious. Beauty arouses spirituality, and vice-versa. Here, too, we need to practice heightening our awareness. Earlier, we noted the ability of great athletes to seemingly "manufacture" time. The nub, however, is not time but mind amplified by spirit. Through an amplified consciousness, trained minds can generate both more effective time and a heightened spirituality. Again, recall the example of Tom Brady. His "secret" is spiritual; focusing on the depth of quietude."

Two characteristics of the Renaissance were to seek truth in time and elevate prudence.[220] Gruden remarks:

> "...those people who can...control and inhabit their own past and future, have a particular dignity... Paradoxically, they can be

---

[219] Gruden, ibid., pg. 8.

[220] See, for example, Titian's "Allegory of Prudence."

approached effectively only when we come to terms...with the one dimension of time which can be studied...directly, the present...We must learn to do this...(sensing) the present (together) with its...coordinates -- house & rooms...loved ones....our work...body, our very spirit..(in order to) appreciate and (perhaps be able to) memorialize every present state...."[221]

Here again is an inspiring passage. The capture of its full meaning requires both perception of essential details and of the wholeness (gestalt) of their contribution to the whole setting in which they lie.

For time and spirituality are close companions. They feed and enrich each other. Realization of the value of a moment may be accompanied by a spiritual rush. A spiritual thought may be coupled with realization of the value and passage of time, even by attaching to some ordinary thing. Spirituality and truth also interact in virtuous circles. I have frequently felt threads of past and future interweaving in the present. Gruden's "particular dignity," however, inheres mostly in anyone's spirituality, which may or may not inform wisdom or prudence. The latter is an old-fashioned name for a woman that is now little used, as name or word. A dictionary definition is: "quality of being prudent; cautiousness...; synonyms: wisdom, judgement, common sense, sagacity, care, forethought..."

Unfortunately, Gruden proceeds to contradict some of his earlier remarks by writing:

"We are continually blinded to process...isolated in the quite unredeeming present...rather than using the totality of the event as a means of understanding..." "[222]

---

[221] Gruden, op.cit., p.13.

[222] Op. cit., p.23.

How many dimensions attach to an "event." What if breaks in the process [the "interrupts" that define time] are entrees to our spirituality? Here is where time and spirituality seem paradoxically to part ways. Spirituality is key to continuity (and vice-versa), along with a host of basic values. But discontinuity awakens us to call upon our spirituality. If one cares to try to attach dimensions to spirituality (as I do not), one is likely to fail. One would lose count. For spirituality is multi…multi (&c) "dimensional." The number is either zero or infinity.

What is "totality"? Consciousness during the event, and spirituality at key junctures -- these are keys to understanding. The connection may also be vice-versa: At least some understanding would have to precede any attempt to grasp whatever totality of an event our consciousness may try or be able to comprehend. The higher level of consciousness that is spirituality may be key to any substantial grasp of some "totality," whether an achievement or realization of a more holistic vision.

Back to Time

It is very important here not to confuse clock measures of time with the value and extent of time. Most important to the latter is realization of the power of human activity to practically create both more value of time and more time of value. A program was mentioned on NPR called "Make Marks."[223] It focused on how parent's time with children helps to enrich kids' lives. Along with the conception of children, this is tantamount to increasing the amount of valuable time in the universe. Within the human segment of the universe, time is life and life is time. The value of time starts with consciousness of self, the sense of "I". This increases with the perception of the otherness of others and of gradually growing, larger worlds; that is, with I = Interrelatedness.

Higher levels of perception and mindfulness lead to I = Integration – of facts and impressions of people and things, how and why they interrelate and what matter and meanings they convey. It takes time to add value and value to add

---

[223] Radio broadcast of March 27, 2017.

time that is truly meaningful and memorable. We have already observed how interrelatedness and integration are among the sources of soulfulness and spirituality.

Over time, Gruden observes, we search for character, value, truth...like listeners perceiving, in different musical instruments at different times, recurring themes and rhythms."[224] What about tuning in to our own spirituality? As shown in a previous chapter, music can be a great help. Gruden again:

> "What we understand best, we understand by renewal -- looking at it internally and externally, walking around it, turning it in our hands, participating in it until some strange spirit(uality) of our being rises from the complexity (and communion) of effort..."

This quote harkens back to our earlier discussion of complex adaptive systems giving rise to higher level developments or insights through "emergence." It also bids forward to our discussion of spirituality and work via "Mens et Manus" – tuning work in our minds while turning it in our hands." What about reflection or meditation -- aspects of our spirituality -- akin to a "strange spirit of our being"? What is "renewal" here? -- of our work? Something we are cultivating or making? Yes!

Gruden further provokes us when he writes:

> "...freedom in space-time is impossible without a larger sense of the larger cycles of experience..."[225]

It seems impossible to imagine the latter without including spirituality as an ingredient essential to any "larger sense," as "a recurring voice in the music of time." Curiously, Gruden makes reference to "Timekeepers" as a source of

---

[224] Op.cit., p.26.

[225] [225]Op. cit., p.28.

help to locate one's "definite position between the entrance and exit of life."[226] It would, however, be better to locate oneself with the help of spirituality, departing from the clock time of any "timekeepers." Gruden mistakenly focuses on "exit", assuming that most of us live lives stricken with the fear of death.

Another quote here is germane:

In space-time, "...the observer sits...as though facing backward in the taut concavity of a wind-stretched sail...(so that he) may look forward only into the void."[227]

This empty, blackened viewpoint is contradicted by life ever after. Gruden is mistaken. He discounts human spirituality, along with its faith and hope. One should be quite sanguine while living fully engaged in the process of living. Even Gruden can be so at some points, as when he writes:

> "...for happy people...the present is so voluminous, so inclusive of the full self and so indivisibly coherent with past and future, that time in the usual sense does not pass for them at all. They are at one with the dynamics of nature: time's motion is implicit in their own."[228]

How is all the above accomplished without strong doses of spirituality? Gruden proposes waiting; that is, allowing for the passage of some time. In this, he follows Montaigne, writing:

> "The best way to wait is...to retire into what Montaigne calls, psychologically, the "back-shop"...to drift fully into our own concerns

---

[226] Op. cit., p.29.

[227] Op.cit., p,30.

[228] Op.cit., p.99.

and away from external tyrannies."[229] (what Gruden cited earlier as a "nest of time").

He then lists nine ways to do so. None of these cite spirituality or meditation. The latter's omission is especially surprising. There is no denying the value of meditative moments in the midst of the sometime madness of everyday life. Such moments are sometimes necessary as well as possible. Spirituality adds value to meditation (and vice-versa). Gruden also fails to acknowledge this. He is focused on time, not spirituality or meditation. His advice in and on "Time and the Art of Living" falls short lacking spirituality.

Conclusion

That's all for our review of Gruden's book on TIME and the ART of LIVING, which provided fodder for and forays into the topic of spirituality and space-time.[230] We found a lot of fodder and many shortcomings in Gruden's treatment.

We also found additional evidence that, unlike conventional religions, a NSB will enable the re-entry of spirituality into every facet of human life – anytime and everywhere at every level -- from the smallest and most ordinary to the largest and most grand. "Every hour eye to eye,", as Dag Hammarskjöld wrote in his journal.

---

[229] Op.cit., p.102.

[230] The interested reader can find a great many books on the subject of time.

Chapter 17

ON the SOUL: Emergent?,

or

from Transformation into Transcendence?

Introduction

The human soul is a work-in-progress. Contrary to the belief of the Catholic Church, we are not born with souls pre-prepared for us by some all-knowing God. Why? – Because there is no soul without consciousness of a self in relationship to others, a state of awareness that fully forms only long after birth. For some, the development of such a state may take a lifetime. Our understanding of what it means to have a soul is diminished, downgraded or distorted by popular culture. Terms like "soul music," "soul mates" and "soul food" are tossed about as if they carry some substantial meaning. Yet, they are little more than labels suggesting some transient good feelings. Real, soulful rivers run deeper. In light of Chapter 6's observations on "emergence," we cannot describe the soul as emergent except over time out of the processes of complex adaptive systems. So, what is the human soul? From whence does it arise? What are its qualities?

Reflections of Others on "Soul"

One of the most influential American attempts to answer these questions can be found in Ralph Waldo Emerson's famous essay on "The Over-Soul." He sees an external heavenly God as cause of soul in all of us as spiritual beings from birth, as in: "Behold...I am born into the great, universal mind...the Supreme Mind...in the closet of God..." As for what soul is: Emerson writes: "All goes to show that the soul of man is not...

> "an organ, but animates...all the organs; is not a function, like the power of memory, of calculation, of comparison, but uses these as hands and feet; is not a faculty, but a light; is not the intellect or the will, but the master of the intellect and the will; is the background of our being in which they lie..."[231]

He goes on to describe an immortal soul as synthesis of all life's particulars:

> "that Unity, that Over-soul, within which every man's particular being is contained and made one with all other...the whole...is the soul;" (but he then states that) "from some alien energy the visions come."[232]

What is missing here from Emerson's high-flown, flowery language is some grounding of soul and practice of soulfulness in everyday life. Immortality is also at issue. How can a soul be deemed immortal if grounded in "life's particulars," including "the revelation of all nature"?

Somewhat opposite from Emerson, the soul can be viewed as the product of deep understandings obtained through life experience, reinforced by reflections on both experience and basic values. The latter are usually assumed to be conveyed through family and traditional family-group cultures

---

[231] Emerson, Ralph Waldo (1841), "The Over-Soul", from **ESSAYS: First Series**, p.2.

[232] Emerson, op.cit., pp.1 &3.

but the larger contexts that surround our growing up often have more influence than familial, conventional or traditional values. Soul emerges when a person comes to realize what is of most matter and meaning and what is the purpose and meaning of his or her life in the contexts in which that life is lived.

Often, these are referred to as a person's "identity," but this term falls far short of "soul." Too often, one's identity is a set of appearances denoted by life-style in terms of house, car(s), clothes, schooling, and social status. Matters of meaning and purpose of one's life are far from superficial. The above surface list is connected to a "will to pleasure" rather than a "will to build a community of faith."[233] But for a rare few, soul builds best together with others, to express shared values and work with them to achieve shared goals.

For the dynamic of soul building lies at the self/other interface. For some well-favored, "other" may embrace the world. For others of much lesser status, it may be a neighborhood adverse to body, mind and soul. Anyone, however, could share the experience of Emerson who:

> "in embracing the worth of someone he admires, writes: "I become his wife...he aspires to a higher worth which dwells in …spirit & so (I am)...receiver of that spirit's influence."[234]

Thus, Emerson believes that anyone can be an "other" as either deliverer or recipient of the "higher worth" of "spirit." The achievement of soulfulness is possible to everyone, whatever the context. "Incarnation of the spirit" enters here as "One mode of the divine teaching." Emerson's divine optimism,

---

[233] The first quote is Freud's; the second from a recommendation I made to Rev. Tim Dobson when he was pastor of St. John's Episcopal Church, Gloucester, MA.

[234] Lopate, Philip (2011), "Between Insanity and Fat Dullness: How I became an Emersonian," **HARPER'S MAGAZINE** (January), p.67.

however, seems to leap ahead of native American practicality, when he writes:

> "All are conscious of attaining to a higher self-possession. It shines for all…a certain wisdom of humanity …common to the greatest men with the lowest…We owe many valuable observations to people who are not very acute or profound. "

Yes, indeed but, apparently, inequality was not a concern for Emerson in 1841.

Souls may emerge in the most terrible circumstances. Some degree of suffering may be required to complete the building and exercise of soul. We have all noticed, even if just from journalistic accounts, how many good people rise to the occasion and come forth to help others in times of emergency, when suffering, death and destruction are all around. The most extreme, inspiring examples have been set forth in Frankl's account of his experience in Nazi death camps during the Holocaust.

In his introduction to Frankl's book, Gordon Allport writes: "to live is to suffer; to survive is to find meaning in the suffering... or as Nietzsche wrote:

> "He who has a why to live can bear with almost any how...What alone remains is the last of the human freedoms – the ability to choose one's attitude in a given set of circumstances... responsible to life for something, however grim... circumstances may be."[235]

The last two of the quoted phrases are most germane to soul building. Reference is to **any** "given set of circumstances" and to one's responsibility **to life – the gift of life that one has been given to live with others.**

---

[235] Frankl, Victor E., **MAN'S SEARCH FOR MEANING**. New York: Washington Sq. Press, p.xiv.

The latter must not be misunderstood. It cannot be read to mean that one is justified in sacrificing another for the sake of oneself; rather the opposite, as human beings have demonstrated through the ages, sacrificing themselves to save others. Exceptions? – extremes of human debasement? Of course; these are also drawn from the Holocaust: "The Capos...

> "drawn only from those prisoners whose characters promised them to make them suitable for...(debased) procedures...prepared to use every means... even brutal force, theft, and betrayal of their friends, in order to save themselves...The best of us did not return."[236]

It is not just sobering but striking to read Frankl's accounts of souls and soulfulness revealed within the incredibly adverse circumstances of Nazi concentration camps – that:

> "it was possible for spiritual life to deepen...(notwithstanding) "the soul-destroying mental conflict and clashes of will power which a famished man experiences."[237]

Note here that expressions of spirituality did not arise because of fears of imminent death and hopes of heaven. They arose in and through prisoners' struggles to live – to survive in spite of all the hour-by-hour threats to their well-being. That "The devil is in the details" of such struggles was evident every day. So, if other human beings have proved themselves able to exhibit soulfulness and spirituality in the context of constant degradation and abomination, what about us? Individuals who have been through trying times often report that adversity or illness have prompted spiritual reflections. More often, these are shared in group settings.[238]

---

[236] Frankl, op.cit., p.7.

[237] Ibid, pp.56 and 48.

[238] As reported to me by Helen Livingston, reflecting on her spinal injury.

Conclusion: Life of Soul

The saying: "These are the times that try men's souls" was exemplified with a vengeance during the last century. And now"? Except in some churches, services and funerals, one hardly hears mention of souls, while soulfulness seems to have currency primarily in high-flown graduation speeches and arias sung in old romantic operas. These are fraught with paradox. On the one hand, soul is idiosyncratic; on the other, generalized. How can something so hardly recognized live on? The answer to such questions lies in both our individual and collective consciousness. We need to heighten awareness of souls and soulfulness at all levels of our lives, starting with our own.

Most critical among the questions that arise here, however, is one of a soul's longevity. Christian belief holds that the soul of a human being lives on after the person dies. This may be a comfort to believers but it doesn't hold up to truth testing. We already have reason and evidence to know that soul and soulfulness arise through processes of development and emergence in the brain. Notwithstanding Hameroff's drawing from quantum theory-, no one has yet found, nor is anyone likely to find, that the brain can remain alive after its bearer has died, or that anything identifiable as the person's "soul" can be extricated from a dead brain. Recall the case vs. "life after death" in Chapter 5.

Though a brain is dead, however, a soul-making process can continue and a human soul can live on to the extent that:

- ✓ During life, the deceased has touched the minds and souls of others so that that his or her qualities, thought and deeds live on in the living memory of others, and
- ✓ He or she has been able to set forth memories of the meaning of life via various media that endure.

These are the most meaningful ways anyone's soul can continue to nurture human life in others. One of the keys to the endurance of such soulfulness is memory, especially that embodied in family histories and the living memories of family members. My father's soul, for example, was rooted in the Great

Depression, science, craftsmanship, gardening and Chinese poetry. Lessons from each were passed on to his son and daughters.

It seems as if only a small minority of people have any confidence in religious beliefs that a man's soul lives on in the arms of a living God. How else can one understand the overflows of material things that provide testimony to the souls of those deceased? These include autobiographies, genealogies, mementos of all sorts, photographs, iPods, YouTube videos, grave sites, artifacts, memorials and honorariums. And yet history is a relentless sifter, culler and filter of even the most soulful individual reputations. Only those of individuals most influential and representative of the basic values of any society survive as, for example, Abraham Lincoln in the U.S.A.

"Soul" emerges as a collective concept of the most precious, deeply rooted values and goals that enable societies to survive long-term. As expressed by Amy Lowell:

> "Our words, our music, who will build a dome to hive them? / In whose belly shall we come to life? A new life, / Beyond submergence and destruction, the implacable life of silent words..."[239]

Another version of this was expressed by Emerson in "The Over-Soul":

> "...that (Transcendentalist) Unity...within which every man's particular being is contained and made one with all other, that common heart..."[240]

Here, "Over Soul" is understood as the collective indivisible soul living on through history. Nevertheless, when push comes to shove (as it did for so many caught up in the brutal madness of the Holocaust), we must recall the

---

[239] Lowell, Amy (1924), op. cit., p.

[240] Emerson, Ralph Waldo (1841), "The Over-Soul", from **ESSAYS: First Series.**

first line of the earlier quote from Nietzsche: "He who has a why to live can bear with almost any how" – pointing to the inevitable, unrelenting locus of responsibility of each of us for the matter and meaning of our own lives and souls.

Chapter 18

Sex, Marriage, Love and Spirituality

Introduction

Arithmetically, 1 +1 = 2; but where love of two for each other is involved, 1 + 1 > 2; that is, the whole is larger than the sum of its parts. Why? – Because the whole, for even as small a set as two, enables the individuals involved to accomplish more and reach for higher levels than they could by themselves. What accounts for the difference? – Love, whose interactivity raises the level of a couple's relationship to a new plateau that is celebrated in song, as in "I was half; now I'm whole." Love is unaccountable. It knows no limit. Thus, the plateaus achieved in a truly open, loving relationship can continue to rise, up to and suffused with spirituality. The higher level is recognized as such by rites of marriage that celebrate a "sacred union", as in "to have and to hold, from this day forward..."

Might we view marriage as a microcosm that reveals essential features of relationships in which spirituality can and should emerge? Yes. Essential features are attention to:

- ✓ Love – of self and other, plus love of difference and love-making;
- ✓ 3C's [Communication, cooperation and collaboration];
- ✓ Family; own and intergenerational;
- ✓ History and living memory;
- ✓ Focus on relationship(s) and the dynamics of their interactivity, nurturing and relationship building;

- ✓ Time frame: long-term;
- ✓ Community: nurturing and building;
- ✓ Togetherness, closeness and intimacy.
- ✓ Synthesis of body, mind and soul;

The latter is the human being's penultimate yearning. Let us pause here to remind ourselves that "body" is the physical existence from whose brain, mind and soul emerge. The latter, in turn, create other bodies besides our own children – bodies in the form of institutions, structures and organizations of all sorts. Neither mind nor soul owe to a hypothetical, external God-in-heaven. The individual's search for matter and meaning in one's life and those of loved others is a fundamental, spiritual driver.

Sex

The architecture of the human bodies spells a procreative sexual union of male and female. Sexual intimacy at its best is potentially, soulfully fulfilling for couples at any age. The author experienced this at age 75 with his loving partner, Helen, two years older. We both felt that our first meeting was a miracle. A remarkable twofold openness and shared views, plus affectionately giving natures spurred a quick, very mutual falling in love. Among several things held in common, we also both felt that spirituality is important and integral to mind and body. And so, our love making was truly transcendent. It continues to rise to new heights.

The sacred union of male and female creates family. Families generate community. Nations and other large political jurisdictions arise from political unions of communities. At each level, the 3Cs [communication, cooperation and collaboration] are instrumental to pro-creative processes of generation and transformation that reaffirm basic values and goals and enable us to adapt them. The latter enable bodies to be both self-governing and self-sustaining. Basic values and goals never fail to include spiritual invocations and justifications.

A colloquial joke line is that "sex sells." Nevertheless, we see and feel that sex is far more fundamental. Intimacy is transcendent as well as procreative, generative and transformative. It is through intimate relationships that we come to know others and thus ourselves. The dimensions and understandings of oneself grow by way of interactivity with others focused on the existence and adaptation of shared meanings, values and goals. This can be observed at all levels, but keep in mind that the terms and meanings of basic features will change from level to level. For instance, "intimacy" differs as the focus shifts from couples to families, friends, coworkers and communities.

Key at every level is the depth of the development of shared learnings and understandings achievable via the 3Cs, supported by levels of resources needed and mobilized to sustain shared efforts. The extent of sharing, however, is likely to depend on actual or perceived levels of equality among the interactants. At the macro-economic level, for example, economic growth has been found to be less among countries where the levels of inequality are greater.[241] At the organizational level, hierarchical structures are too often an impediment to the 3Cs, innovation, learning and growth.[242] At the species level, sex can be considered the greatest innovation of evolution. Why? – Because sex generates differences that enable greater flexibility and adaptability of species to changing circumstances, thus fostering greater likelihood of species' survival. It spells love of difference above love of self or love for a same-sex, clone-like or self-similar "other."

Unfortunately, the latter seems to be far more prevalent among young people than among their parents and elders. Young boys and girls are making out with same sex "friends." Kids 11-13 years old are declaring they are gay or lesbian, long before they have enough knowledge and experience to make any fundamental choice. What's going on here? Is sex education deficient, and/or youth behavior-twisting media too influential? What are the consequences of

---

[241] Aghion, Philippe, E. Caroli and C. Garcia-Peñalosa (1999), "Inequality and Economic Growth: The Perspective of the New Growth Theories, **JOURNAL of ECONOMIC LITERATURE** (December).

[242] Senge, Peter (1990), **THE FIFTH DISCIPLINE: The Art and Practice of the Learning Organization**. New York, Random House.

a society that treats "sex" as a matter of "choice"? Have not the meanings of both words (and the ideas they connote) been distorted?

Marriage

In this context, the meaning of another word has been misconstrued and also, terribly distorted, that of "marriage." Fierce debates over "gay marriage" have not been foreclosed by a careless legislative mandate akin to untruth in labeling. The questions raised herein have been addressed, but not resolved, by countless speakers and many other authors.[243] Hopefully, others will pick them up and help with their resolution.

Conclusion

Our focus on sex, love, marriage and their interrelationships also helps to underline the importance of the factors cited earlier for spirituality as it may or may not be exhibited in and among organizations. Marriage, too, is an institution even though a little bit of love goes a long way anywhere. On the other hand, our focus here has shed no light on how to achieve the dream of "synthesis." The work of Moore has helped somewhat to overcome the difficulties for couples, as discussed in his book on **SOULMATES**.[244] As for organizations, the work of Senge on "learning organizations" is most helpful.[245]   **SYTHEISM** provides a comprehensive approach, but one

---

[243] For example, see: Diamond, Stephen (2014), "The Psychology of Sexuality," **PSYCHOLOGY TODAY** (May 10); "The Power of Human Sexuality," **YOUTUBE** (September 30, 2010); and/or: **Scientific American MIND**, Vol.25, No. 1 (2016), "The Sexual Brain: What Really Goes On In There, especially "Do Gays Have a Choice?", p. 56.

[244] Moore, Thomas (1994), **SOULMATES**: Honoring the Mysteries of Love and Relationship. New York: Harper Collins.

[245] Senge, Peter(1994), **THE FIFTH DISCIPLINE FIELDBOOK.** New York: Random House.

sometimes difficult to follow; and the book's conclusion, that "God is the Internet" is quite unsatisfactory and unacceptable.[246]

---

[246] Bard, Alexander, and J. Soderqvist (2014), **SYTHEISM:** Creating God in the Internet Age. Stockholm: Stockholm Text.

Chapter 19

A Spiritual Politics

Introduction

Today's politics struggles to find common ground. They also seem to caste debate down to its lowest common denominators. This lowering, however, has been part and parcel of another downward trend – in people's political participation. How are "We the People" to take back what should be ours – our politics – if we can neither find common ground nor raise ourselves up to participate in the political process? There is a vicious circle here that must be broken.

One answer is to recognize that each of us is a spiritual person with a soul that is ever a work-in-process. Spirituality is clearly a higher common denominator. Another is to appreciate that a NSB is needed if we are to overcome artificial barriers between peoples and cultures. A focus on a God of life -- the life force in all living things -- would be a major factor in weaning people away from reliance on their own, segregating versions of a God-in-heaven. Another fundamental issue is that "Americans lack the tools to comprehend the scope of what's gone wrong...a complete failure of democratic governance."[247]

---

[247] **WALL ST. JOURNAL's REVIEW** "Bookshelf" of February 22, 2017.

The prime currency of politics – power – needs to be fused with spirituality. Unfortunately, the language of politics is bottom-line secular; some would even label it "vulgar." What if politicians felt they had to address the spiritual souls of constituents? Instead of power seen as arising from campaigns in terms of prize fights, battlegrounds and trying to cut the other guy down, we might hear talk of reconciliation, forgiveness, togetherness, and raising our sights as to what we could accomplish together. We might even try to redefine what political power means – from a zero-sum [I win; You lose] game to a process of a developing community working together [win-win]. Much of the work of the Kettering Foundation on deliberative forums points the way.[248]

Exemplary Spiritual Political Leadership

Striking examples of spiritual political leadership in our own country are relatively few. They include Martin Luther King, Jr. and Abraham Lincoln. An enormous literature is available on both. Sometimes, though, we need to step down from our "America First" throne long enough to recognize that some foreign leaders provide great examples of how to mix spirituality with politics. One of these is the late Vaclav Havel, former President of Czechoslovakia, who advocated a "spiritual politics" in words and action. He wrote:

> "We must recollect our original spiritual and moral substance. I believe this is the only way (of) a genuine renewal of our sense of responsibility for ourselves and for the world...We must discover a new respect for what transcends us: for the universe, for the earth, for nature, for life and for reality...Above all, it is a task for politicians."[249]

---

[248] See Kettering Foundation reports on National Deliberative Forums...

[249] Havel, Vaclav (1995), "Civilization's Thin Veneer", **HARVARD MAGAZINE** (July-August) [Excerpts from Havel's Harvard Commencement address].

How many, however, would agree with the last sentence? Very few, which points to the urgency of this book. Recognition of a God of Life and our spirituality are essential to raising the level of our politics so that "renewal of our sense of responsibility" becomes indeed "a task for politicians."

Another fine example of a spiritual politics is provided by Nelson Mandela, former President of South Africa. He spent over 25 years in jail for fighting apartheid. As reported by the editor of **TIME**:

> "He looked around at the green and tranquil landscape and said something about how he would be...joining his "ancestors." "Men come and men go," he later said. "I have come and I will go when my time comes ...I never once heard him mention God or heaven or any kind of afterlife. Nelson Mandela believed in justice in this lifetime."[250]

He once said that every man should have a house in sight of where he was born. Much of Mandela's belief system came from his youth in the Xhosa tribe, raised by a local Thembu King after his own father died. As a boy, he lived in a grass hut with a dirt floor. He learned to be a shepherd. He fetched water from the spring. He excelled at stick fighting with the other boys. He sat at the feet of old men who told him stories of the brave African princes who ruled South Africa before the coming of the white man.

The first time he shook the hand of a white man was when he went off to boarding school. Eventually, little Rolihlahla Mandela would become Nelson Mandela and get a proper Methodist education. But for all his worldliness and his legal training, much of his wisdom, common sense, and joy came from what he had learned as a young boy in the Transkei.

---

[250] This and much that follows is drawn from: Stengel, Richard (2013), "Nelson Mandela, 1918–2013: Remembering an Icon of Freedom," **TIME** (December 5).

In a free and nonracial South Africa, Mandela would have been a small-town lawyer, content to be a local grandee. This great, historic revolutionary was in many ways a natural conservative. He did not believe in change for change's sake. One thing turned him into a revolutionary – the pernicious system of racial oppression he experienced as a young man in Johannesburg. When people spat on him in buses, when shopkeepers turned him away, when whites treated him as if he could not read or write, that changed him irrevocably. For deep in his bones was a basic sense of fairness: he simply could not abide injustice. If he, Nelson Mandela, the son of a chief, tall, handsome and educated, could be treated as subhuman, then what about the millions who had nothing like his advantages? "That is not right," that simple phrase — that is not right — underlay everything he did, everything he sacrificed for and everything he accomplished.

His life followed the narrative of the archetypal hero – of great suffering followed by redemption. But as he said to me and to many others over the years, "I am not a saint." And he wasn't. As a young revolutionary, he was fiery and rowdy. Prison was the crucible that formed the Mandela we know. The man who went into prison in 1962 was hotheaded and easily stung. The man who walked out into the sunshine of the mall in Cape Town 27 years later was measured, even serene.

It was a hard-won moderation. In prison, he learned to control his anger. He had no choice. And he came to understand that if he was ever to achieve that free and nonracial South Africa of his dreams, he would have to come to terms with his oppressors. He would have to forgive them. So, what was different about the man who came out of prison compared with the man who went in? He said simply, "I came out mature."

Because he was not a saint, he had his share of bitterness. He famously said, "The struggle is my life," but his life was also a struggle. This man who loved children spent 27 years without holding a baby. Before he went to prison, he lived underground and was unable to be the father and the husband he wanted to be. Though pursued by thousands of police, he secretly went to tuck his son into bed. His son asked why he couldn't be with him every night. Mandela told him that millions of other South African children needed him too. It's amazing that he was not bitter. It was with enormous self-control that he learned to hide his bitterness.

A 3rd great example is Bishop Desmond Tutu of South Africa.[251] Though raised in a poor family, Tutu excelled in his studies and rose to become Archbishop of Cape Town, the most senior position in southern Africa's Anglican hierarchy. Earlier, as Bishop of Lesotho, he began taking an active role in opposition of South Africa's apartheid system. He emerged as one of South Africa's most prominent anti-apartheid activists. As such, he stressed non-violent protest and foreign economic pressure to bring about change, brought women into the priesthood, emphasized a consensus-building model of leadership, and played a role as mediator between rival black factions.

Later, Nelson Mandela selected him to chair the Truth and Reconciliation Commission – established to uncover, investigate and report past human rights abuses. Tutu also campaigned for gay rights, and unlike the U.S. Preacher, Billy Graham, spoke out on a wide range of foreign conflicts, including the Israeli-Palestine conflict and the Iraq War (in opposition), while publicly criticizing South African Presidents Mbeki and Zuma.

Tutu courageously stood his ground when confronted with severe opposition from many in his home country. Apartheid supporters despised him. Many white liberals saw him as too radical. Like Bernie Sanders, he was a declared socialist. Communists scorned him for his anti-communist stance. Internationally, however, he was praised for his anti-apartheid activism and awarded the Nobel Peace Prize. The keystones of Tutu's religious/political activism were prayer and forgiveness.

He saw prayer as an essential link between physical and spiritual well-being. His spirituality was rooted in his strongly Christian upbringing, but it found its true expression via his personal magnetism and social/political activism, much more so than through the activities of the religious institutions over

---

[251] This brief review of Bishop Tutu is drawn and paraphrased from **WIKIPEDIA**.

which he held sway as a church leader. He spoke in opposition to the old saw "Don't mix religion with politics. He characterized it as:

> "very much the...position of dualists. And just look at the tangle we have got into...embarrassed with our physicality...we have found it attractive to engage in the...dichotomies as between the sacred and the secular..."[252]

Imagine a Tutu shed of unsupportable Christian myths and you have a man who might well have been celebrated as the founder of a NSB. For he was a man nurturing and celebrating human life all his days. His older sister, Sylvia, called him Milo ("Life"), a name given to him by his paternal grandmother. Indeed. He worked tirelessly to raise people up – not only to provide succor in their suffering but, most important, to enable them to fight, altogether, the evil forces that kept them down and shackled their ability to raise themselves up.

Billy Graham

The main lesson we can derive from these examples is that truly great political leadership expresses and demonstrates spirituality as well as political canniness. There is a spiritual politics. Unfortunately, even following the great legacies of Martin Luther King, Jr. and Abraham Lincoln, there is no spiritual political leadership in view in the U.S.A at this time. In light of the dramatic, nationwide memorials honoring Billy Graham following his passing on February 21, 2018, however, many folks may beg to differ. So, let us turn some attention to him.

No question: Billy was a great preacher, inspiring millions worldwide during his crusades for Christ. He also sought to influence the most powerful political and governmental leaders of his time, including U.S. Presidents Eisenhower, Kennedy, Nixon, LBJ and Carter. He enjoyed the patronage of powerful media titans. The broadcasting of his message through the Hearst

---

[252] Quoted from Archbishop Tutu's sermon at Southwark Cathedral, Feb. 6, 2004 at 3:30 p.m.

empire was instrumental to putting him on the national media map early in his career.

The blossoming reputation, however, initiated a pattern akin to hypocrisy not unlike what we have seen exhibited by so many in public life -- using and being used by the powers-that-be. Though registered as a Democrat, Billy courted and was courted by Republican Party leaders in Washington. His persistent denial of any interest in politics seemed quite disingenuous, as with other leaders of the evangelist movement.[253]

The true test of spiritual political leadership is breadth and depth of influence. The scope of Billy's leadership was broad but not deep. It was broad and great in terms of numbers. George Will commented:

> "Americans respect quantification, and Graham was a marvel of quantities. He spoke...to more people directly, about 215 million – than any person in history...except that follow-up studies revealed that the percentages of people who would make "professions of faith" as a result of his crusades were always in the single digits..."[254]

As for depth, consider scope and context. The scope of Billy's message was actually quite narrow in the context of his time. The latter featured the rising state-political power of communism, the nuclear arms race, the steadily growing influence of science and technology, and the civil rights movement. His bow to the latter was significant but not surprising given the relatively conservative caste of black churches. He allowed that blacks should attend his crusades. As for other major issues, he supported the powers-that-be with his

---

[253] See Carter, Neil (2018), "Billy Graham Was Not a Great Man," www.patheos.com/blogs/godlessindixie (March 5). Carter claims that "Evangelism was always about politics... (even though) Graham insisted...that he had no interest in politics. In truth, he was a Machiavellian backroom operator." Op. cit., p.7.

[254] Quoted in Carter (2018), op. cit., p.6.

virulent anti-communism and support of armaments and other means of violence against opposing forces.

To the extent that Billy otherwise recognized the nature of human nature and the real world, it was to over-simplify to the extreme. As in:

- o **"God's Word,"** the Bible is the ultimate source of "truth;"
- o **Man is born in sin** and must be "saved" so he can enter into "heaven" (or otherwise be damned forever in a counterpart "hell");"[255] He can be saved only by accepting Christ as his savior;
- o **Science?** – recognized only as a source of the technologies that enabled Billy's message to be broadcast worldwide.
- o **Sin?** – an individual thing, remediable only by experiencing a "born again" conversion.[256]
- o **The ills of this world?** – not to be remedied until the end of times, when Christ would come again.
- o **Politics and power?** Instruments of an unexamined elite caste that Billy served as sycophant.
- o **"Soul"** – Also an individual thing, as if there were nothing distinctive, larger or higher about the spirit of life, community or America.[257]
- o **Prayer:** Billy frequently testified to the power of prayer but here, too, there was a divide between intention and action. A major newspaper alleged that Billy had initiated the National Prayer Breakfast in 1953. Its true founder was Abraham Vereide, a truly humble man unknown

---

[255] Billy's heaven was a place where "...the angels will wait on us, and we'll drive down the golden streets in a yellow Cadillac convertible." Quoted from Moser (2028), op. cit., p. 4.

[256] Yet authentic, individual conversions were experienced by relatively few of those attending Graham's crusades and, of these, most slipped their conversion moorings after a few years.

[257] See: Moser, Bob (2018), "The Soul-Crushing Legacy of Billy Graham," **ROLLING STONE** (February 23).

to nearly everybody who also exemplified widespread and beneficial influence on political leaders, often in spite of the constitutional separation of church and state.[258]

Thus, Billy served to exemplify rather than resolve an artificial divide between spirituality and politics – a divide that supported injustices that only his limited personal, individualized [not his mass broadcasts') counseling helped to ameliorate. Unfortunately, notwithstanding all the heightened hype and hoopla surrounding his funeral, Billy raised neither the level of our spirituality nor that of our politics.

Wole Soyinka

A final, much less well known, unattached to any religion but nevertheless fine example of spiritual political leadership is Wole Soyinka.[259] Wole is a Nobel Prize-winning Nigerian writer (resident in the U.S. for more than 50 years) whose work is international in scope and inspiration. His first overt political work was an act of great courage for such a young man in such a place in the 1960's -- unilaterally desegregating a swimming pool in Atlanta, Georgia.

As a writer, of course, his work has been far more influential as well as prolific. He is the author of 2 novels and translations, 3 movies and short stories, 5 memoirs, 8 poetry collections, 13 essays and 30 plays.

Politically, he has taken an active role in Nigeria's political history and its struggle for independence from Great Britain. In 1965, he seized the Western Nigeria Broadcasting Service studio and broadcast a demand for the

---

[258] See **WIKIPEDIA** on the National Prayer Breakfast and The Fellowship Foundation on Vereide.

[259] This section draws from a memorable article co-authored by Soyinka and Henry Louis Gates Jr. (2019), **"There's One Humanity or There Isn't a Conversation," NEW YORK REVIEW of Books** (March 21).

cancellation of the Western Nigeria Regional Elections. In 1967 during the Nigerian Civil War, he was arrested by the federal government of General Yakubu Gowon and put in solitary confinement for two years.[260]

Soyinka has been a strong critic of successive Nigerian governments, especially the country's many military dictators, as well as other political tyrannies, including the Mugabe regime in Zimbabwe. Much of his writing has been concerned with "the oppressive boot and the irrelevance of the color of the foot that wears it".

The thoughtfulness and depth of Soyinka's work are revealed by the **NEW YORK REVIEW** number already cited.

Conclusion

There is a prior, still lingering problem that we need to face – the fact that there is no politics in the U.S. overall that earns little but a curse at this time. Another book might be needed to fully document the fact. One recent example comes to mind – from a Fox News broadcast of October 30, 2017. The newscaster had been troubled by seeing an article in the November 3, 2017 number of the ECONOMIST, a "Lexington" editorial piece on "America's love affair with uniformed men..."

The newscaster remarked on the context of the piece: That Americans now distrust all other major institutions, including the Congress, and so it is heartening to know that the military is held in such high regard. This observation, however, is very troubling. It denies the importance of politics

---

[260] This section borrows from Wikipedia on "Wole Soyinka." Wole's accomplishments in the face of severe opposition and great struggles reminds me of two articles. One is entitled "Despite Perils, Decide to Hope," by Anne Lamott in the **NATIONAL GEOGRAPHIC** number of October, 2018, The other is Curnutte, Mark (2018), MLK's America remains a world of trouble,' USA Today (January 14).

and a representative Congress to the health, well-being and future of a democratic republic.

Unfortunately, in light of their low rates of political participation, most Americans seem to deny the importance of politics. A recent number of **THE ATLANTIC Magazine** reported that "Only One Percent of Americans Are Really Politically Active. Go to:

https://www.theatlantic.com/business/archive/2014/05/only-one-percent-of-americans-are-really-politically-active/425286/

Then let us recall Aristotle: "A citizen is one who participates in power."

The Fox newscaster noted above had also brought in a woman to join her who happens to be from a military family. Her two brothers are U.S. Marines. Besides deriding the editorial, she remarked how she gets "warm and fuzzy" feelings whenever there's a flyover of military jets. Is this an example of spirituality? If so or even if not, its fuzziness further helps to veil the problem raised by the piece.

This adulation of the military reveals a problem not recognized by any of the comments provided online by magazine readers as of 10/30/17. Worship of the military in a situation where civil institutions are held in such low esteem is a red flag for a democratic republic and should be read as such. The danger is that a President bent on growing presidential power already great could serve to destroy the foundations of our democratic republic. Then the lack of any meaningful politics, spiritual or otherwise, could well prove disastrous.

Chapter 20

NSB and Similar Religions

Introduction

"Similar Religions" are those that do not rest in belief of the existence of an external, all powerful god-in-heaven. As indicated earlier (Chapter 4), atheism is not considered a religion.

QUAKERS

Analysis of Quakerism reveals remarkable similarities and some differences with a NSB. The Quaker faith differs primarily with regard to:

- o Emphasis on dress or other specific styles of behavior (like Quakers emphasis on "plain dress"; and
- o Refusal of "tithes, oaths and other "worldly courtesies."

What are "Quakers"? Quakers are members of the Religious Society of Friends, a faith that emerged as a new Christian denomination in England during a period of religious turmoil in the mid-1600's and is practiced today in a variety of forms around the world. To members of this religion, the words "Quaker" and "Friend" mean the same thing.

Quakers are: an active, involved faith-based community living in the modern world. They are a diverse people consisting of several distinct branches who continue traditional testimonies of pacifism, social equality, integrity, and simplicity These are interpreted and expressed in a variety of ways. Today, many Friends include stewardship of our planet as one of the major concerns expressed in their testimonies.

Quakers are not: Amish, Anabaptists, Shakers or Puritans. These come from a separate tradition. Quakers do not dress like the man on the box of oats anymore, and they hardly ever address people as "thee." Quakers and Shakers, however, both honor simplicity, as in the old Shaker song: "Tis a gift to be simple; tis a gift to be free..."

The Quaker Information Center works on behalf of the Religious Society of Friends to answer questions from Friends and non-Friends alike. It directs inquirers to information and resources from and about the Society of Friends. Until July 2010, the Center was located in Philadelphia under the capable leadership of Chel Avery. The Quaker Information Center is now a virtual center provided as a service of the Earlham School of Religion [ESR].

ESR is a Christian graduate theological school in the Quaker tradition. ESR prepares women and men for leadership that empowers and for ministry that serves. This mission grows out of the Quaker's Christian belief that God calls everyone to ministry. Using a transformative model of education, ESR encourages students to explore the intellectual, spiritual, and practical dimensions of their calls to ministry.

From the very beginning, the "public testimonies" of Friends included plain speech and dress, and refusal of tithes, oaths, and worldly courtesies. In a few years. Friends added an explicit renunciation of participation in war; bankruptcy delayed (up to and within the next century), and marriage not blessed at a Quaker meeting. Smuggling, dealing in or owning slaves also became practices for which an unrepentant Friend would be disowned. These latter, especially those relating to slavery, became matters for discipline -- even if testimony from no more than a minority of Friends persuaded the rest that they were inconsistent with Friends' principles.

But not all social concerns were corporate in this sense or were enforced by sanctions. Friends' relief work, for example, has usually arisen from individuals' responses to suffering, often as the result of war. From the time of the American Revolution Quakers have been active in ministering to refugees and victims of famine—so much so that the entire Society of Friends is sometimes taken for a philanthropic organization. Yet this work, recognized in 1947 by the award of the Nobel Peace Prize to the American Friends Service Committee and the (British) Friends Service Council, has mobilized many non-Quakers. This exemplifies the interaction between the Quaker conscience and the wider world. Quakers reach out to others not of their faith. They do not live in a self-contained box.

Yet the Society of Friends is grounded in the experience of an external God out of which philanthropic activities flow. There have always been Friends whose concerns went well beyond what meetings were willing to adopt. Most Friends were not abolitionists before the American Civil War. They probably did not approve of the Underground Railroad nor share the early feminist views of Lucretia Mott and Susan B. Anthony. Yet most of the early suffragist leaders in America were Quakers. There were two American presidents of Quaker background, Herbert Hoover and Richard M. Nixon.

Often the issue has been the relationship between private witness and public policy. Some Quaker pacifists make an absolute personal stand against war; for example, by refusing to register for selective service and thus forfeiting conscientious objectors' status. Others are more willing to sacrifice absolute purity by working for an alleviation of international tensions even at the cost of a less rigorous application of their principles.

In sum, there is much to admire in Quakerism except its major difference with our NSB – devotion to an external God.

UNITARIAN-UNIVERSALIST [UU]

> As between a NSB and UU, there are both remarkable similarities and differences. In general, overall terms, UU is a religion alike to the NSB in being engaged in a:
> Search for truth and meaning, especially via the guidance of reason and the discoveries of science.
> Search for spiritual growth.
> Eclectic selection of insights from all major world religions.

- ➤ Retention of some Christian traditions such as Sunday worship with a sermon and the singing of hymns.
- ➤ Nurture of a creedless, non-dogmatic approach to spirituality and faith development.
- ➤ Rejection of the Trinitarian belief in the tri-personal godhead; assertion of a unitary notion of God without recognition of Jesus as God.

A note re the latter: Non-Trinitarianism was prevalent during the Reformation. A Spanish physician, Michael Servetus, concluded that the concept of the Trinity was not biblical. He was arrested, convicted of heresy and burned at the stake in 1553 under the order of John Calvin.

A NSB differs from the Universalist side of UU in <u>not</u> having:

- ✓ A defining doctrine of universal salvation for all souls through Christ,
- ✓ Belief in an end point of time leading to the "restitution of all things;" nor
- ✓ Belief in an external loving God on high..

There were different forms of Christology early in the Unitarian movement, but the dominant view became that Christ was a man with a unique relationship to God.[261] But a NSB differs from the Universalist side of UU in not having a defining doctrine of universal salvation for all souls through Christ, leading to the "restitution of all things;" nor belief in a loving God "on high."

The defining character of UU is that religion is a matter of individual experience. Each person is free to search for his or her personal truth on issues such as the existence, nature and meaning of life; deities, creation and afterlife. What binds UUs together is a belief in the power and sacredness of unconditional love and in a God of all-inclusive love. Many subscribe to deism, pantheism or polytheism. Many also reject the idea of deities

---

[261] Courtesy of **WIKIPEDIA** (2017).

altogether and instead, like NSB, speak of the "spirit of life" that binds all life on earth.

Seven UU Principles were created by committee, affirmed democratically by a vote of delegates from member congregations, and adopted in 1960. They are:

1) The inherent worth and dignity of every person.
2) Justice, equity and compassion in human relations.
3) Acceptance of one another and encouragement of spiritual growth.
4) A free and responsible search for truth and meaning.
5) The right of conscience and use of the democratic process.
6) The goal of world community with peace, liberty and justice for all.
7) Respect for the interdependent web of all existence of which we are all a part.

The latter (#7) was deemed to have five sources, nearly all of which resonate with a NSB:

i. Spiritual teachings of earth-centered traditions which celebrate the sacred circle of life and instruct us to live in harmony with the rhythms of nature.
ii. Direct experience of that transcending mystery and wonder, affirmed in all cultures, which moves us to a renewal of the spirit and openness to the forces that create and uphold life.
iii. Words and deeds of prophetic men and women challenge us to confront powers and structures of evil with justice, compassion and the transforming power of love.
iv. Wisdom from the world's religions.
v. Jewish and Christian teachings which call us to respond to God's love by loving our neighbors as ourselves.
vi. Humanist teachings which counsel us to heed the guidance of reason and the results of science, while warning us against idolatries of mind and spirit.

These sources of UU are among those that have also informed and inspired the formulation of a NSB. So, too, have UU practices which are based on the assumption that truth and spiritual meaning can be found in all faiths. There exists great variety of both practices and how congregations conceive of themselves. UU gatherings include churches, societies, fellowships or congregations. Fellowships are traditionally a lay-led worship model. The Bible is not seen as sacred.

UU practices employ Buddhist-style meditation groups, Jewish Seder, Yom Kippur & Passover dinners, Iftar meals (marking breaking of the fast for Muslims), and Christmas Eve/Winter Solstice services. Youth religious education classes teach about the divinity of our world and the sanctity of world religions. Many more people (by a factor of four) identify as UUs than actually attend UU churches.

Similar variations are anticipated for the NSB, but the primary difference identified by this review – rejection of an external god – is quite fundamental.

THE BAHAI FAITH

Summary: The Bahai religion is similar to a NSB only in having no specific rules regarding the practice of religion or limits on the ordinary conduct of everyday life. Bahā'i is a religion teaching the essential worth of all religions, the unity of all peoples, and the equality of the sexes.

Bahái's around the world annually elect local, regional, and national Spiritual Assemblies that govern the affairs of the religion, and every five years the members of all National Spiritual Assemblies elect the Universal House of Justice, the nine-member supreme governing institution of the worldwide Bahá'í community, which sits in Haifa, Israel near the shrine of Bahá'u'lláh

Basic Principles

Shoghi Effendi, the Guardian of the religion from 1921 to 1957, wrote the following 13 point summary of what he considered to be the distinguishing principles of the teachings of Bahai's founder, Bahá'u'lláh, which, together with the laws and ordinances of the Kitáb-i-Aqdas constitute the bedrock of the Bahá'í Faith. These are the:

✓ Independent search after truth, unfettered by superstition or tradition;

- ✓ Oneness of the entire human race, the pivotal principle and fundamental doctrine of the Faith;
- ✓ Basic unity of all religions;
- ✓ Condemnation of all forms of prejudice, whether religious, racial, class or national;
- ✓ Harmony which must exist between religion and science;
- ✓ Equality of men and women -- two wings on which the bird of humankind is able to soar;
- ✓ Introduction of compulsory education;
- ✓ Adoption of a universal auxiliary language ;
- ✓ Abolition of the extremes of wealth and poverty;
- ✓ Institution of a world tribunal for the adjudication of disputes between nations;
- ✓ Exaltation of work, performed in the spirit of service, to the rank of worship;
- ✓ Glorification of justice as the ruling principle in human society, and of religion as a bulwark for the protection of all peoples and nations; and
- ✓ Establishment of a permanent and universal peace as the supreme goal of all mankind—these stand out as the essential elements.

History

Established by Bahá'u'lláh in 1863, Bahai initially grew in the Middle East and now has between 5-7 million adherents spread out into most countries of the world. The Bahá'í Faith formed from the Bábí religion, itself a 19th century outgrowth of Shia Islam, when Bahá'u'lláh declared himself He whom God shall make manifest, a messianic figure in the religion of Bábism. Bahá'u'lláh was imprisoned and exiled from his native Iran and spent time in Baghdad, where he founded the Bahá'í Faith, and was further exiled to Istanbul, Edirne, and finally Akka in the Ottoman province of Syria, in what is now Israel. Following Bahá'u'lláh's death in 1892, leadership of the religion fell to his son `Abdu'l-Bahá (1844-1921), and later his great-grandson Shoghi Effendi (1897-1957). Since 1963, the Universal House of Justice has been the elected head of the Bahá'í Faith.

Beliefs

Bahá'í beliefs are sometimes described as syncretic combinations of earlier religious beliefs. Bahá'ís, however, assert that their religion is a distinct tradition with its own scriptures, teachings, laws, and history. While the religion was initially seen as a sect of Islam, most religious specialists now see it as an independent religion, with its religious background in Shi'a Islam being seen as analogous to the Jewish context in which Christianity was established. Muslim institutions and clergy, both Sunni and Shia, consider Bahá'ís to be deserters or apostates from Islam, which has led to Bahá'ís being persecuted. Bahá'ís describe their faith as an independent world religion, differing from the other traditions in its relative age and in the appropriateness of Bahá'u'lláh's teachings to the modern context. Bahá'u'lláh is believed to have fulfilled the messianic expectations of precursor faiths.

Bahá'í teachings are in some ways similar to other monotheistic faiths: God is considered single and all-powerful. However, Bahá'u'lláh taught that religion is orderly and progressively revealed by one God through Manifestations of God who are the founders of major world religions throughout history. Buddha, Jesus, and Muhammad are the most recent Manifestations preceding the Báb and Bahá'u'lláh.

Three core principles establish a basis for Bahá'í teachings and doctrine: the unity of God, the unity of religion, and the unity of humanity. From these postulates stems the belief that God periodically reveals his will through divine messengers whose purpose is to transform the character of humankind and to develop, within those who respond, moral and spiritual qualities. Religion is thus seen as orderly, unified, and progressive from age to age. Thus, Bahá'ís regard the major religions as fundamentally unified in purpose, though varied in social practices and interpretations. There is a similar emphasis on the unity of all people, openly rejecting notions of racism and nationalism

God

The Bahá'í writings describe a single, personal, inaccessible, omniscient, omnipresent, imperishable, and almighty God who is the creator of all things in the universe. The existence of God and the universe is thought to be eternal, without a beginning or end. Though inaccessible directly, God is nevertheless seen as conscious of creation, with a will and purpose that is expressed through messengers termed Manifestations of God.

Bahá'í teachings state that God is too great for humans to fully comprehend, or to create a complete and accurate image of, by themselves. Therefore, human understanding of God is achieved through revelations from his Manifestations. In the Bahá'í religion, God is often referred to by titles and attributes (for example, the All-Powerful, or the All-Loving), and there is a substantial emphasis on monotheism. Bahá'ís do not expect a new manifestation of God to appear within 1000 years of Bahá'u'lláh's 1863 revelation.

Bahai and Humanity

To Bahá'ís, the Ringstone symbol represents humanity's connection to God. The Bahá'í writings state that human beings have a "rational soul", and that this provides the species with a unique capacity to recognize God's station and humanity's relationship with its creator. Every human is seen to have a duty to recognize God through His messengers, and to conform. to their teachings. Through recognition and obedience, service to humanity and regular prayer and spiritual practice, the Bahá'í writings state that the soul becomes closer to God

This is the spiritual ideal according to Bahá'í belief. When a human dies, the soul passes into the next world, where its spiritual development in the physical world becomes a basis for judgment and advancement in the spiritual world. Heaven and Hell are taught to be spiritual states of nearness or distance from God that describe relationships in this world and the next, not physical places of reward and punishment achieved after death.

Bahá'í writings emphasize the essential equality of human beings, and the abolition of prejudice. Humanity is seen as essentially one, though highly varied; its diversity of race and culture are seen as worthy of appreciation and acceptance. Doctrines of racism, nationalism, caste, social class, and gender-based hierarchy are seen as artificial impediments to unity. The Bahá'í teachings state that the unification of humanity is the paramount issue in the religious and political conditions of the present world.

Conclusion

Major religions similar to our NSB, especially Bahai and the Quakers, share many of its beneficial, humane features. Their worship of an external god-on-high, however, means that they differ from a NSB -- fundamentally. Their ability to attain spirituality leaves much to be desired.

Chapter 21

A NSB and Strictly Non-Christian Belief Systems

BUDDHISM

This is an Indian religion that encompasses a variety of traditions, beliefs and spiritual practices largely based on teachings attributed to the Buddha.[262] Buddhism originated in ancient India sometime between the 6th and 4th centuries BCE, from where it spread through much of Asia. Thereafter, it declined in India during the middle ages. Buddhists do not believe that the Buddha is a god, but that he is a human being who has awakened to see the true way the world works.

They believe this knowledge totally changes the person. Some say this puts them beyond birth, death, and rebirth.[263] Two major extant branches of Buddhism are generally recognized by scholars: Theravada Pala ("The School of the Elders") and Mahayana ("The Great Vehicle"). Buddhism is the world's

---

[262] This paragraph and others are drawn or paraphrased from Wikipedia in some parts; PBS and Diamond Way in others. Diamond Way Buddhists are lay people, often with families and regular jobs, who incorporate Buddhist methods into their daily lives.

[263] Rebirth is explained further on.

4th largest religion, with over 500 million followers. 7% of the global population are known as Buddhists.

Practices of Buddhism include:

- Taking refuge in the Buddha,
- Taking refuge in the Buddha,
- Reading of scriptures,
- Observance of moral precepts,
- Renunciation of craving and attachment,
- Practice of meditation, and
- Cultivation of wisdom, loving-kindness and compassion.

In Theravada the ultimate goal is the attainment of the sublime state of Nirvana, achieved by practicing the Noble Eightfold Path (also known as the Middle Way), thus escaping what is seen as a cycle of suffering and rebirth. Theravada has a widespread following in Sri Lanka and Southeast Asia.

Mahayana, which includes the traditions of Zen, Pure Land, Nichiren Buddhism, Shingon and Tiantai (Tendai), is found throughout East Asia. Rather than Nirvana, Mahayana instead aspires to Buddhahood via the bodhisattva path, a state wherein one remains in the cycle of rebirth to help other beings reach awakening. Early Buddhist canonical texts and early biographies of Buddha state that Gautama, the young Buddha-to-be, studied under Vedic teachers, learning meditation and ancient philosophies, particularly the concept of nothingness/ emptiness" and "what is neither seen nor unseen".

Gautama was moved by the innate suffering of humanity. He meditated on this alone for an extended period of time, in various ways including asceticism, the nature of suffering, and means to overcome suffering. He attained a state of enlightenment, discovering the Middle Way, a path of spiritual practice to end suffering. Perceived as an enlightened being, he attracted followers and founded a monastic order.

As the Buddha, he spent the rest of his life teaching the Dharma he had discovered, and died at the age of 80. The Buddha's teachings were propagated by his followers, which in the last centuries of the 1st millennium BCE became over eighteen Buddhist sub-schools of thought, each with its own texts containing different interpretations and teachings of the Buddha. Over time, these evolved into many traditions, of which the more well-known and widespread in the modern era are Theravada, Mahayana and Vajrayana Buddhism.

Dukkha is a central concept of Buddhism and part of its Four Noble Truths doctrine. It is viewed as a central characteristic of life in this world. It can be translated as "incapable of satisfying" -- the unsatisfactory nature and the general insecurity (or possibly "painful" nature) of life. Dukkha refers not to literal suffering, but to the ultimately unsatisfactory nature of temporary states and things, including pleasant but temporary experiences.

The Four Truths express the basic orientation of Buddhism. We crave and cling to impermanent states and things, which is dukkha, "incapable of satisfying" and painful. This keeps us caught in an endless cycle of repeated rebirth, dukkha and dying again. But there is a way to liberation from this endless cycle by achieving the state of nirvana – following the Noble Eightfold Path.

The truth of dukkha is the basic insight that life in this "mundane world," with its craving for impermanent things, is unsatisfactory. This premise, by the way, runs against the grain of Western beliefs. Dukkha goes on to state that, though we might expect happiness from states and things which are transitory, we cannot attain any real happiness. Our clinging and craving produce Karma, which ties us to samsara, the round of death and rebirth. Craving includes kāma taṇhā samsara , craving for sense-pleasures -- craving to continue the cycle of life and death, including rebirth –not craving to experience the world and painful feelings. Dukkha ceases, or can be confined, when craving and clinging cease or are confined. This also means that no more "karma" (see below) is being produced. Rebirth ends. Then we achieve nirvana, "blowing out," and peace of mind.

By following the Buddhist path to liberation, one starts to disengage from craving and clinging to impermanent states and things. The term "path" is usually taken to mean the Noble Eightfold Path, but other ways of "the path" can also be found. The Theravada tradition regards insight into the four truths as liberating in itself. Buddhism, like other major Indian religions, asserts that everything is impermanent, but, unlike them, also asserts that there is no permanent self or soul in living beings. The ignorance or misperception, that anything is permanent or that there is a "self" in any being, is considered mistaken. Such denial of selfhood is contrary to the American way and to our NSB.

Samsara is another basic Buddhist concept, Saṃsāra, means "wandering" or "world", with the connotation of cyclic, circuitous change. It refers to the theory of rebirth and cyclicality of all life, matter, and existence. As with all major Indian religions. Samsara in Buddhism is considered to be dukkha – unsatisfactory and painful, perpetuated by desire and ignorance and their resulting bad karma. The later Buddhist texts assert that rebirth can occur in six realms of existence – three good realms (heavenly, demi-god, human) and three evil realms (animal, hungry ghosts, hellish). Samsara ends if a person attains nirvana, the "blowing out" of desires and the gaining of true insight into impermanence and non-self-reality.

Rebirth refers to a process whereby beings go through a succession of lifetimes as one of many possible forms of life, each running from conception to death. In Buddhist thought, this rebirth does not involve any soul, because of its no-self doctrine, which rejects the concepts of a permanent self or an unchanging, eternal soul. According to Buddhism there ultimately is no such thing as a self in any being or any essence in anything. Buddhist traditions have traditionally disagreed on what it is in a person that is reborn, as well as how quickly the rebirth occurs after death.

The majority of Buddhist traditions assert that a person's consciousness, though evolving, exists as a continuum and is the mechanistic basis of what undergoes rebirth, re-becoming and re-death. The rebirth depends on the merits or demerits gained by one's own karma, as well as those accrued on one's behalf by a family member. Each rebirth takes place within one of the six supernatural realms according to Theravadins, noted earlier. In East Asian and Tibetan Buddhism, rebirth is not instantaneous, and there is an intermediate state between one life and the next. The orthodox Theravada position rejects the wait and asserts that rebirth of a being is immediate. Note that rebirth as conceived here is tantamount to life after death in the form that NSB denies.

Karma does not refer to preordained fate. It refers to good or bad actions a person takes during his or her lifetime. Good actions, which involve either the absence of bad actions or actual positive acts, such as generosity, righteousness, and meditation, bring about happiness in the long run. Bad actions, such as lying, stealing or killing, bring about unhappiness in the long run. The weight that actions carry is determined by five conditions:

1) frequent, repetitive action;
2) determined, intentional action;
3) action performed without regret;
4) action against extraordinary persons; and
5) action toward those who have helped one in the past.

Finally, there is also neutral karma, which derives from acts such as breathing, eating or sleeping. Neutral karma has no benefits or costs.

Enlightenment: There is no essential difference between the Buddha and us. We all have minds. We can all attain liberation and enlightenment by working with our minds. Our body, thoughts, and feelings are constantly changing. Buddhism views them as "empty"-- empty of any lasting essence, meaning that they are no basis for a real, separate ego or self. The state of liberation comes when we not only understand this intellectually but experience it in a deep, lasting way.[264] Then we stop taking things personally. We gain an enormous space for joyful development, without the need to react to every negative emotion that comes by.

---

[264] The "one (true) way" to enlightenment and liberation is set forth in Buddha's **LOTUS SUTRA**, a "true dharma" or revelation, in **THE WALL ST. JOURNAL** (WSJ, Dec.16).

Enlightenment (without science) is the ultimate goal in Buddhism. All positive qualities – especially joy, fearlessness, and compassion – are now attainable. Here, our awareness becomes all-encompassing, and not limited in any way. And it becomes so without us having to betake ourselves to a monastery or a nunnery. Our heroes in this process are not monks or nuns but those who see the truth and stay behind in the world "to help others cross to the far shore of peace."[265] With no confusion or disturbance in our minds, we are better able to benefit others.

Nirvana: The nirvana state has been described in Buddhist texts partly in a manner similar to other Indian religions, as the state of complete liberation, enlightenment, highest happiness, bliss, fearlessness, freedom, permanence, independence, unfathomable, indescribable. It has also been described in part differently, as a state of spiritual release marked by "emptiness" and realization of non-self. The Buddha explains that the cultivation of the path to Nirvana rests on one or the other of two ways – the quest for right knowledge and insight (again, without science), or liberation or release. Nirvana literally means "blowing out, quenching, becoming extinguished."

In early Buddhist texts, it is the state of restraint and self-control that leads to the "blowing out" – the ending of the cycles of sufferings associated with re-births and re-deaths. Many later Buddhist texts describe nirvana as complete "Emptiness, Nothingness". In some texts, the state is described with greater detail, such as passing through the gate of Emptiness – realizing that there is no soul or self in any living being, then passing through the gate of signlessness – realizing that nirvana cannot be perceived. This is inconsistent with an NSB.

Finally, one may pass through the gate of wishlessness if one believes that nirvana is the state of not even wishing for nirvana. [Quite a contradiction here, wouldn't you say?] While Buddhism considers Nirvana, or liberation from Samsara, as the ultimate spiritual goal; in conventional practice, the

---

[265] WSJ, op. cit. But what does the "far shore of peace" mean? Life after death?

primary focus of a vast majority of lay Buddhists has been to seek and accumulate merit through good deeds, donations to monks and various Buddhist rituals in order to gain better rebirths rather than nirvana. Here, majority Buddhist behavior seems oddly similar to that of most "desac" Christians. Read on.

There are some overlaps of Buddhism with NSB, but the differences are highly significant. Most gaps are attributable to substantial differences between eastern and western cultures and/or lack of scientific support for some Buddhist beliefs.

On the side of similarity, NSB:

- ✓ Is open to learning about the most effective means of meditation;
- ✓ Supports the aversion to "ignorance" and the emphasis on "knowledge," and
- ✓ Is adaptable to a variety of settings and situations.

But unlike Buddhism...

- ➢ NSB emphasizes the importance of the individual – selfhood disallowing "non-self-emptiness" while affirming the existence of souls and soulfulness, both personal and collective.
- ➢ NSB does not recognize the existence of "demigods" and "other (supernatural) realms."
- ➢ Would no more support rebirth cycles after death than life after death.

"Adaptable" may seem an understatement but for the fact that Americans' diverse modifications of Buddhism exemplifies the word. It is no surprise that American culture glories in variety while reducing spirituality to "desac" therapeutic catch phrases. This is the main gist of a new book entitled "Why Buddhism is True." Its author, Robert Wright, offers a Buddhism "cleansed of supernaturalism" [good!], but "His Buddha is conceived as a wise man and self-help psychologist." The secularization of American society has struck again. Wright's version of Buddhism offers no "divine being – no miraculous birth...no reincarnation." Also good, but the author tries to finesse the contradictions built into Buddhism with feints tantamount to "evasion of analysis."[266] Here again, no science.

In so doing, he departs from the individualism basic to Americanism. He comes close to denying ("blowing out") the "self" in favor of "emptiness" and "not-self." Ironically, this line of thinking focuses too much on self-development by way of meditations that take the meditator ever inward into his or her "self." There is no attention to the congregate group aspects of spirituality.

As far as the latter is concerned, Richard Rorty claims that -Buddhism was "betrayed into Brahmanism....; the open-ended artisanal practice of meditation became a caste-bound dogma..."[267] And so it would appear that inequality also strikes again. American experiments with Buddhism reveal more about America than Buddhism. "Desac" commercialization of religion strikes again.

HINDUISM... is a major religious and cultural tradition of South Asia, developed from Vedic religion.[268] Nine beliefs of Hinduism direct believers' thoughts and attitudes about life, which in turn direct their actions. By their actions, Hindus create their destiny. Beliefs about sacred matters--God, soul and cosmos--are essential to one's approach to life. Hindus believe many diverse things, but there are a few bedrock concepts on which most Hindus

---

[266] Quotes here are from a review article on the book by Adam Gopnick (2017) in **THE NEW YORKER** (August 7 & 14).

[267] Gopnick, op. cit., p. 72.

[268] Vedic religion developed in Persia during 1200-2000 B.C. Its devotees worshiped a central god of might and victory along with subsidiary gods of fire, rivers and heroes via hymns and sacrifices. They believed in cosmic order. There is a Vedic spa in the U.S. (Ellicott City, Maryland). Find more in the forthcoming section on "Vedic Culture."

concur. The following nine beliefs, though not exhaustive, offer a simple summary of Hindu spirituality.[269]

1) Hindus believe in a one, all-pervasive Supreme Being who is both immanent and transcendent – a Creator and Reality that is not made manifest to us.

2) Hindus believe in the divinity of the four Vedas, the world's most ancient scripture, and venerate the Agamas – primordial hymns that convey God's word – the bedrock of Sanatana Dharma, the eternal religion.

3) Hindus believe that the universe undergoes endless cycles of creation, preservation and dissolution. [Scientific evidence?]

4) Hindus believe in karma, the law of cause and effect by which each individual creates his own destiny by his thoughts, words and deeds.

5) Hindus believe that the soul reincarnates, evolving through many births until all karmas have been resolved, and "moksha" – liberation from the cycle of rebirth – is attained. Not a single soul will be deprived of this destiny.

6) Hindus believe that divine beings exist in unseen worlds and that temple worship, rituals, sacraments and personal devotionals create a communion with these devas and Gods.

7) Hindus believe that an enlightened master, or Satguru, is essential to know the Transcendent Absolute, as are personal discipline, good conduct, purification, pilgrimage, self-inquiry, meditation and surrender in God.

8) Hindus believe that all life is sacred, to be loved and revered, and therefore practice non-injury in thought, word and deed.

9) Hindus believe that no religion teaches the only way to salvation above all others, but that all genuine paths are facets of God's Light, deserving tolerance and understanding.

---

[269] As presented by the Himalayan Institute.

Hinduism, the world's oldest religion, has no beginning--it precedes recorded history. It has no human founder. It is a mystical religion, leading the devotee to personally experience the Truth within, finally reaching the pinnacle of consciousness where man and God are one. Hinduism has four main denominations--Saivism, Shaktism, Vaishnavism and Smartism.

NSB agrees with #'s 8 and half of #4; also agrees #3 is not an unreasonable theory, but disagrees with #'s 1, 5,6,7 and partly differs on #'s 2 and 4. In #2, "divinity" is a stretch too far, since it insinuates creation or influence by an external god. It is sufficient to call the documents containing ancient hymns "holy." No.4 is right to acknowledge the importance of an individual's thoughts, words and deeds towards the shaping of his or her destiny but not to attribute that shaping to an individual's "creation of." Also, "cause and effect" is far too simplistic a view in a world of growing interconnectedness and complexity.

As Charles Colson said of Christianity, a NSB "cannot be simply a file drawer in our crowded lives. It must be the central truth from which all our behavior, relationships and philosophy flow."[270] Hindus probably see their belief system the same way. Even apart from Hinduism's reliance upon an external god, however, Hinduism represents a huge gap between belief and reality, largely because it fails to recognize science as the major source of search for "central truth".

VEDIC CULTURE

This belief system is grounded on the Vedic philosophy that proclaims the primacy of personality in every sphere of life and knowledge. Vedic teachings are summarized in SRI ISOPANISAD, authored by His Grace A.C. Bhakti Vedanta, founder of the International Society for Krishna Consciousness, The

---

[270] Quoted by Billy Graham in his book **HOPE FOR THE TROUBLED HEART.**

p. 39.

latter, translated from Sanskrit, means "The knowledge that brings one closer to the Supreme Person, Krishna...the fountainhead of all energies and all happiness." Vedic belief in large part stands contrary to modern science and directly vs. NSB in relying on an external god. Though it resonates with the NSB's support for the being and becoming of individual personality, it runs contrary to philosophies that focus on sharing, community and commonalities that characterize other Asian religions.

ISLAM

The core of Islam's message is that: "There is no one to be worshiped and obeyed except The One and Only One God, Allah," which, in Arabic, is the name of God. "All the most beautiful names belong to Him." Every Prophet sent by God was to be followed by his people. God also told his prophets that if he sent another Prophet, they were obligated to follow the new Prophet.

Some other important points about Islam:

- It is an unforgiveable sin to believe that there are gods other than Allah. That was told by all the prophets of God.
- It is not enough to believe that God exists. He must be worshipped and obeyed.
- Worship and obedience of God must be according to the Prophets of God.
- Muhammad is the last Prophet of God sent for all mankind. All must follow him now to believe in the one and only True Religion of God for mankind. Muhammad's Message is timeless, universal and is for all of humanity.

The Holy Quran is the last Book sent by God. It is the only Book of God which is in its original form provided text in Arabic. It testifies what was sent to earlier Prophets and makes belief and obedience clear. The Quran and teachings of Prophet Muhammad are the two primary sources of knowledge in Islam.

From the Quran, 6:151-153, it is said:

> "Come I will tell you what your Lord has really forbidden you. Do not ascribe anything as partner to Him; be good to your parents; do not kill your children in fear of poverty; We will provide for you and for them; stay well away from committing obscenities, whether openly or in secret; do not take the life Allah has made sacred, except by right. This is what He commands you to do; perhaps you will use your reason...We do not burden any soul with more than it can bear...when you speak, be just...keep any promises you make in Allah's name. This is what He commands you to do, so that you may take heed: This is my path leading straight, so follow it. Do not follow other ways; they will lead you away from it."

There is much here to guide the living of human life.

Allah sent His final Messenger as Rahmah (love, compassion and mercy) for all mankind. Prophet Muhammad was sent to all mankind with the message and mission to help save themselves from the Hell-fire. Islam's message is to be humble to Allah, and be compassionate, loving, giving and caring for all creation. Those who go out and shoot randomly and kill are submitting to the rejected Satan. Such acts are acts of disobedience to Allah and His Prophet Muhammad. Evil does not justify evil.

Most of the above gives an impression that Islam differs little from Christianity. A 2017 article on Islam, however, states that:

> "Islam is unique...in at least one regard. Whereas...Jesus was a dissident executed...the Prophet Muhammad was a political leader who founded a polity...(with) the Koran as (its) constitution..."[271]

Democracy was not one of Muhammed's prescriptions.

---

[271] "Muslim democrats, inshallah," article in TIME (August 26, 2017), pp. 18-23.

In other words, the separation of church and state is practically meaningless to Islam. This helps to explain the uncompromising conflicts both within Islam and between Muslim and non-Muslim polities. The mixing of state and religion translates to unrelenting, often bloody, battles for political power. Thus:

> "The fear that secularists would try to undermine their governments convinced elected Islamists that they needed to grab as much power as possible...(& so) In nearly all places where Islamists are politically active, there are checks on how much power they can amass."[272]

The divide between Sunnis and Shia is the largest and oldest in the history of Islam. Members of the two sects have co-existed for centuries and share many fundamental beliefs and practices. But they differ in doctrine, ritual, law, theology and religious organization. Their leaders also often seem to be in competition. From Lebanon and Syria to Iraq and Pakistan, many recent conflicts have been based on the sectarian divide, tearing communities apart.

Who are the Sunnis?

The great majority of the world's more than 1.5 billion Muslims are Sunnis. Estimates suggest the figure is somewhere between 85% and 90%. In the Middle East, Sunnis make up 90% or more of the populations of Egypt, Jordan and Saudi Arabia. Sunnis regard themselves as the orthodox branch of Islam.

The name "Sunni" is derived from the phrase "Al al-Sunnah", or "People of the Tradition". The tradition in this case refers to practices based on what the Prophet Muhammad said, did, agreed to or condemned. All Muslims are guided by the Sunnah, but Sunnis stress its primacy. Sunni life is guided by four schools of legal thought, each of which strives to develop practical applications of the Sunnah.

---

[272] Previous reference to **TIME**, p. 19.

Who are the Shia?

Shia are also guided by the wisdom of Muhammad's descendants, passed down through his son-in-law ad cousin, Ali. Shia constitute about 10% of all Muslims, and globally their population is estimated at between 154 and 200 million. Shia Muslims are in the majority in Iran, Iraq, Bahrain, Azerbaijan and, according to some estimates, Yemen. There are also large Shia communities in Afghanistan, India, Kuwait, Lebanon, Pakistan, Qatar, Syria, Turkey, Saudi Arabia and the UAE.

In early Islamic history, the Shia were a movement - literally "Shiat Ali" or the "Party of Ali". They claimed that Ali was the rightful successor to the Prophet Muhammad as leader (Imam) of the Muslim community following his death in 632. Ali was assassinated after a five-year caliphate marred by civil war. His sons, Hassan and Hussein, were denied what they thought was their legitimate right of accession to the caliphate. Hassan is believed to have been poisoned in 680 by Muawiyah, the first caliph of the Sunni Umayyad dynasty, while Hussein was killed on the battlefield by the Umayyads in 681. These events gave rise to the Shia concept of martyrdom and their rituals of grieving.

There are three main branches of Shia Islam today - the Zaidis, Ismailis and Ithna Asharis (Twelvers or Imamis). The Ithna Asharis are the largest group. They believe that Muhammad's religious leadership, spiritual authority and divine guidance were passed on to 12 of his descendants, beginning with Ali, Hassan and Hussein.

The 12th Imam, Muhammad al-Mahdi, is said to have disappeared from a cave below a mosque in 878. Ithna Asharis believe the so-called "awaited imam" did not die and will return at the end of time to restore justice on earth.

What role has sectarianism played in recent crises?

In countries which have been governed by Sunnis, Shia tend to make up the poorest sections of society. They often see themselves as victims of discrimination and oppression. Sunni extremists frequently denounce Shia as heretics who should be killed.

The Iranian revolution of 1979 launched a radical Shia Islamist agenda that was perceived as a challenge to conservative Sunni regimes, particularly in the Gulf. Tehran's policy of supporting Shia militias and parties beyond its borders was copied within Sunni-ruled Gulf states. This strengthened their links to Sunni governments and movements elsewhere.

Today, many conflicts in the region have strong sectarian overtones. In Syria, Iranian troops, Hezbollah fighters and Iranian-backed Shia militiamen have been helping the Shia-led government battle the Sunni-dominated opposition. Sunni jihadist groups, including Islamic State (IS), have meanwhile been targeting Shia and their places of worship in Syria and Iraq. In January 2016, the execution by Saudi Arabia of a prominent Shia cleric who supported mass anti-government protests triggered a diplomatic crisis with Iran and angry demonstrations across the Middle East.

Major Differences Between Islam and the NSB

In strong contrast with the NSB, Islam is primarily undemocratic, intolerant and devoted to an all-powerful, external God-in-heaven [and Hell headed by Satan] whose authority, as interpreted by Islamic prophets, cannot be questioned. The NSB does not countenance an all-powerful, external God, nor insist on strict "obedience" to it or to the Koran and teachings of Mohammed – "the two primary sources of knowledge." Nor does it countenance undemocratic institutions.

Chapter 22

Non-Religious Belief Systems and the NSB

Introduction

There are also belief systems that reject belief in an external god and overlap the NSB in certain other respects. It may seem unnecessary to include them but it's at least interesting to do so. Why? – Because:

- They have attracted many adherents or practitioners;
- Their features challenge our basic assumption: that human beings need a more explicitly spiritual or higher order system of belief to help guide their lives; and yet...
- They also represent challenges to outright, individualistic atheism.

The two selected for review are Humanism and Taoism.

Humanism[273]

Humanism is the particular glory of the Renaissance. The recovery, translation, and dissemination of the literature of antiquity created a new excitement, displaying so vividly the accomplishments and capacities of humankind, with consequences for civilization great beyond reckoning.

The disciplines that came with this awakening all bore the mark of their origins -- the mastery of classical languages, the reverent attention to pagan poets and philosophers, the study of ancient history, and the adaptation of ancient forms to modern purposes, Yet they served as the robust foundation of education and culture for centuries until the recent past. In muted, expanded, and adapted forms, these Renaissance passions still live on among those of us who honor the humanities. Nevertheless, the utility of the Humanities is now in question, despite their having been at the center of learning throughout the period of the spectacular material and intellectual flourishing of Western civilization.

Science now prevails. We are now less interested in equipping and refining thought, more interested in creating and mastering technologies that will yield measurable enhancements of material well-being -- at least for those who create and master them,.[274] Now we are less interested in the exploration of our glorious mind, more engrossed in the drama of staying ahead of whatever

---

[273] This essay on humanism has been excerpted, but presented here edited and paraphrased, from Chapter 1 on "Humanism" by Robinson, Marilynne (2015), **The Givenness of Things.** London: Farrar, Straus and Giroux. Sections that immediately follow – those on "Science' and 'Neuroscience" especially – also owe much to Robinson's writing.

[274] See: Chubin, Daryl E. (2017), "Polarization and Participation," AAAS Trellis: "Technology has created a human problem. Silicon Valley and the media, themselves scorned, have a role to play. But they thrive on their polarized audiences. That means it's all up to us in our local communities, not them."

it is we think is pursuing us. Or perhaps we are just bent on evading the specter of entropy.

The spirit of the times is one of joyless urgency, many of us preparing ourselves and our children to be means to inscrutable ends that are not our own. In such an environment, the humanities seem to have little place. They are poor preparation for economic servitude. This spirit is not the consequence but the cause of our present parlous state of affairs. After all, we have as good grounds for exulting in human brilliance as any generation that has ever lived.

SCIENCE

The antidote to our gloom is to be found in contemporary science – not to be confused with technology. Technology is a means of doing science, not an end. Science is a process of truth-seeking and discovery. Even though many people are now likely to say: "I believe in science," it is not a system of belief. Science could even be viewed as a stance from which to defend the humanities. Do we want to undervalue contemporary art, literature, music or philosophy? After all, these, too, seek truth and offer discovery. But it is difficult to recognize the genius of a period until it has passed. Milton, Bach, Mozart all suffered long periods of eclipse, beginning before their lives had ended.

Science can also assert great achievements and insights, however tentative, during our present age as well as over 500 years prior. The last century and the beginning of this one have transformed the understanding of Being itself. "Understanding" is not quite the right word. The mysterious old category, Being, fundamental to all experience past, present, and to come, is by no means understood. However, the terms in which understanding may now be attempted have changed radically. This in itself is potent information. The phenomenon called quantum entanglement, relatively old as theory and thoroughly demonstrated as fact, raises fundamental questions about time, space, and causality, and therefore what it means "to be."

Particles that are "entangled," however distant from one another, undergo the same changes simultaneously. This fact challenges our most deeply embedded habits of thought. To try to imagine any event occurring outside the constraints of locality and sequence is difficult enough. Then there is the problem of conceiving of a universe in which the old rituals of cause and effect seem a gross leap beside the physically elegant sleights of hand of emergence. Discussed earlier in Chapter 5, these operate discreetly beyond the reach of all but the most rarefied scientific inference and observation. However pervasive and robust quantum entanglements are or are not, they imply a cosmos that unfolds or emerges on principles that bear scant analogy to a universe consonant with either scientific theory or common sense.

This complexity is abetted by string theory, which adds seven dimensions to our familiar four. And those four seem suddenly tenuous when the fundamental character of time and space is being called into question. Mathematics, ontology (the Science of Being), and metaphysics have become mixed and melded.

Einstein's universe seems almost mechanistic in comparison; Newton's, the work of a tinkerer. Galileo shocked the world by removing the earth from its place at the center of our universe. Now, a polyglot army of mathematicians and cosmologists offer new grounds for new conceptions of absolute reality that should dazzle us all, freeing us at last from the circle of old compasses. But we are not free.

There is no discipline for which the nature of reality is a matter of indifference. One ontology or another is always being assumed even if not expressed. Great questions are as open now as they have been since Babylonians began watching the stars. Certain disciplines, however, are still deeply invested in a model of reality that is as simple and narrow as ideological reductionism can make it. For example, the dominant schools of economics and Republican politics focuses on a "free market" which is not free.

Consider science of another kind. The study of brain and consciousness, mind and self-associated with so-called neuroscience asserts a model of mental functioning as straightforward as a game of billiards. It prides itself on just this fact. It is by no means part of the science that addresses ontology. The most striking and consequential changes in ontology have generated little or no change in neuroscience. Let us therefore address the shortcomings of the field.

NEUROSCIENCE

The gist of it is an assumption that the adverbs "simply" and "merely" can exorcise the mystifications that have always surrounded the operations of the mind/brain. Can one "simply" expose the complex of subtleties that produces emotion, behavior, and all the rest as one can describe a piece of machinery? Inquiries into the substance of reality reveal further ever more subtle relationships that are utterly new to our understanding.[275]

Yet neuroscience tells us that the most complex object we know of -- the human brain – can be explained sufficiently in terms of activations of "packets of neurons" bequeathed to us by an evolutionary process in service to homeostasis -- an organism's stability. The amazing complexity of the individual cell is being pored over in other regions of science, while neuroscience persists in declaring that the brain – with complexity vastly compounded -- is no more complex than a computer. If this could be true -- if this most intricate and vital organ could be "simply" described as a computational device -- this would be one of the wonders of scientific discovery.

Yet, it is not true, as we discovered early in this book. The brain is not just a computer. The work of Stuart Kaufman has shown that the most important work of the brain is "non-algorithmic" -- not reducible to computation. Why? Because there is no way to pre-define the set (space of) computable possibilities. Note that neuroscience has, as its primary resource, technology that captures images of processes within the living brain. Fear lights up a certain area, therefore fear is a function of that area which developed for the purposes of maintaining homeostasis.

---

[275] See, for example, Ikemoto, Satoshi (2019)m "Regulation of Negative Behavior," **SCIENCE** (29 November).

Fear prepares the organism to fight or flee. Well and good. But fear is rarely without context. People can be terrified of spiders, dentists, the Last Judgment, germs, speaking in public, the number 13, extra-terrestrials, mathematics, hoodies, or the discovery of a fraud in their past. All of these fears and many others are the creatures of circumstance, innumerable and often undefinable, of the history and state of health of a specific brain -- that of a specific, unique person.

Neuroscientists identify threat and its context in highly individual terms. These, not threat in the abstract, trigger alarm, and they are the products of parts of the brain that do not light up under technological scrutiny and would elude interpretation if they did. If they are not taken into account, the mere evidence of a fearful excitation has little descriptive and no predictive value. A fearful person might take a pill, faint, or commit mayhem. The assumptions behind the notion that the nature of fear and the impulses it triggers could be made legible or generalizable for the purposes of imaging would have to exclude complexity—the factor that introduces individuality with all its attendant mysteries. Yet the neuroscientists seem well content with the technology they have, extrapolating boldly from the data it yields. Refinements that introduced complication might not be welcome.

This all appears to be a straightforward instance of scientists taking as the whole of reality that part of it their methods can report. These methods are as much a matter of vocabulary as of technology, though the two interact and reinforce each other. Here is an example: Many neuroscientists seem predisposed to the conclusion that there is no "self." This would account for indifference to the modifying effects of individual history and experience, and to the quirks of the organism that arise from heredity, environment, interactions within the being as a whole, and so on.

What can the word "self" mean to those who wish to deny its reality? It can only signify an illusion we all participate in, as individuals, societies, and civilizations. So it must also be an important function of the brain, the brain aware of itself as it is modified by the infinite particulars of circumstance like those experienced by others. But this would mean the self is not an illusion at all but a product of the mind at work other than the one most neuroscientists are inclined to acknowledge.

Of course, the physical brain is subject to every sort of impairment of the areas that light up during imaging. Impairments that seem to compromise the sense of self may be taken to demonstrate that it is rooted in the physical brain. If the physical disruption of the sense of self is taken to prove that the self is an experience created by the physical brain, then there are no better grounds to call the existence of selfhood into question – any more than there would be to question equilibrium or depth perception. Obviously, there is a conceptual problem here—equilibrium does not "exist" except in the moment-to-moment orientation of an organism to its environment. Say as much of the self and it is granted the same kind of reality.

But it is absurdly contradictory of neuroscientists who insist on the category "physical," but also argue that outside this category nothing exists, to dismiss the reality of the self on the grounds that its vulnerabilities can be said to place it solidly within the physical category. How can so basic a contradiction survive? There is a certain presumptuousness, even unto arrogance, in a branch of science that could rescue us from entrenched error but does not. Questions that undermine its presumptions might seem a betrayal of science as rescuer. Thus, tenets of neuroscience seem to enjoy a singular immunity from criticism. Proponents feel buttressed rather than undermined by doubts and objections when critique comes from those whose underlying motives might seem to lie in some hostility to science.

Under greater scrutiny, however, the physical is as elusive as anything to which a name can be given. The physical as we have come to know it frays away into dark matter, antimatter, and by implication on beyond them and even beyond our present powers of inference. But for many neuroscientists, it is a business of nuts and bolts, a mechanics of signals and receptors of which no more need be known. Their assertions are immune to objection and proof against information. One they dismiss and the other they ignore. Neuroscience is remarkable among the sciences for its tendency to bypass theory and go directly to assertion

A major implication of this approach takes us back to the very beginning of this book. Recall that we opened with a focus on the soul. But here and now, suddenly, there is no soul. Why? – Because neuroscience views the soul as totally non-physical, as a core of self that stands apart from it. What a contradiction! Such ignorance, such avoidance of emergence! – that even matters most spiritual are emergent from the physical networks of the human brain.

The soul is claimed to be nonphysical, therefore sacred and sanctifying as an aspect of being human. It is the self that stands apart from the self. From a narrowly neuroscientific perspective, the soul suffers injuries of a moral kind when the self is but then is not when a human being lies or steals or murders, untouched by the accidents that maim the self or kill it. This intuition cannot be dispelled by proving the soul's physicality because such proof has been disallowed by an overly narrow definition. On these same grounds, its non-physicality is no proof of its nonexistence. This might seem a clever evasion of skepticism if the character of the soul were not established in remote antiquity, in many places and cultures, long before such a thing as science was brought to bear on the question.!

WHAT HAVE WE DISCOVERED?

The soul is a valuable concept, a statement of the dignity of a human life and of the unutterable gravity of human action and experience. I would add that I find my own soul interesting company, if this did not seem to cast doubt on my objectivity. This is not entirely a joke. I am not prepared to concede objectivity to the arbitrarily reductionist model of reality that has so long claimed and been granted a presumption of "objectivity." The new cosmologies open so many ways of reconceiving the universe(s) that all sorts of speculations are now respectable.

If most or all these speculations are only flaunting new definitions of the possible, the exercise is valuable and necessary. Possibility has been captive to a narrow definition for a very long time, New cosmologies preclude almost nothing except "the physical" as a special category. The physicality enshrined by neuroscientists as the measure of all things is not objectivity, but instead a pure artifact of the scale at which, and the means by which, we and our devices perceive. So to invoke it as the test and standard of reality is quintessentially anthropocentric.

We are complex enough, interesting enough. What we have learned, limited as we must assume it to be, is wonderful even in the face of its limitations. This is no proof, of course. Be that as it may. It is not anthropocentricity that is a problem here, but the fact that it is unacknowledged and misapplied, all the while imputed to the other side of the controversy as if it were a flagrant error. The objectivity claimed by neuroscience implies that it is free of this bias. Yet there could be no more naive anthropocentricity than is reflected in the certainty and insistence that what we know about the nature of things at this moment makes us capable of definitive judgments about much of anything.

That we have come to this place is not a failure of science but a glorious achievement, the continuous opening of insights that science itself could never have anticipated. Nothing can account for reductionist tendencies except a lack of rigor and consistency, a loyalty to conclusions that are prior to evidence and argument and indifferent to science as a whole.

This kind of criticism is conventionally made of religion. The point is simply that neuroscience, at least in its dominant forms, greatly overreaches the implications of its evidence. It is tendentious. Its tendency is to insist on the necessity of a transformation of our conception of human nature—to make it consistent with a view of reality that it considers clear-eyed and tough-minded, therefore rational and true. Its presumption seems to be that we all really know better than to subscribe to the mythic foolery that sustains us in a lofty estimation of ourselves and our kind.

The evidence it offers is secondary to this conclusion and inadequate to it, because it is based in a simplistic materialism dosed with nostalgia. The profound complexity of the brain is an established fact. The depiction of a certain traffic of activation in it can only understate its complexity. One might reasonably suspect that the large and costly machines that do the imaging are very crude tools whose main virtue is that they provide the kind of data their users desire and no more.

This school of thought is directed against humanism. The old humanists took the works of the human mind—literature, music, philosophy, art, and languages—as proof of what the mind is and might be. Out of this has come the great aura of brilliance and exceptionalism around our species that neuroscience would dispel. If Shakespeare had undergone an MRI, there is no reason to believe there would be any more evidence of extraordinary brilliance in him than there would be of a self or a soul. Except that he left a formidable body of evidence that he was both brilliant and singular.

Yet, from a narrow, neuro-scientific perspective, this is not deemed germane. Why? -- Perhaps because this places the mind so squarely at the center of the humanities. After all, where did our high sense of ourselves come from? From what we have done and what we do. And where is this awareness preserved and enhanced? In the arts, other humane disciplines, and the fecundity of science.

If there is a scientific mode of thought that is crowding out and demoralizing the humanities, it is not research in the biology of the cell or the quest for life on other planets. It is a neo-Darwinism that claims to cut through the dense miasmas of delusion to what is mere, simple, and real. Since these "miasmas" have been the main work of human consciousness for as long as the mind has left a record of itself, their devaluing is a major work of dehumanization – not unlike Gasset's "Dehumanization of Art" noted in Chapter 13. Humanistic explorations are a great measure of our distinctiveness as a species. It is what we know about ourselves. It has everything in the world to do with how we think and feel, with what we value, despise or fear. All these things are refracted through cultures and again through families and individuals.

If the object of neuroscience was to describe an essential human nature, it would surely seek confirmation in our history and culture. But these things are endlessly complex. They are also continually open to variation and changing interpretations. So the insistence on an essential simplicity is understandable, but here it is not fruitful. If Neuroscience is essentially neo-Darwinist, it is attached to a model of reality that has not gone through any meaningful change in a century, except in the kind of machinery it brings to bear in asserting its worldview.

A nematode is more complex than a human being was thought to be fifty years ago. Now biology is in the course of absorbing the implications of the fact that our bodies are colonized by specialized microorganisms, all of them certainly complex in their various ways and in their interactions.[276] It is the elegance of nature that sometimes creates the appearance of simplicity. The double helix as a structure expedites fluent change, modifications induced by the genetic alphabet it contains. These baffle any deterministic associations.

Elegance of this kind could be called efficiency if that word did not have teleological implications. The prohibition against teleology (goal-seeking) must be an arbitrary constraint. We hardly know what time is. It may not be respectable to say that an organism is designed to be both stable as an entity and mutable in response to environment. Yet it must be said that this complex of equilibrium and disequilibrium is an amazing and beautiful paradox, everywhere repeated in a wealth of variations that can seem like virtuosity regaling itself with its own brilliance.

I am a nondenominational theist, so my habits of mind have a particular character. Such predispositions, long typical in Western civilization, have been carefully winnowed out of scientific thought over the last two centuries in favor of materialism, by which I mean a discipline of exclusive attention to the reality that can be tested by scientists. The scientific project has been very necessary and very fruitful. The greatest proof of its legitimacy is that it has found its way to its own limits.

Scientific inference has now moved past the old assumptions about materiality and beyond the testable. Presumably, it would prefer not to have gone beyond its classic definitions of hypothesis, evidence, demonstration. No doubt it will continue to bring great ingenuity to bear on the questions that exceed any present ability to test them, as it has done so often over the past 500 years.

Nevertheless, science may never find a way to confirm or reject the idea of multiple universes (now designated "multiverses"), or to arrive at a satisfactory definition of time or gravity. We know things in the ways we

---

[276] Recent research has focused on microbiota and connected some of them to depression.

encounter them. Our encounters, and our methods and assumptions, are determined by our senses, techniques and intuitions.

The recent vast expansion and proliferation of our models of reality bring with them the realization that our situation on this planet and our ability to understand it, is radically exceptional even though our capacity for awareness is therefore parochial in ways and degrees we can hardly estimate. To have arrived at this point is not a failure of science but a spectacular achievement.

That said, it might be time to pause and reflect. Holding to the old faith that everything is in principle knowable or comprehensible by us is a little like assuming that every human structure or artifact must be based on yards, feet, and inches. The notion that the universe is constructed, or we are evolved, so that reality must finally answer in every case to the questions we bring to it, is entirely as anthropocentric as the notion that the universe was designed to make us possible. Indeed, the affinity between the two ideas should be acknowledged. While the assumption of the intelligibility of the universe is still useful, it is not appropriately regarded as a statement of doctrine and should never have been.

Science of the kind criticized here tends to assert that everything is explicable, that whatever has not been explained will not only be explained, but that the explanations will be brought forth by its methods. Its practitioners have seen to the heart of it all. So mystery and miracles are banished. They are no more than whatever scientific methods cannot capture yet. They also include those aspects of reality whose implications are not always factors in a scientific worldview; for example, the human mind, the human self, history, and religion – the broad terrain of the human.

We now know that chromosomes are modified cell by cell, and that inheritance is a mosaic of differentiation within the body, distinctive in each individual. Therefore, the notion that one genetic formula, one script, is elaborated in the being of any creature must be put aside, along with all the determinist assumptions it has seemed to rationalize. Moreover, the impulse toward generalization that would claim to make the brain solvable should be rejected. For we need some grasp of the deeper sources of this complexity and order, the causal factors that lie behind this infinitesimal nuancing. The brain is more profoundly individuated than our science can yet reveal.

If selfhood implies individuality, or if our undeniable individuality justifies the sense of selfhood, then there is another mystery to be acknowledged. Why should any impulse to deny the existence; indeed, the value of the human self, still persist and flourish among us? Where slavery and other forms of extreme exploitation of human labor have been general, moral convenience would account for much of it. Where population groups are seen as enemies or even as burdens, certain nefarious traits are attributed to them as a whole that are taken to override the qualities of individual members. Again, moral convenience.

Both cases illustrate the association of the denial of selfhood with the devaluation of the human person. This would seem too obvious to be said but for the fact that the denial of selfhood persists under the wing of neuroscience. That is, it appears to be authorized by the methods of neuroscience and by the generalized reports it offers of the profoundly intricate workings of the brain. That such "science" may also provide convenient, morally obtuse rationalizations of mans' inhumanity to man should be obvious. The Holocaust proved that mankind can rationalize anything, no matter how brutal or inhumane.

Fortunately, there are other scientists whose science resonates with the both the value and meaning of individual selfhood and the collective richness of human life. One of these is Douglas Hofstadter. His book, **I AM A STRANGE LOOP**, illuminates the real world, macro-level, multivariate dimensions of "I" in ways consistent with the infinitesimal level of particle physics.[277]

---

[277] See Hofstadter, Douglas (2007), **I AM A STRANGE LOOP**. New York: Basic Books, especially Chapter 13, "The Elusive Apple of my "I"", pp. 177-191.

There are so many works of the mind, so much humanity, that to disburden ourselves of the essence of our selves might be viewed an understandable temptation. Open a book and a voice speaks. A world, more or less alien or welcoming, emerges to enrich a reader's store of hypotheses about how life is to be understood. As with scientific hypotheses, even failure is meaningful, a test of the boundaries of credibility. So many voices, so many worlds, we can weary of them.

The Humanist Association of Canada, part of a "growing secular movement," has distilled humanism down to ten (10) tenets. Edited and paraphrased, they are as follows. Each is followed by my commentary.

1) **The human species has evolved - and remains - as part of nature**. Thus, like all living organisms, human life is limited in duration and scope – one of the standpoints of this book.

2) **Human consciousness emerges from the activity of the human brain.** Being aware of the rest of nature - and of the universe and our place within it -- is characteristic of humankind's mental functioning that is perhaps unique and certainly wonderful. Nevertheless, consciousness is another aspect of natural life, not a force or essence instilled into humans by an outside deity or intelligence. An individual's conscious-ness ends when that person dies.

3) **Human beings require a system of belief in order to function.** So far, most belief systems have revolved around the idea of an external god or gods. However, the same need to believe can be equally served by alternative systems of philosophy. The Humanist system employs the scientific method to establish the factual basis of its beliefs. It also bases human behavior on reasonable conduct and democratic principles.

4) **Humanists believe in supernatural myths in all their forms**. NOT OK. This book recognizes the downside of the supernatural.

5) The human species is capable of achieving a great deal using collaboration and creativity. The results often benefit our species and planet. We are also capable of using the same abilities in acts of destruction and cruelty. Humanists recognize that the awful potential for destruction is part of the human repertoire. "Acts of mass aggression, killing and war are results of tendencies built into human behavior, not simply the result of the acts by a few abnormal and aberrant individuals. Heaven and hell are constructs of human beings here on earth, not of any external "God" above or "Satan" below.

6) Humanists do not believe that the range of human behavior has been pre-ordained or that the rules of human conduct have been set by any deity or external intelligence. No single religion has been able to show that it has exclusive access to the secret of peaceful and cooperative co-existence of life on earth. There is much merit in the idea that there is no such thing as an extrinsic set of rules imposed from outside humankind governing all human behavior.

7) Humanists believe that individuals who are aware of the consequences of their actions -- on other individuals, on the community and on the species --are likely to behave in more reasonable and more ethical ways. Indisputable, especially without the guidance of a supernatural god.

8) **Humanists believe that equality of opportunity is a fundamental principle on which humankind can base its behavior.** Agreeable up to a point but arguable as to "fundamental" and "base." Equality is not just a matter of opportunity, nor does equality of opportunity provide assurance of social or economic equality.

9) **Life on earth is relatively fragile. It requires nurturing care and careful attention to carry on.** There is nothing protecting the human species against all causes of potential extinction. Our own activities may threaten our existence. So we need to organize and regulate what we do if the human race is to survive as a species.

10) Humankind's destiny is not predetermined or preordained much of it lies in our own control. There is hope. It is up to all human beings to look after each other and themselves."[278] Here there is wholehearted concurrence.

Altogether, these tenets are honorable, estimable and eminently humane. There is little to disagree with among the ten. They substantially overlap the features of a NSB. Together with the preceding Chapter, they reveal that our NSB is also truly humane in ways recognized by our humanist friends, even more so.

Unfortunately, they do not address the fundamental issue of human spirituality or related ethical concerns. Nor do they explicitly recognize the "dark side" of human nature or of technology except indirectly, as with "tendencies built into human behavior." There is also no mention of Gaia.

Another major ethical concern not cited is the Golden Rule, variants of which are found in every major religion. Thus, notwithstanding its substantial "overlap" with a NSB, humanism provides an insufficient basis for our efforts to attain higher levels of human development and spirituality. Overall and above all, it fails to measure up to a NSB sufficient to sustain human life.

Taoism[279]

Taoism is a Chinese philosophy based on the writings of Lao-tzu (6th century BC), advocating humility and religious piety. Taoism teaches a person to follow their breathing, to embrace wonder and the joy in living gracefully with style. A practical guide to Taoism follows.

---

[278] Humanism Association of Canada, **"Ten Core Beliefs of Humanism,"** https://www.humanistcanada.ca [no date].

[279] Excerpted, with minor editing from **Taoism 101: Introduction to the Tao.** Source: PersonalTao@gmail.com.

To many people, a confusing aspect of Taoism is its very definition. Many religions will happily teach a system of belief which helps to define a person living in the context of that system. Taoism flips this around. It starts by teaching a truth: "The Tao" is indefinable. It then follows up by teaching that each person can discover the Tao in their own terms. It's puzzling at this point to sense a possible contradiction here – A "truth" on one's "own terms"?

Indeed, teaching like this can be very hard to grasp when most people desire very concrete definitions to guide their own life. A simple way to start learning the definition of Taoism is to start within yourself. Here are three easy starting steps to learning Taoism:

    i.   Don't concentrate on the definition of the Tao ("indefinable"?; hopefully, this will come later).

    ii.   Understand what Taoism really is. Taoism is more than just a "philosophy" or a "religion." Taoism should be understood as being a system of belief, attitudes and practices set towards service to others and towards helping a person live up to his or her own, true nature.

    iii.   The path of understanding Taoism is simply accepting yourself. Live life and discover who you are. Your nature is ever changing and yet always the same. Don't try to resolve the various contradictions in life, instead learn acceptance of your nature.

Practicing Taoism: Taoism teaches a person to "go with the flow" of life. Over the years Taoism has become many things to many people. Hundreds of variations in Taoist practice exist. Some of these practices are philosophical in nature, others are religious. Taoism makes no distinction among labels applied to its own nature. This is important since as a person, we are each a blend of many truths. The truth taught in Taoism is to embrace life in actions that support you as a person with, hopefully, a long life to live. Taoism teaches a person to live up to the meaning of their soul (for which there is no definition).

Here are some simple starting tips to help a person live as a Taoist. Having a set of basic guidelines can be helpful. However realistic, guidelines don't determine how you can or should live; Instead Taoism teaches how you can express your soulful nature in the course of living. Some personal guidelines are the following.

- First, view persons around you as extended expressions of your own nature. Then, with care, aid them in order to --
- Second, be true to yourself and connect to the world as you want to be treated, and
- Third, connect to those outside your nature with decisive action.

Remember: You own nothing; you are merely a passing custodian of items outside of your nature.

Discover a set of practices to aid keeping the mind, body and spirit engaged and strong. Remember practices should support your essence with activities fitting the needs of the moment. Which means a shifting balance of activities relative to your needs. You could, for example:

- ✓ Practice martial arts to keep your body strong,
- ✓ Do yoga to make your body subtle,
- ✓ Meditate to clear your mind, and
- ✓ Bike around simply to fly about and lift your spirit.
- ✓ You might also try to read or write poetry as a lens of self-examination and expression. All these and more are practices that can be shifted to support your essence. In doing each, we are helped to learn more about ourselves in relation to the rest of the world.
- ✓ Take time, relax and just explore and poke around. Taoism has no plans. Taoism is based upon following your gut feelings and trusting your instincts. It's within the pause of a breath that each step of living becomes visible for your larger life to improve and follow upon. So:
- ✓ Smile when needing to pick a possible next step. To smile is to open possibilities.
- ✓ Breathe when needing a break. To breathe is to be at one with yourself.
- ✓ Alternate the two and your path will become free and clear for an entire lifetime of wonder to explore.

This may sound simple, but you would be surprised how many people cannot embrace this most basic aspect of Taoist practice! People think it cannot be that simple!, but truly it is this simple. This is all one needs to fully embrace Taoism. Anything becomes possible with this simple practice. However, most people need time to let go of old attitudes, habits, practices and expectations. It's OK to dig deeper. Taoism has many levels of teachings to help people from all perspectives move smoothly through their lives.

We can summarize Taoism as: --

> Taoism is acceptance of your life.
> Taoism is following your breath to find peace.
> Taoism is opening up a smile to enable possibility.

If you embrace these three ideas, everything else follows in Taoism. Some people start here. Others take a longer more colorful path. That's fine also, since you get to experience more color in your life. No wrong path exists. It is all about experiencing life.

Practical Taoist Advice

❖ At times the process of learning Taoism is also a process of healing. Take time to heal. Don't rush and hurt yourself more in the rushing. Taoism teaches to embrace your body with patience.

❖ There are over 7 billion people in the world. This means over 7 billion paths to Taoism! Every person can teach us something.

❖ Sometimes you need quietness. At times, it's ok to take time off to only hear yourself and not the noise of civilization. While listening, sing or hum "The Sound of Silence" and "The Sound of Music."

❖ People think that the goal of life is perfection. It's not. You should desire to be good at something. Also learn to recognize and embrace the various little imperfections that often end up being defining characteristics of each of us. Little bits of imperfection are elements of variety that give each person individuality and distinction! Without our little flaws we wouldn't be individuals at all! Taoism teaches us how to accept both the best and worse parts of our lives. Remember: "The perfect is the enemy of the good."

❖ Taoism teaches a person to drop expectations. The more expectations you have for your life, the less you will become. A Taoist lives life without expectations, living fully in the here and now. Since most people need a few expectations, especially when approaching important future possibilities, here is a trick. Create only a single expectation at a time. Leave room for future experience. For example: An expectation you will smile or have some fun. That's it! Don't invest any learning or changing into expectations. If you do, this actually plants the seed for the opposite to occur. By creating a single simple expectation such as smiling, this then becomes something you can always fulfill since you can easily enable that action to happen. Any expectation more complicated or relying on something outside of yourself just sets up a future that may not meet your needs. Dropping expectations is very important within Taoism.

❖ Lather, Rinse and Repeat, then toss the instructions away to do what is right for yourself… This is Taoism at the very elemental level, so be open, experiment and embrace what works for you. Taoism has teachers who work with students on an individual basis. In the end no guide or Master can be right for everyone. For this reason, we are always our own best teacher. Give yourself credit and patience to be such a teacher during your own life.

Explore Your Essence

○ **First:** Learn how to trust your own intuition.
○ **Second:** Let go of judgments that hold you back.
○ **Third:** Remove conflict and anger from your relationships.
○ **Fourth:** Be kind to yourself and pace your life to match your essence (soul?) as a human being.

Comparison with a NSB

These tenets overlap substantially with those of a humane NSB, but they are nevertheless questionable and inadequate in several respects. Some even appear to be contradictory within the set. Consider the differences as follows.

- Wholesale "acceptance of own nature" ignores the existence of a "dark side" in each of us.
- Practices and activities to "fit the needs of the moment" – These are far too oblivious to future hopes and contingencies. There is also a seeming contradiction with the recommendation that "Each step (be) visible for a "larger life."
- The latter is inconsistent with "No plans," just follow "gut feelings," "trusting your instincts," "No wrong path exists" and "drop expectations."
- The most heralded virtue of Taoism, its "simplicity" is mistakenly simple to an extreme in failing to present a system of belief adequate to helping any of us to deal with the growing complexity of human life worldwide. Taoism is a very simple two-step dance: "smile" and "breathe." Note this judgment comes from one who has repeated said to others: "The only answer to complexity is simplicity."

Notwithstanding, there are two substantial, overlapping agreements: (1) There is no external "God" or "heaven", but (2) There is at least partial (but insufficient) recognition that soul and soulfulness exist.

Chapter 23

Spirituality and Work

Introduction

We would be terribly remiss to not consider this theme. Before and after all, we spend most of our waking time working to make our livings. On the one hand, much of work would be a terrible grind and pox on our lives if there were no ways to enable the realization of spirituality in the course of a workday or week. On the other, we cannot help but notice that for at least a significant minority among us, work is hardly distinguishable from play. Along the whole wide range and diversity of work activities, time is indeed of the essence. Some realization of the value of time expended or invested is fundamental. Our work, however routine, creative or in-between it may be, comprises an important part of our search for matter and meaning in our lives.

Thus, this chapter includes an interview with Scott McLennan who, before retiring in 2000, spent 14 years as the Dean for Religious Life at Stanford University.[280] There, among other things, he interviewed the Dalai Lama and worked to create a campus meditative center. Upon his return to teach at Stanford Graduate School of Business, the Unitarian Universalist minister sat

---

[280] For more see: Nash, Laura, and S. McLennan (2001), **CHURCH on SUNDAY, WORK on MONDAY: The Challenge of Fusing Christian Values with Business Life.** Jossey-Bass.

down to discuss the benefits of quiet reflection, and why people do not need to check their religion at the door whenever they start work.

Attempts to deal with the matter of work pay little or no attention to the spiritual aspects of human nature. Not that the nature of work necessarily negates spirituality. Far from it. The best work is recognized for its attentiveness to whole products in service to other human beings and whole cultures – their craft, precision, beauty, quality, &c. The spiritual temper of the work to create such products enters in and around work as a process of design, creation and craft.

To the extent that any of the contexts of our lives are counter to spirituality, then it is our responsibility as both citizens and souls to work with others to change them. Our individual abilities to fulfill our potentials are constrained, and thereby limited by the settings in which we find ourselves. Here is another instance where reliance on the market and the choices and contexts that marketplaces present to us don't work. Most folks will say: 'Don't like the company you work for? – Just go get another job.' But any job requires us to invest time – the signature of our mortality – and most of us would like to be investing in our work to produce something of matter and meaning. Work should have such spirit. The attitude of 'just get a job' treats work as a transactional choice, not an investment over the precious time of our lives.

Religious practices in workplaces – Is this what we're pointing to here? Only in small part. We've already recognized that "religion" and spirituality don't necessarily equate. Followers of Mohammed, for example, may demand and receive time for their prayers while at work. Fine, but what about other workers, and the quality of work itself? I sat next to an ironworker in Harry's Bar, in Carrabelle, FL. He had spent his life helping to build tall buildings. He recalled the spirit of his work in two ways. One was the thrill of standing on girders high above the ground. The other was the act of building, making something that would last. We should all have work that raises our spirits.

Now for the interview. Author's note: Some of the features mentioned herein are also aspects of Taoism, Buddhism and Taoism, discussed earlier. The interview text has been slightly edited

Interviewer (hereafter designated "V"):

Many successful business people integrate religion into their careers.[281] Taking a coffee break on the job can increase productivity. Setting aside 10 minutes for meditation can do the same. When visiting Windhover Contemplative Center at Stanford, which you had a key role in creating, I noticed that some visitors could not help but chat with each other, and one was even texting on her mobile phone.

Why is it so difficult for us to be still, even in a center intended for that purpose? Windhover is meant to be a technology-free zone, knowing that our mobile phones and other electronic devices can not only be addictive, consuming our attention, but also can keep us tense, stressed, and even unable to relax and sleep, as much current research is confirming. They can also be disturbing to others. Of course, we're social beings, so chatting with each other and chatting online are normal and routine.

Meditation is meant to break the normal and the routine in order to radically expand one's breadth and depth of experience – to generate an enhanced awareness and mindfulness. It's not easy, though. It takes discipline, precisely because it takes us far from our normal, routine life. You actually have to sit still and do nothing. Ideally, you have to concentrate on only one thing, like following your breath in and out, rather than being scattered and consumed by many other things. See Chapter 26 for more.

McLellan (hereafter designated "M"): I have been an activist in many ways – physically, intellectually, politically, spiritually. But learning how a great activist like Gandhi found his strength in quiet meditation helped me try it out, and the Hindu priest I lived with one summer in India insisted on it as a daily exercise. Practice makes perfect. Or makes it easier, since it's certainly never been perfect for me.

---

[281] See Peterson, Deborah (2015?),**"How to Bring Your Spiritual Side to Work Every Day"**

The more I meditated, the more I learned the value of stillness in many realms: listening to others more patiently and empathetically, smelling the flowers rather than passing them in a rush, becoming slower to anger and breathing intentionally when I feel stressed, while feeling connected to the larger universe or to the ultimacy of life.

V: Meditation is a central practice for many Buddhists and Hindus. In America, we often attribute it to traditions other than Judaism, Christianity and Islam. Yet, all religious traditions (and many humanistic, secular ones) show something akin to meditation, especially through various forms of centering prayer. And also through silent recitation of scripture or poetry, veneration of icons, handling prayer beads, rocking rhythmically, mental visualization, muscle relaxation, contemplating nature, and enjoying art, to name a few techniques and methods. No one has a lock on quietude, reflection, stillness, and serenity. I think some people are surprised to know that a minister teaches at a business school. How do these lessons translate to business?

M: Business people spend the majority of their waking hours at work, and many of them want to find it meaningful. Many also want to conduct their business affairs ethically. Most of us worldwide learn our ethics through our religious traditions or through philosophical understanding of morality that we inherit from our families, education and surrounding culture. I wrote a book with a colleague at Harvard Business School where we tried to help readers integrate their spirituality and ethical commitments into their daily work lives. Ultimately, I believe this leads to more successful businesses and to greater satisfaction of customers and other stakeholders. That this belief is well-founded is attested by some research studies on the matter.[282]

---

[282] For example, see: Stillman, Jessica (2015), "An Entrepreneur's Secret Weapon: Spirituality," INC magazine, INC.com (March 10), and Burack, Elmer (1999), **"Spirituality in the Workplace," JOURNAL of ORGANIZATIONAL CHANGE** (Vol.12.4), pp.280-292.

V: There seems to be a renewed interest among business people to make space for finding their inner calm, such as through the practice of mindfulness. But how do you convince CEOs and other high-achieving leaders that it is a worthwhile thing to do?

M: It doesn't take much to convince business leaders and others that they should take a coffee break from time to time. Taking 10 or 15 minutes off ultimately increases productivity rather than decreasing it. How much more useful and fulfilling to stimulate one's "relaxation response" through a meditational or prayer practice during one of those break times. If nothing else, there's good medical evidence that it helps you to reduce stress, limit negative emotions, lower blood pressure, restore calmness, and increase your overall sense of well-being.[283]

V: You are just finishing up a sabbatical before you return to lecture at Stanford Graduate School of Business. How did you spend your time off? What will you teach at Stanford GSB?

M: I've used my leave to travel and write and explore areas of interest that I've had for a very long time but not been able actively to pursue. These include listening to classical music, spending time outdoors in nature, learning about digital photography, watching great movies, and catching up on developments in constitutional law. I've been developing two new courses. One is tentatively titled "Business Biography: Finding Spiritual Meaning at Work." We'll look at biographies of respected people in business to see how they integrate what ultimately really matters to them with their business careers, and how they fail in this regard.

---

[283] For reports of research providing evidence supporting these observations, see: Melnick, Meredith (2013), "Meditation Health Benefits: What the Practice Does to Your Body," **HUFFINGTON POST** (May 2), and Dienstmann, Giovanni (2017), "Scientific Benefits of Meditation," www.liveanddare.com.

In the other course, I want to help students understand the etiquette of doing business in quite different cultures: say, Japan, China, India, Egypt, Israel, Russia, Brazil, and Great Britain. They will learn about the deeper cultural ethos from which that etiquette emerges, and finally be introduced to the dominant religious traditions which I believe underlie both etiquette and ethos.

V: Which biographies are on your short list?

One is serial entrepreneur Noah Alper's **BUSINESS Mensch** (2009). Among other ventures, the natural foods chain Bread and Circus, now owned by Whole Foods, was founded by Alper, as well as the Noah's New York Bagels chain, which he sold to Einstein Brothers for $100 million in 1995. Alper tried to run his bagel business on traditional Jewish religious principles, including keeping kosher. He took the ethical dimensions of Judaism very seriously, as well. For example, he describes in detail, with examples, how important being a mensch (an honorable, decent person) is to elicit and earn employee dependability and customer loyalty. He cites the importance of keeping the Sabbath holy – shuttering the business for a full day each week. He also stresses taking personal time every day, like a scheduled half-hour walk, for personal reflection.

Another biography I'm considering is basketball coach Phil Jackson's **Eleven Rings**.[284] Jackson brought his Zen Buddhist ideas and practices into his work with his teams, the Chicago Bulls and the Los Angeles Lakers. He explains how Buddhism helped his teams move from being disconnected and ego-driven to being unified and selfless. He tried always to relate to his players as full persons as well, not just as cogs in a basketball machine, helping them develop their personal moral qualities and spirituality. He incorporated

---

[284] Jackson, Phil, and H. Delehanty (2013), **ELEVEN RINGS: The Soul of Success**. New York: Penguin.

mindfulness meditation into practices and used rituals to infuse work with a sense of the sacred.[285]

V: What are some ways people can integrate religion into their work lives?

M: In the book I co-authored with Laura Nash of Harvard Business School[286], we distinguished between conventional religion, which we counsel against bringing to work, and catalytic and foundational religion. The catalytic is personal and includes practices like meditation and prayer, while the foundational emphasizes generalized statements of religious wisdom that cross boundaries and traditions, like the Golden Rule and Ten Commandments, or stories of love and sacrifice like that of Rev. Martin Luther King. It can be very important and helpful to bring catalytic and foundational religion to work, from the CEO level on down, while espoused religion should be left at the door.[287]

We also cite business educator and consultant Stephen Covey's emphasis on practicing spirituality at work as part of "sharpening the saw," one of his Seven Habits of Highly Effective People. Since spirituality, often directly derived from one's religion, lies at one's core and involves commitment to one's value system, it is critical to nurture those sources as much in the workplace as in private life. That can be done through the likes of personal

---

[285] Though not part of the interview, it helps here to note remarks of Scott Rogers in his article on "The Mindful Lawyer, published in **THE FLORIDA BAR**: "In practicing mindfulness, we work on cultivating the capacity to be simply aware of our thoughts and mental activity – just knowing that the thoughts are happening, without getting fixated on their content or needing to figure them out."

[286] Nash and McLellan, (2001), op. cit..

[287] This resonates with earlier observations distinguishing religion from spirituality.

rituals, applying scripture to workplace situations, and developing corporate credos and sagas that can affect a business's culture.

V: What lessons does literature offer to the contemporary workplace?

M: Hermann Hesse's title character in Siddhartha struggles throughout his life to combine business and spirituality. He becomes a rich merchant who is at first unattached to material success, concentrating on putting his customers first and acting ethically with all stakeholders. Then he becomes covetous, succumbs to the "soul sickness of the rich," and becomes not only mean-spirited but also suicidal. Late in the book he finds equilibrium in a daily business of ferrying travelers across a river, providing spiritual mentoring to some, then finding that most people simply want good transportation services.

Bharati Mukherjee's Jasmine portrays a Hindu immigrant's journey through a variety of jobs and experiences as she seeks the American Dream from Florida to New York to Iowa to California. Takeaways include how to balance new-world selfishness and personal freedom with old-world selflessness in familial duty. Major concerns include examining whether there is a stable self (or Self) to rely upon in each of us, or an ever-changing identity as we change our environments; also, the foundation of morality in karma, reaping what one sows; and the struggle between fate and will.

V: Name a CEO who is successfully bringing his or her spirituality to work every day.

M: Jeff Weiner, the CEO of LinkedIn, has spoken and written about how he has been influenced by the by the Buddhism of the Dalai Lama. He considers the number one management principle in his own work life and for his company to be managing compassionately. This goes beyond empathy. It extends to walking in another's shoes and taking collaborative action together. Some papers cited among this book's references provide some evidence of how collaboration incites or encourages spirituality.

He is convinced that compassion can be taught not only in school, but also in corporate learning and development programs. A fellow minister who heard Jeff Weiner speak on "The Art of Conscious Leadership" at the 2013 Wisdom 2.0 conference in San Francisco described Weiner as making the most inspiring contribution to the conference. Not only was his spiritual commitment to his employees and customers strongly in evidence; he also has a business leadership dream to expand compassion worldwide through his powerful social media company. The interview ended with McLellan's introduction of gut-wrenching challenges.

Spirituality in the Workplace: References, Trends and Follow-up

A movement in this direction began in the early 1920s. It slowly emerged as a grassroots movement with individuals seeking to live their faith and/or spiritual values in the workplace. One of the first publications to mention spirituality in the workplace was Business Week, June 5, 2005. The cover article was titled "Companies hit the road less traveled: Can spirituality enlighten the bottom line?" Prior to that, William Miller wrote an article titled "How Do We Put Our Spiritual Values to Work," published in New Traditions in Business: Spirit and Leadership in the 21st Century, 1992, San Francisco: Berrett-Koehler.

Gilbert Fairholm wrote Capturing the Heart of Leadership: Spiritual Community in the New American Workplace in 1997 and Jay Conger wrote Spirit at Work: Discovering the Spirituality in Leadership in 1994, both considered germinal works in the field. Spiritual or spirit-centered leadership is a topic of inquiry frequently associated with the workplace spirituality movement. For more, see citations to Benefiel, 2005; Biberman, 2000; Fry, 2005; and Giacalone & Jurkiewicz, 2003 or June, 2006 under the References to this chapter.

The movement began primarily as U.S.-centric, but it has become much more international in recent years. Key supporting organizations include:

- o The International Center for Spirit at Work (ICSW)
- o European Baha'i Business Forum (EBBF)
- o World Business Academy (WBA)
- o Spiritual Business Network (SBN)
- o Foundation for Workplace Spirituality

Pragya M. Kumar and his co-authors have analyzed of the influence of Indian philosophy on the teaching of management. Writing in 2010, they state that about 10% of the professors at top US business schools are of Indian descent, noting the vision of C. K. Prahalad, in which (some) corporations "simultaneously create value and social justice."

The authors cite an article characterizing the "spirituality in the workplace movement" as having become a "mini-industry." With regards to the Indian component of this industry, they state "A large number of Vedant scholars are on a whistle stop tour of the U.S. counseling executives on the central message of the **Bhagavad Gita** to put purpose before self," a mantra that resonates with that of Rotary International: "Service before self."

Key factors that have led to this trend include:

- ✓ Mergers and acquisitions: that destroyed the psychological contract whereby workers had a job for life. This led some people to search for more of a sense of inner security rather than looking for external security from a corporation.
- ✓ Baby Boomers hitting middle age, resulting in a large demographic part of the population asking meaningful questions about life and purpose.
- ✓ The start of a new millennium, which created an opportunity for people all over the world to reflect on where the human race has come from, where it is headed in the future, and what role business plays in the future of the human race.

In the late 1990s, the Academy of Management formed a special group called the Management, Spirituality and Religion Interest Group. This is a professional association of management professors from all over the world who are teaching and doing research on spirituality and religion in the workplace. This action by the Academy of Management was a significant step in legitimizing spirituality in the workplace as a new field of study. One problem I discovered, however, is attempts by both the Academy and its International Center for Spirit at Work (ICSW) to establish what I consider to be an artificial, misleading divide of spirituality between "horizontal" and "vertical" components.

The Selection Committee of the (ICSW) employs a set of criteria in their application form for the International Spirit at Work Awards. These include the following broad interpretations of spirituality overall and of spirituality in the workplace as starting points for consideration, with the recognition that each individual may have his/her own personal definitions:

The innate human attribute: All people bring this as an integral part of themselves to the workplace. Spirituality is a state or experience that can provide individuals with direction or meaning, or provide feelings of understanding, support, inner wholeness or connectedness. Connectedness can be to themselves, other people, nature, the universe, a god or some other supernatural power. [But recall that a NSB would deny the latter.]

The "vertical" component in spirituality: A desire to transcend the individual ego or personal self. The name you put on the vertical component might be God, Spirit, Universe, Higher Power or something else. There are a great many names for this vertical dimension. This dimension is experienced as a conscious sense of profound connection to the Universe/God/Spirit. This might be experienced internally as moments of awe or peak experiences. [Yet, an NSB puts into question nearly the entire "vertical" component.] A strong, sustained "vertical" component: (redefined "horizontal" according to a NSB) reflects in outer behaviors as a person (or group) who is centered and able to tap into deep inner strength and wisdom. I have felt especially blessed by folks with whom I have had what most would call ordinary, "businesslike" interactions, like that with Renee at the County Courthouse.

The feeling of being blessed: is beyond individualistic. Generally quiet time, time in nature, or other reflective activities or practices are needed to access the presumed "vertical" component of our spirituality. Examples of what helps us to foster this component of spirituality include meditation rooms, time for shared reflection, silence before meetings, ecumenical prayer, and support for employees to take time off for spiritual development. Organizational spirituality examples include: meditation time at the beginning of meetings, retreat or spiritual training time set aside for employees, appropriate accommodation of employee prayer practices, and openly asking questions to test if company actions are aligned with higher meaning and purpose. Also note the potential of participation in organized groups such as choral societies, prayer groups or Habitat for Humanity – learning by doing!

The horizontal component in spirituality connotes a desire to be of service to other humans and the planet. In the horizontal dimension, we seek to make a difference through both words and actions. This dimension is manifested externally. A person with a strong, so called "vertical" connection who is also able to demonstrate the "horizontal dimension" has a clear grasp on his/her mission, ethics and values. He and/or she would be much better enabled to pull these pieces together via the integrative capability of a NSB. A strong horizontal component is demonstrated by a service orientation, compassion, and well-aligned vision/mission and values that are carried out by way of productive, effective services and products – a spirituality well-rooted in the real world. Companies with a strong sense of the horizontal will generally demonstrate some or all of the following: caring behaviors among co-workers; a social responsibility orientation; strong service commitments to customers; environmental sensitivity; and a significant volume of community service activities. The prime question to ask here, however is: To what extent are these values incorporated into any company's mission statement? A recent article revealed that most company mission statements are either weak tea, or even if they try to be otherwise (e.g., Facebook and Google), their implementation bows to their bottom line concern "of turning them a profit."[288]

Spirituality in the workplace: therefore, means that employees find nourishment for all dimensions of their spirituality at work. Spirituality in the workplace is about individuals and organizations seeing work as a spiritual path, as an opportunity to grow and to contribute to society in a meaningful way. It is about care, compassion and support of others; about integrity and people being true to themselves and others. It means individuals and organizations attempting to live their values more fully in the work they do.

---

[288] Tarnoff, Ben, and M. Weigel (2019), "Next Gen: The Battle for Silicon Valley's Soul," **THE NEW REPUBLIC** (March).

The various dimensions should be well integrated, so that both motivations and actions are well linked. We should be honoring organizations that are focused on greater meaning and purpose as well as being financially sound, sustainable, and effective. We believe that when done properly, Spirit at Work enhances the overall value of the organization.

The phrase "explicitly nurture spirituality" means that the topic of spirituality is openly discussed, not just assumed or implied. In the past some groups have called their initiatives "team Building" or "leadership," yet what they really wanted was to create a more spiritual work environment. The drive to make a difference in the world for them was a spiritual hunger. Now they are willing to discuss this openly."[289]

Spirituality is evident in a workplace when the following activities are included:

- Bereavement programs.
- Wellness, including spirituality, information displayed and distributed.
- Employee Assistance Programs.
- Programs to integrate work and family.
- Management systems that encourage personal and spiritual transformation.
- Servant leadership – the desire to first serve others in preference to oneself.
- Stewardship – leadership practices that support growth and well-being of others.
- Diversity programs that create inclusive cultures.
- Integration of core values and core business decisions and practices.
- Leadership practices that support the growth and development of all employees [see the chapter on "Servant Leadership" for more.] Our complicity in world making is a source of awesome and sometimes painful responsibility as well as a source of profound hope for change.

---

[289] From a 2008 International Spirit at Work Award Application, p. 2.

It is the ground of our common call to leadership – the truth that makes leaders of us all.

Above all, a leader is someone with the power to project either shadow or light onto some part of the world and onto the lives of the people who dwell there. A leader shapes the ethos in which others must live, an ethos as light filled as a heaven or as shadowy as a hell. A good leader is intensely aware of the interplay of inner shadow and light, lest the act of leadership do more harm than good.[290] Good examples include:

- ➢ **Graham Wilson (minister):** A workplace chaplain
- ➢ **Dominic Steele:** His ministry includes workplace Bible groups
- ➢ **Swami Sukhabodhananda:** Nicknamed "the Corporate Guru"
- ➢ **John Sentamu:** An advocate for faith in the workplace

Such leadership also now has greater leverage enabled by three tools:

- ✓ The Benefit corporation: A relatively new type of corporation, "corporate "B" form," whereby corporations are enabled to do good as well as profit]
- ✓ Workplace Religious Freedom Act: 2005 US bill requiring employers to make reasonable accommodation for an employees' religious practice or observance
- ✓ A Practical Reference to Religious Diversity for Operational Police and Emergency Services

Concluding Remarks

The theme of this chapter is symptomatic of the challenge we face at every level – that of nurturing spirituality in the settings of an increasingly secular society. It is gratifying to see how open many business leaders are to allowing time for employees to express their spirituality during workdays. Even at the

---

[290] Palmer, op. cit., p. 78.

level of large corporations, however, the issue extends more deeply into the design of work itself.

How can work elicit the higher, more spiritual faculties so often left latent or repressed in every human being? Labor laws and regulations need to be liberalized. Work needs to be redesigned. The legal thresholds that constrain creativity and innovation during work should be removed. Spirituality is no respecter of firm size. Human spirituality is eternal. The fight to enable it, however, is time-bound by constraints of contexts and by the virtue or lack of such in processes of change.

Scott McLennan's interview is strongly supportive of a NSB. It has been gratifying to see his emphasis on spirit and spirituality, as well as many practical prescriptions as to how they can be brought into work and business life. The only qualifier is his unqualified stress on a strong "vertical" component that a NSB either denies or would not necessarily require. It appears to derive from McLennan's position as an ordained minister of a church that worships an external god-on-high.

References

- Benefiel, M. (2005). Soul at work: Spiritual leadership in organizations. New York: Seabury Books. ISBN 1596270136
- Biberman, J. (Ed.).(2000). Work and spirit: A reader of new spiritual paradigms for organizations. Scranton, PA: University of Scranton Press. ISBN 0940866897
- Bowman, T.J. (2004). Spirituality at Work: An Exploratory Sociological Investigation of the Ford Motor Company. London School of Economics and Political Science Fairholm, G.W. (1997). Capturing the heart of leadership: Spirituality and community in the new American workplace. Westport, CT: Praeger. ISBN 0275957438
- Fry, L.W. (2005). Toward a paradigm of spiritual leadership. The Leadership Quarterly, 16(5), 619-722.
- Giacalone, R.A., & Jurkiewicz, C.L. (2003). Handbook of workplace spirituality and organizational performance. New York: M.E. Sharpe. ISBN 0765608448

- Jue, A.L. (2006). Practicing spirit-centered leadership: Lessons from a corporate layoff. In Gerus, C. (Ed.). Leadership Moments: Turning points that changed lives and organizations. Victoria, BC: Trafford. ISBN 1412099641
- Miller, D.W. (2006). God at work: The history and promise of the faith at work movement. New York: Oxford University Press. ISBN 0195314808
- Palmer, Parker J. (2000) Let Your Life Speak: Listening for the Voice of Vocation. San Francisco: Jossey-Bass. Ch 5 "Leading from Within." ISBN 978-0-7879-4735-4.
- Russell, Mark L., ed. (2010). Our Souls at Work: How Great Leaders Live Their Faith in the Global Marketplace. Boise: Russell Media. ISBN 9780578039893
- Marques, Joan, Dhiman, Satinder, and King, Richard, ed. (2009) The Workplace and Spirituality: New Perspectives on Research and Practice SkyLight Paths, Woodstock, VT.
- N.T., Sree Raj. (2011). Spirituality in Business and Other Synonyms: A Fresh Look at Different Perspectives for its Application, 'Purushartha' A Journal of Management Ethics and Spirituality Vol.IV, No.II, pp 71–85
- Mitroff, I.I, and Denton, E.A. (1999) A Spiritual Audit of Corporate America, A Hard Look at Spirituality, Religion, and Values. San Francisco: Jossey-Bass.

External links

- Spirituality in the Workplace - The Living Organization
- Catholic Servant Leadership
- Foundation for Workplace Spirituality
- Global Dharma Center
- International Center for Spirit at Work
- The High Calling of Our Daily Work
- Theology of Work Project
- Seven Principles of Spirituality in the Workplace
- Faith and Work Initiative
- www.theologyofwork.org

Chapter 24

On the Power of Life, Love, Faith, Hope and Spirituality

This chapter might as well been titled more tersely: "NSB & Power." For all existing major systems of belief have managed to construct or become integral parts of hierarchical systems of power over others. A notable, admirable exception is the "Society of Friends," or Quakers. As indicated in the previous chapter, it is the author's heartfelt hope that the NSB might avoid the fate of previously initiated major systems. Life, Faith and Hope have been included in the title, therefore, because they not only offer the possibility of such avoidance, they also provide leaven for the raising of real power of real people in real places, contexts or settings.

Casually placing the adjective "real" before "power" means that we cannot avoid coming to grips with what the word really means. This varies with level or numbers. For an individual, it is the ability to do something, to act on one's own initiative. Group-wise, it is the capacity to work together and, possibly, to influence others in order to change the course of events. With respect to political authorities or governmental organizations, it is the monopolization of force to compel people to do what is authorized under law.[291] The latter applies primarily at all levels from local to national, but extends to international matters only insofar as countries have agreed to have issues adjudicated by the U.N. or the International Court of Justice.[292] From the standpoint of spirituality, however, the key to power is a system of belief.

So, the key question to face is how love, faith, hope and spirituality affect or effect people's beliefs, the application of power oneself, or acceptance of the application of power by others. This, in turn, immediately brings subsidiary or related questions to mind. For example, with respect to "faith: Is there a trade-off between faith in an external god and faith in people? A Christian may pray to God for and/or to give thanks for, His love, without praying to give and receive the love of others. Unfortunately, this example may be all too familiar. Too often, the faithful of a "God in Heaven" are praying for godly intervention to effect solutions to problems that can only be solved by the prayerful on behalf of themselves and/or others.

How long will it take for people to realize that, even if there is a God, it cannot be a personal god? That it can only be a god of the universe in no way willing or able to comprehend, let alone respond to or resolve, personal petitions, or even persons' collectively, ranging from individuals to worldwide mankind? Better to pray for those in our lives, leaders or human institutions for ways to resolve disputes so that we can live in peace.

While participating in prayer circles, I am constantly surprised how, invariably, people ask for prayers to God to intervene on behalf of themselves, friends or relatives suffering from some ailment or another,

---

[291] These observations are consistent with the definition of "power" provided by the **CONCISE OXFORD ENGLISH DICTIONARY** [11th Edition, Revised, 2008].

[292] The U.S. is not a signatory to the Court even though the most crucial issues facing the human race need to be decided at the international level. Shame on US!

instead of praying for one another to work together to deal with any sort of issue, personal or otherwise[293]. Power, and the responsibility of its exercise, are thus devolved only upon an unknown other, above and external to us rather than placed where it belongs and must be brought to reside – in and among ourselves.

We need to realize and exercise such power. Instead, "We the People" have too often yearned for hero-leaders in whom we invest the powers that are truly ours. This tendency is seen at all levels and in many ways in our history. The illusion of a personal, external "God" is replicated up and down the line by Fuehrers, Presidents, Governors, Mayors, heads of committees, teachers and countless others. In all such cases and the contexts they command, our impulse should be diminish the vertical and go horizontal. This means reaching out to all and sundry to get together to seek solutions to common problems, including those of poverty or "the weak and the weary." As Pink Floyd has been known to sing:

> "Just a world that we all must share. It's not enough just to stand and stare. Is it only a dream that there'll be, no more turning away?"[294]

Do not let the foregoing observations in any way diminish the power of faith. Oft-times, this is all we've got. From where does this power come? Our reading of Frankl's experience in Nazi concentration camps indicates that god (with or without a capital "g") had little to do with survival. Rather it had to do with the obdurate, tenacious faith in whatever powers of life could be

---

[293] For example, after personal testimony of serious difficulty during the concluding prayer circle of Seafarer's Chapel, only one offer of help emerged. I know of no other example but I am sure the reader can recall others.

[294] Song title: "On the Turning Away;" written by Dave Gilmour (words) and Anthony Moore (music) and featured in the1987 Pink Floyd album: "A Momentary Lapse of Reason." Learn to sing it!

summoned in order to survive.[295] This, in turn, draws from a love of the life with which we have all been blessed.

Even those who would most vehemently fight for claims of the non-existence of God do not deny the power of faith. It would be paltry of any of us to deny this power simply because of disagreements over the "existence of god" question. And yet, neither can expostulations over others' "evidence" of the power of faith be accepted as evidence of the existence of God. Faith is rooted in human life via the emergent qualities of the human brain and the transcendent powers of human consciousness and human love.

Faith and hope are displaced and degraded by their attachment to an external god. So, too, is spirituality. The examples are legion. Most notable are those that feature media or public officials. A broadcaster on Fox News recently stated that "The Pope has a line to the Big Guy. I don't."[296] This amounts to a dumb and destructive denial of responsibility for faith, hope and spirituality at both individual and community levels.

Along with spirituality, love is a primary, emergent feature of human consciousness, It also provides both inspiration and core of responsibility. And yet, even after thousands of years of experience with it and musings over it, love is still deemed to be a mystery, Nevertheless, it seems to this author that the first half of the theme song from the movie **THE ROSE** is still an inspiration:

"Some say love, it is a river than drowns the tender reed.

---

[295] Also see Shaer, Matthew (2017), "The Holocaust's Great Escape," **SMITHSONIAN** (March), testimony of Ponar, where: "...at least 80,000 people (were) shot...90% of those were Jews...(and yet) the escape tunnel... was a tale of hope...it proved how resilient humans can be."(pp.45 & 50) [even in the face of bestiality]

[296] TV broadcast of "Fox and Friends" on December 16, 2017.

Some say love it is a razor that leaves the heart to bleed.
Some say love it is a hunger, an ever-aching need.
I say love it is a flower and you the only seed." [emphasis mine]

The connections of love to spirituality and religion are well documented, even intimately. Christian marriage services, for example, are memorable for recognizing the bonds of marital love as a:

"sacred union...to have and to hold...from this day forward...for better or worse, in sickness and in health, for richer or poorer, to love and to cherish, forsaking all others..."

Lovers everywhere attest, not only to the orgasmic but also to the immanent, transcendent qualities of love-making, culminating in the euphoric, enrapturing transcendence of their coming together into what is truly a sacred union.[297] It helps to recognize that such rapture is a human creation, not the gift of a great God-in-heaven. For when, inevitably, problems arise in relationships even among the most loving couples, it hardly helps to pray to an external God-on-high if either or both partners...

- ❖ Do not fully know him- or her-self, and thus have not learned how to fully love the other;
- ❖ Have gotten so used to the patterns of day-to-day life that he or she fails to hear or see signals of problems arising in their life together.
- ❖ Fail to appreciate, let alone understand, the deep undercurrents and complexities, not only of each other's personalities, but also of their souls.[298]

---

[297] That such realizations are not age-dependent is attested by the author's deeply loving relationship with his partner, Helen, which began through mutual discovery at a jazz concert at, respectively, ages 75 and 77.

[298] For more, see Moore, Thomas (1994), **SOULMATES: Honoring the Mysteries of Love and Relationship.** New York: Harper Collins. By contrast, the book by Arielle Ford on the subject, entitled **TURN YOUR**

In other words, as Moore reports:

> "I have learned from talking to many couples whose marriages have survived at least 50 years – when I ask them "How?" – they invariably say some variation on: "It takes work, and we found ways to make it work."[299]

Thus, truly long-term, meaningful love relationships require devotion and hard-work, with couples deep-diving into each other's psyches and souls. They are the work of a lifetime. This essential truth is made especially clear if one recognizes the exceedingly small odds of finding one's "one true love." As Randall Munroe writes in the science book **WHAT IF:**

> "Given that you have 500 million potential soul mates, you would find true love only in one lifetime out of 10,000...Tolkien blamed our obsession with soul mates on the Romantic chivalric tradition: "Its weakness is...that it began as an artificial courtly game (that takes) the young man's eye off women as they are... companions in shipwreck, not guiding stars. True soul mates are made, not born."[300]

The "hard work" starts at day one and only ends "when death do us part." Simply going to church each week and/or praying to God for aid and grace will not suffice. For the god we seek lies within, not without. "Interiority", as Moore terms it, is the starting point of self-knowledge, without which love of others is superficial and so not likely to bear up under challenge of circumstance or difference. The god within is the realization of the preciousness, depth and complexity of our own human life, buttressed by love

---

MATE INTO A SOULMATE: A Practical Guide to happily ever after (Harper Elixer, 2015) is saccharine and superficial.

[299] Moore, op. cit., p.??

[300] Calhoun, Ada (2017), "Searching for a soul mate is futile: The ideal partner is one you create." **TIME** (5/29).

of life and hope that life's potential can be realized. It is hard to see that this love and potential can be accomplished by sole reliance upon one's own wits or those of more than a few; that is, without some support from a NSB and additional others.

It is also hard to imagine such realization without hope. The old saw says: "Hope springs eternal," but from where does it spring? Again, it is an emergent quality of the human mind, deeply rooted in the life-force of heart and soul, reinforced by love, faith and spirituality. And so we can now can draw a diagram to illustrate the positively reinforcing virtuous cycles linking all three, supported by a NSB. See Fig. 15, below.

Fig. 15

Before closing this chapter, let us take a few minutes to review what the linked pairs shown above represent. First, recall that they are all long-term in nature. No "quickies" here! Each following comment bears on the creation of a NSB.

LINKS:

- FAITH to LOVE: Faith(fullness) is essential to the maturation and endurance of love. A NSB embraces love.
- LOVE to FAITH: Without the expectation of a full love, faith(fullness) may wither. A NSB in suffused with faith.

- FAITH to HOPE: Faith may not long be sustained without hope, individual or collectively. As for the latter, another factor is trust. Faith may be deeply shared, group-wise, but an element of trust must be present among individuals working together towards shared goals. Hope in trust and trust in hope are essential.
- HOPE to FAITH: Faith embraces hope in most systems of belief, including a NSB. Hope in better futures supports faith in the efforts of shared ventures.
- LOVE to SPIRITUALITY: Love is contagious. A keyword here as earlier is "suffused." The practice of love raises the spirits of one and all, and the latter can be felt and expressed as a form of spirituality.
- SPIRITUALITY to LOVE: Similar to hope in faith and faith in hope, spirituality necessarily incorporates love. Shared spirituality can also induce love.
- SPIRITUALITY to HOPE: Similar to hope in faith. Since spirituality is so suffused with faith, it also necessarily incorporates hope. Shared spirituality can also induce a shared hope.
- HOPE to SPIRITUALITY: Hope can exist without spirituality per se; nevertheless, hope is an essential element of spirituality via faith. As the love of my life, Helen (a.k.a. Elena) remarked: "You don't have hope without faith in something" (including oneself).

As stated in the Christian Bible, in Paul's 1st letter to the Corinthians: "And now faith, hope and love abide, these three, and the greatest of these is love..."[301] On the latter, note that: "It matters less, whatever else you do, as long as you walk in love."[302]This is a distillation of the meaning of Christianity. Since love and spirituality are fundamental to any system of belief and all the elements noted earlier overlap, they should also be fundamental elements of any NSB.

---

[301] 1 Corinthians 13:13-13:13.

[302] Oral remark to the author from Helen Cleaveland (June 18, 2017).

It is also worth noting that love between a man and a woman can and should be viewed as an important beginning and foundation to the potential realization of a more societal and worldwide virtue and sense of value: The love of differences. Few couples are perfectly matched.

Chapter 25

NSB and Syntheism

Introduction

The chapter title elements represent the two newest attempts to formulate a new system of belief; thus, it is high time to present, contrast and compare them. First, let us note and contrast the context and origins of each. An essential similarity is that each is a response to a felt society-wide situation of growing political and governmental dysfunctionality and social alienation threatening breakdowns at almost every level. An important common denominator is the exponential growth of Internet utilization and connectivity.

Irony in such a situation is unavoidable. As Charles Handy recognized many years ago, we live in a society of paradox -- so many opposing ideas can be simultaneously true and in conflict. So, the world is rife with pressures and opportunities to design new systems, even extending to revising systems of belief that now prove inadequate to the challenges of our time. Such is Syntheism, three years old, now followed by the New System of Belief [NSB] that is the focus of this book.[303] We start by highlighting the features of each.

---

[303]   Bard, Alexander, and Jan Soderqvist (2014), **SYNTHEISM: Creating God in the Internet Age.** Stockholm: Stockholm Text.

NSB

✓ Life is sacred; Life is the core of human ontology (of its being and becoming), and so God is Life and Life is our God.
✓ Institutionalized religion has done little to nurture spirituality.
✓ Spirituality is a quality of the consciousness of the human brain emerging from a complex adaptive system [CAS].
✓ Human history reveals us to be a species of life with an inherent need to create spiritual beliefs, gods, religious institutions and all the rituals thereof. "At no point in history has Man been able to or chosen to live without gods. Man can never be liberated from religion unless he ceases to be human."[304]
✓ While "spirit" thrives in most sectors of activity in the U.S., and "feelings of spirituality are on the rise," "Americans have become less religious..."[305]
✓ Several higher levels of consciousness lead one to God, but "God" arises within us, not from without.
✓ Every cusp in one's life provides an opportunity to stop, pause and reflect in ways that may invoke our spirituality; major divides are most challenging.
✓ Though one can imagine a God of the Universe of Life, it is and can never be a personal god. This God, though suggested by at least six fine-tuned parameters necessary to the sustenance of life, "plays dice." See Chapter 5 for more.
✓ Rituals, rites and holy days are important times for the renewal and invocation of spirituality in human life. Physical, strategically located facilities for meditation, singing, reading, study, teaching or other

---

[304] Bard and Söderqvist, op. cit., pp.137, 138

[305] Masci, David, and M. Lipka (2016), "Americans may be getting less religious, but feelings of spirituality are on the rise," Pew Research Center [PewResearch.org, January 21], and Yaden, David Bryce (2016), "The Future of Spirituality," **HUFFPOST: THE BLOG** (May 7).

related learning activities are also needed. Study or reflections of a NSB would be necessary but not sufficient.

✓ There must be leadership and activism to fight for renewal of the sacred and to battle against the desacrilization of life and society.
✓ The need for a NSB arises, most fundamentally, from revolutionary changes in human history and life.
✓ A NSB would support the aspirations of "We the People" towards increased democratization of life, society & government, and the building of an increasingly broad, people-based participatory culture.

SYNTHEISM

Syntheism purports to be a radically new religion for the Internet age. It does away with God and Heaven as irrelevant concepts external to human life. Its new god is the Internet or possibly the Universe-as-Network. Like most established religions, however, it embraces churches, rituals, religious holidays and monasteries. It points to "The One" as a one and only god, yet also embodies a set of divinities called Atheos, Pantheos, Entheos and Syntheos and Utopia.

> "The One" is defined as the Syntheist Utopia. Thus, the Syntheistic religion appears to be pantheistic rather than unitary – worshiping many gods rather than just one. The synthetistic divinities are "immanent, finite and mortal, rather than transcendent, eternal and immortal"-- gods that reveal themselves "only to those that seek gods."

Syntheism is a purely intellectual construct. As such, it is phrased in words foreign to ordinary folks, including new words invented by its authors. There are so many of these that the authors needed to include a Glossary of definitions of 120 terms in the back of their book. For example, note the following:

1) **Ontology:** The nature of being."
2) **Immanence:** Wherein a divine presence is manifest in the material world; i.e. the spiritual world permeates the mundane.

3) **Mobilism:** Part of the process-philosophy, constructed "reality" at one end of a dialectic: between eternalism and mobilism, a constantly mobile chaos in all directions and also within itself.
4) **Mimetics:** The sociology of signs and other expressive gestures without words, including body language.
5) **Fictive:** The smallest component in the authors' extensive mimetics, and the unit to which every little aspect of a meme is attributable.
6) **Consumptariat:** The Internet age's pathetic underclass – those who are left behind or outside the digital world, isolated in their minimal social activities and reduced to the lowest common denominator. Also embracing the vulgar, passive consumption of mass-produced goods and services. In my view, this attitude is quite snobbish and elitist and an attempt to rationalize a class society, Eternalist: One who adopts a philosophical approach to the ontological nature of time whereby all points of time are equally real, as opposed to the...
7) **Presentist:** Idea that only the present is real, or the block universe theory in which present and past are real but the future is not.

Syntheism is grounded on a large number (15) of underlying assumptions. These are:

i. There are no eternal, external laws originating in an eternal, external world to which we have no access; i.e., God-in-heaven does not exist independently of Man. He is a creation of Man. Comment: The NSB agrees.

ii. The rise of the Internet is the most recent of four revolutions. What is revolutionary is the Internet's generation of overloads of information and multiplicities of connectivity. The overload makes the 'Net "the only credible metaphysical system for the intellectual human being of the 3rd Millennium" The holy Internet is a new basis for religion. Comment: The NSB strongly disagrees.

iii. A new religion should be based on science. More specifically, Syntheism is at least consistent with the theory of loop quantum gravity, which regards space as an elastic phenomenon subject to network dynamics. Multidimensional space is a maximally entangled pure geometry where nodes lack substance. Also: It is based on a new metaphysics grounded on quantum physics and a world made up of entanglements, fundamentally plural phenomena rather than discrete objects. The overwhelming majority of all connections are indirect. Comment: NSB says, in part, "Yes, but only in part. Our earlier discussion seriously questioned reliance upon quantum physics. Read on.

iv. An innermost core in each human being that regards everything that exists as an endless multitude of expression of and for The ONE [similar to Buddhism]. Comment: The NSB sees this as highly speculative, questionable and scientifically unsupportable.

v. The One is equivalent to a Syntheist utopia, always in the future. Comment: Such a "utopia" is un-imaginable, unconstructable, undesirable and doomed to failure in light of past experience with utopian experiments and the NSB. This assumption also appears to contradict "presentist."

vi. The future is its "point of departure." Comment: Nonsense as per the above.

vii. "At no point in history has Man been able to or has chosen to live without gods..." Comment: Indeed; one of only four points of agreement.

viii. The Holy Spirit is all that is left from the death of Christianity. Comment: Not true in light of the largely Christian roots of the NSB.

ix. Pauline Christian theology and the law manifest the death drive. Comment: "Manifest but not resting on Life as does the NSB.

x. Existence is an "open entirety." Comment: Agreed

xi. Abandon individual identity (and individualism): Shift focus to the Universe. Time =Change. Change and time are fundamental to existence, and the Arrow of Time points forward to infinity. Comment: Agreeable only with respect to the "Arrow…;" otherwise mistaken or disputable, especially as to "identity" and "Change." The equivalence of Time and Life is fundamental to the NSB.

xii. Truth is an Act. Comment: Wrong; reverse the two according to the NSB, which then enables us to beg the question of any act.

xiii. The Cosmos is a dynamic, indeterministic, multiverse network. Comment: Agreed; as also one of the foundational assumptions of the NSB.

xiv. Everything that exists is holy. Comment: No so; omits recognition of the "dark side."

xv. A religion grounded upon trans-rationalism: A concept of existence as an open entirety -- not rationalism, which is a closed logical construct. Comment: Quite agreeable.

The major features of Syntheism consistent with these assumptions can be highlighted as follows.

> A passion for activism which is a foundation for Syntheist ethics.
> A sanctuary and protection vs. capitalist and consumptive stress.
> A religion that the Internet created; the 'Net is its God.
> Synonymous with theological anarchism and atheism.
> A religion of immanence and multiple finitudes...
> Provides for a syntheistic monastery as the central agent for truth.
> A radicalized atheistic ideology designed to maintain and maximize the dynamics of existence.
> What else should we know about Syntheism? [Author's warning:
> Take a deep breath here; there are 48 points to follow!] Syntheism:
> Traces back to Zoroaster. Origin in Iran ~ 1700 B.C.
> Opens the way for a genuinely sensual and thereby also spiritual understanding of immanence.
> Is a logical consummation of Christianity.
> Provides the basis for a deep ethics constructed on the basis of intentions rather than on consequences.
> Emerges from the right lobe of the brain and is holistically oriented, producing a "mobilist,," emotionally driven and culturally explorative epoch.
> Lacks all forms of nostalgia or theory of a lost paradise.
> Projects a Utopia where the law is no longer recognized and allowed to exercise its power.
> Is a living religion that moves away from lonely alienation and towards the resumption of community [Question: Similar to Taoism?].
> Is like art, implicit rather than explicit, open to contingencies and emergencies.
> Believes that divinities are immanent, finite and mortal rather than transcendent, eternal & immortal. [Question: Human values, too?]

- Leads to a conclusion that if God exists, then God must be the Universe, but God is immanent rather than transcendent.
- Posits that transcendence is entirely subjective, an experience that takes place in a completely immanent world.
- Says that Utopia in itself is divine. The Internet-as-God designates the collective utopia.
- Is a divinity of theological anarchism – suffused with a Holy Spirit that is independent of the other two parts of the Christian Trinity and indifferent to death on the horizon as a creator of meaning.
- Is the basis for a "New Age" or Renaissance for the critically thinking man.
- A belief in the impossible being possible. The Syntheist "agent" represents pure joy – a pure form of activism.
- Reveals a divine dissolution of the self in the collective, of the self in the cosmos.
- Is a quest for the genuine religious experience – for a life intensity so strong that it bridges the gap from the present moment to eternity – the infinite now.
- Enables us to enjoy the philosophical creation and redesign of models of fleeting reality in a never-ending flow.
- Is a new religion providing the contraction of information necessary to existence in a world of information overload.
- Assumes there are no discrete objects in the Universe; what really exists is relations without their own inner substance.
- Aims to make life and its intensification the divine foundation.
- Posits activist ethics of survival as the propelling principle, not immortality.
- Is a process religion – a collective name for immanent spiritual experience.
- Encourages a credible spirituality that can only arise within the confines of an imminent process religion.
- Includes "Will to Power", not as a cosmic drive, but as a necessary ethical principle.
- Abandons the individual identity and shifts focus to the Universe. Shifts from the human to a universal center.

- Defines the key role of a syntheist agent – working to create a radically different utopian future.
- Posits "agential" realism as a new kind of objectivity made possible by agential separability, where "agential" means an agent of the new Syntheist Church.
- Places transcendence in becoming, not being.
- Realizes that internalisation of a mobilist chaos is in itself the original sacrilisation of existence. Syntheism contributes spiritual experience through its production of infinity in the present that defeats drawn out and lifelong suffering...
- Its fascination is not with life itself but with the enormous and expanding complexity of our world(s) [what Syntheism is based on and what gives its agents and phenomena their value]. Life is really not much to speak of...mostly lots of death! based on self-sacrifice.
- Means that the role of victim fades away [No need for sacrifice!]. Worship of the NW as event.
- Offers a saving grace in providing a correct overall picture of man's world – life as context for an engaged presence.
- Is grounded on relationality, a state where no objects exist, where differences on top of differences create relations between the differences without fixed objects ever arising. Syntheism embraces what Bohr calls a field and Whitehead a process – a world of relationalisms where the object is dissolved.
- Is based on a new ontology -- where the Universe and not the human being is primary...The inhuman God lives...Universe as a glittering network: God is a network!
- Comes from the world of quantum physics, governed by complementarity, entanglement, chance and non-locality.
- Abandons the anthropomorphic fixation on a special status for human life in the world. Replace vitalism of life with one based on physics' intensity – a world of constantly vibrating, interactive bodies (human & non-) rather than isolated things.
- Inspired by Zoroastrianism's Haurvatat: A state combining sacred perfection with simultaneous dynamism, and so unable to fixate – synonym for Syntheism's infinite now. Places holiness in the mutable rather than immutable. Universe is contingent.

- Believes that there are no things whatsoever to relate between. Only human relationships are primary. Syntheistic phenomena are not stable objects at all. There are lots of local subsystems but no isolated systems anywhere in Universe. Sees that theories of everything are impossible. The only ethical imperative remaining: Go with the flow!
- Conceives the Universe as a constantly mutable entity that evades us – The ONE as GOD. The equivalent-in-being is the gigantic, expanding and incalculable flow of words and signs that confront us.

For the sake of brevity and simplicity [two qualities that SYNTHEISM lacks even in summary], let us abbreviate the systems we are covering as "S" (for Syntheism) and "N" (for New System of Belief). First, a number of basic and remarkable similarities between the two need to be noted against the backdrop of a few, more powerful differences that stand out in sharp relief. S and N are alike in emphasizing the need for a belief system that:

- ✓ Claims that life is sacred [N] or "infinitely valuable" [S] and helps to sustain life;
- ✓ Is grounded in, or at least consistent with, science; and so denies the existence of supernatural forces
- ✓ Assumes a Universe that is an open system "infinite in all directions," an engine of constant, indeterministic change, and a progenitor of life;
- ✓ Rests on qualities of human consciousness, including the most transcendent, emergent from the human mind;
- ✓ Assumes, as revealed throughout human history and pre-history, that mankind has a deeply rooted proclivity to invent gods that represent the deepest yearnings of our species;
- ✓ Consistent with scientific methods and findings, there is no external, god-in-heaven governing our and any other worlds. Even though the possibility of such is acknowledged, it would be an infinitely distant, wholly impersonal god exhibiting unpredictable behavior – one to whom we could not pray, nor one to whom we could look for sanctuary, deliverance, grace or mercy of any kind whatsoever – the god of an Einstein who refused to believe that "God plays dice."

S and N, however, <u>differ crucially</u> on points essential to the imagination and construction of a system of belief truly capable of sustaining human life. These points focus on:

- Implications of the importance attributed to life in general and human life in particular:

S – "Life is really not much to speak of; it is mostly lots of death... based on self-sacrifice (& so we should) view life as large-scale, duplicate non-life...in a line of pure complexities."

N – Life is truly sacred, as in the prayer: "As it was then, as it is now, as it shall ever be, world without end. Amen".

The major implications of these contrasts will be discussed further on.

- o **The importance of individualism and individual responsibility:** S not only disparages the latter; S foresees "the divine dissolution of the self in the collective"; while N would foster them.
- o **The building and nurture of the human "community":** Though S is seen by its authors as a: "Living religion that moves away from alienation and towards the resumption of community;" the "dissolution...in the collective" (cited above) suggests that an S-community would be more of a utopian tribe than an American community as under N.
- o **The politics and governance of human communities:** S is a highly elitist vision. N encourages democratic politics and self-governing communities. These concerns are discussed at length further on.
- o **The nature of truth and consequences:** S posits "Truth as act" relying on intentions with no regard given to consequences; moreover, S' view is similar to that of the Catholic Church in stating: "The...monastery is the central agent of truth." N disagrees on both counts. Apparently, the authors of S have not heard or disbelieve the old saw: "The road to hell is paved with good intentions." Truth resides in consequences.
- o **Ethical implications of the two belief systems:** S – It is not apparent that a "passion for activism (is the) foundation for S-ethics" unless S-

believers buy into their elite agents' vision of utopia. Nor is it apparent that a "deep ethics" has been or can be "constructed on the basis of intentions rather than on... consequences." S provides an "ethics of survival" that raises "Will to Power" to "a necessary ethical principle." N-ethics are strongly contrasting --fundamentally those as set forth by Christ in his Sermon on the Mount, especially the Beatitudes.

- o **The scope of holiness, divinity and the nature of God:** S regards things as holy and the Internet as God; N does not.
- o **Important differences in the interpretations of key terms** such as "immanence," "transcendent" and "holy." These were touched upon earlier and will be further discussed in due course.

Conclusion

Except for their reinterpretation of human history, the authors of S deny its value to and influence on human behavior, preferring to focus on "the infinite now", at best conflating history to the present moment.[306] The authors also deny the importance of individual behavior in decision-making by abandoning the individual ID and shifting focus to a collective ID all the way up to the Universe. How do they justify such conflating and refocusing? – By viewing the "revolutionary" historical moment as providing opportunities for a new elite to take charge by offering a "sanctuary and protection against capitalist and consumptive stress."

The rest of us would be relegated to a 2nd to 4th place "consumptariat --the pathetic underclass" – tied up in our TVs and devoted to consumption of the infinitely variable consumables advertised on TV. The new elite, presumably and presumptuously to be led by S' authors as the key S-agents, would work to keep the consumptariat focused on a Utopian future [a Marxian future resting on an "opiate of the masses" put forth by S-Agents].

---

[306] It is either puzzling or contrarian, therefore, to also read: "Memory generates ethical substance."

S would also demand an ethics that is constructed on the basis of good intentions oblivious to consequences, an ethics whose byline is "Go with the flow!" For all its elaborate philosophizing, S is an arcane, purely intellectual, rather inhumane construct.

S can also be seen as providing a convoluted basis for promoting a revolution against the capitalist organization of economy and society. This has some merit as an end to be sought over an indeterminate long-term, but only if the means to help achieve the goal are democratic. A philosophy that, in effect, is based on an assumption that "the end justifies the means" has effectively debased itself as a credo for human action. The assumption is all too familiar and too much at work in a corrupted politics dominated by "them" to the extent that "us" (we'uns) cast off or betake themselves AWOL from responsibility.

Thus, we conclude that our NSB if much more preferable than Syntheism as a new system of belief.

Chapter 26

Spirituality, Mind and Soul

+

Spiritual Discipline and Practices

Introduction / Recapitulation

Where does spirituality reside in such a way that it is continually accessible to us at any time and over the full range of human experience, from the mundane (and presumably superficial) to the critical (life or death moments)? Remember, human life is a trilogy. Each of us has a body, mind and soul. Spirituality belongs to the latter, so it could be equated to soulfulness. And yet, the latter may be aimless without mindfulness. So, spirituality springs from the higher consciousness of mind. There lies the soul. Since all of any life that has a chance to endure the ravages of time is the highest and best of that to which we have been devoted, soulfully, we have here discovered the only sign of life in the hereafter with a real chance to live on. It is that which represents our soul.

Our soulfulness, however, cannot exist in the realm of a "heaven" other than that which we help to create here on earth. The memory of what we best represent is only retained over time by our family or other historians, depending on the scope of good works. John Steinbeck's character Ethan wonders: "Maybe it is Ellen (his daughter) who will carry and pass on whatever is immortal in me."[307] So do I wonder, too. Recall the *OXFORD ENGLISH DICTIONARY* definition of "soul" as "The spiritual or immaterial part of a person, regarded as immortal." Our recasting soul at the center of mortal human life is nonetheless consistent with this definition.

Realizing that the placement of the soul is in the mind [which a surge of research on the brain is in the process of discovering[308]] also roots spirituality in the body as well – things incarnate, even unto the glorification of the carnal and all things ordinary. In other words, there is an unbroken connection, via a variety of neural links, among all aspects of human life from the ordinary to the extraordinary. What is the nature of this connection? It is a self-similar pattern visible in nature at all levels and scales from low-to-high – the pattern that Benoit Mandelbrot called "fractal."[309] This essential similarity offers the possibility that soulfulness can be associated with any old thing. As it has, in countless households!

---

[307] Steinbeck, op.cit., p.192.

[308] For useful references, see Graves, Mark (2016), **MIND, BRAIN and the ELUSIVE GOAL: Human Systems of Cognitive Science and Religion.** New York: Routledge, Ashgate Science and Religion Series, or Moreira-Almeida, Alex, & F. Santana-Santos (eds., 2012), **EXPLORING FRONTIERS of the MIND-BRAIN RELATIONSHIP**, especially Chapter 6: "Neurological Correlates of Meditation & Mindfulness. Also see Chapter 21 here and Chapter 5 in Sole', Richard & B. Goodwin (2000), **SIGNS of LIFE.** New York: Basic Books.

[309] See Mandlebrot, Benoit (1986), **THE FRACTAL STRUCTURE OF NATURE.**

Spirituality, Things and Moments: A Fractal Paradigm

There's no limit to those material things to which we attach special meanings of a spiritual nature.[310] Likewise, there's no limit to the applicability of fractals, in either direction, from the very small as seen in powerful microscopes, to the extremely large, as glimpsed through the most powerful telescopes scanning the universe. Recall Richard Muller's report that the director of one of his research projects "devised an innovative way to transmit data over slow international networks...using the math of fractals to facilitate data compression."[311]

Like other segments of human life, spirituality has been allocated its quantum of space and time, mostly on Sunday according to locations and times that have been set, mostly by others, that have become accepted and habitual. A key point arising from our earlier discussions, however, is that, for the meaning of spirituality to be realized and assimilated, people need to be conscious of its continuity so that it can leaven and elevate life at any time. In other words, spirituality itself needs, in a way, to become a good habit, too, but one in which the "way" brooks no barriers of time, space or occasion. Rather than a barrier, any occasion becomes an opportunity for the insightful and transformative power of one's spirituality to be brought to bear.

A fractal paradigm can help to enable adults to fulfill the great potential of their spirituality. It's basis lies in any individual's ability to heighten his or her consciousness at the point of any cusp – any break in a routine pattern.[312] The

---

[310] For more, see: Cochran, Tracy (2014), "Living as Spiritual Practice," **PARABOLA** (July 27).

[311] Muller, Richard, op. cit., p. 154.

[312] Recall that a fractal pattern is a set of patterns that are self-similar from top to bottom, from the macro-scale to the tiny. A good example is the branching structure of trees from roots to branches and leaves. My personal version of a fractal paradigm is represented by a formula: $I/X \sim SP * 3\{AIM\}$; where I/X represent the edge of a cusp. I is start; X is end. SP= strategic

first reaction should be one of heightened awareness, mindfulness, humility, empathy and care -- not reactionary. Again: Stop. Pause. Think or meditate. Then ask: What do I need to obtain or do? What have I forgotten? If another is involved, think how to elicit his or her spirituality so to bring forth "the better angels of our nature."[313]

Practices

Spiritual discipline begins with physical exercise. PhysEd instructors usually recommend that people perform an exercise regimen daily for at least half an hour. One's mind and spirit need exercising, too. So, we should recognize that one can be thinking, praying or wondering while working out. Then, it's easy to extend ½ hour to a whole hour, adding selective reading and spiritual reflection to the "work out." Which hour of any given day will vary from day to day and person to person depending on a number of factors well-known to us. What's most important is that time be so dedicated for at least 5 days of every week.[314]

Steinbeck's Ethan reflects on waking up:

> "Coming out of sleep, I had the advantage of two worlds (as) the layered firmament of dream and the temporal fixtures of the mind awake...First, I referred to my remembered dreams...Then I explored the coming day for events...Next, I followed a practice learned from...Charley Edwards...he opened his mind and his heart to his

---

pause; A ~ alertness, attentiveness and/or awareness; I ~ intermediacy, intensity or intimacy; M ~ mind, mindfulness or mentality. Note that **Soule's DICTIONARY of ENGLISH SYNONYMS** specifies "soul, spirit..." as the first two synonyms of "mind."

[313] From the 2nd Inaugural Address of Abraham Lincoln.

[314] A woman speaking recently on NPR recommended 3 hours of restful meditation each day.

family. He went over each one in turn...he caressed them and reassured them of his love. It was though he picked precious things one by one..."[315]

Reflections are often prompted by questions. We all know the old saying: "If you don't ask the right questions, you don't have a snowball's chance in hell of finding the right answers." Questions and answers have an inevitable way of differing among people, sooner or later (as they should). What's a good set of starters? – questions that reflect on our vulnerability and defensiveness, those that probe deeper meanings, and some that ask: "Who am I? – the answer to which may provide the deepest and most salient answers of all." Try these:

- Do I have at least one friend with whom I can talk about the serious questions of life that we share?
- Do I have a spiritual side to my life? If so, what arouses it? If not, why not? What kind of life am I trying to build for myself and significant others? Is there any place or value for spirituality in that picture?
- Who do I love and who loves me? What are the qualities of my close relationships and how can I elevate them? How much love do I bring to my relationships with others?
- How is my love of life expressed in my relationships with others?
- How do I mark my love of life at the beginning and end of each day in the life of (YOUR WIFE, HUSBAND or PARTNER'S NAME)?

What do such questions have to do with spirituality? Note that the questions have to do with one's self-understanding and realization of the qualities of life among the living, along with remembrances of those whose life and love have been influential in making us who we are. For what is spirituality if not one's ability to reflect what is most important to living a good life? Spirituality makes us aware of the dangers of letting ourselves get caught up in, sometimes even overwhelmed by, the messy minutia of daily living. It's what enables us to step back and see things from a new angle, using a different set of lenses. Even to speak or hear messages of a higher level.

---

[315] Steinbeck, John (1962), **WINTER of OUR DISCONTENT**, p.190.

Yet, we should not see a once-a-day meditational moment as sufficient to either the need or challenge of our spiritual natures. Every cusp, break or pause in our day-to-day routines provides, if not a special need, then an opportunity to bring the power and revelation of spirituality to bear; i.e., to invoke our higher and better natures. For example, hunger may signal the need for food at lunch, but we can and should use the opportunity to entertain a higher thirst – for spiritual moments that enable and empower us to recall the higher aims we would like to serve and put our work into that more spiritual context; like, a blessing before a meal.

Some moments at work, home or anywhere during any given day may have been stressful. Thus, our spirituality is a call for understanding, grace and forgiveness. Any church worth its salt should realize and provide training to enable folks to engage their spirituality at any moment when the latter three qualities are called for. Too often, there are conflicts in either home or work. Spirituality must enter then as a call for peace. Then an old song may flood into memory, the opening line of which is: "Let there be peace on earth and let it begin with me..."

The Democratic Spirit

Our spirit should never stand aside from any aspect of life as if it were only accessible by way of a higher-level figure like a priest or bishop. No, the holy spirit is ever alive and near to us – the spiritual version of a public good accessible to all, anytime. It is the spirit of the Reformation, which democratized religion by infusing it with the spirit of "We the People" – the first three words of our Constitution – contra to the authority of the priesthood. Thus, religion became a driver of democracy.

Democratic movements, in turn, helped to focus and reinforce people's attention on the individuality of conscience informed by the universality of the human holy spirit. The spirit of "We the People" was thereby strengthened. Some may be wont to deprecate the beliefs of our Founders because some of them were 'merely' Deists. They might thereby be considered flabby religious believers, but the spirit of "We the People" among them cannot be denied.

How do we come to recognize and cultivate the spiritual side of human nature? Traditionally, this starts with the rite of baptism. This is a fine feature of conventional religion in that it informs the guardians of a newborn as to the child's potential human spirituality and engages them to share responsibility for training the child in spirit-building exercises. Nevertheless, years may pass before a child comes to recognize, appreciate and train his or her own spirituality. This suggests that a joyous event might be a later-in-life re-baptism when a young man or woman, fully conscious of his or her spirituality, joins with family and friends to celebrate the recognition.

In the meantime, a new form of religious education should be publicly recognized as a necessary and important, nonsectarian aspect of public education.[316] After all, spirituality flows from and enables the highest and deepest expressions of human life. A question here remains, however: Do we want NSB to be institutionalized?-- reified?, as has democracy in America? Probably not, but we may need to return to the question sooner or later.

Adaptations

Here is where there's little new but tremendous potential for both nominal and creative adaptations of what already exists. Most of us grew up in the context of existing religious practice. There's some familiarity with hymns or other religious songs, rites, rituals, prayers and texts. Most of this can be readily adapted to our NSB. Even the change of one word in a hymn can serve to shift the focus from an all-powerful, external god to the power of life within us all. Some hymns and a few psalms can be used unchanged.

---

[316] Here we need to confront the all-to-frequent misinterpretations of the 1st Amendment to our U.S. Constitution regarding church and state, which opens "Congress shall make no law respecting an establishment of religion". This implies that what is being proposed here should not be declared un-Constitutional. Why? – Because a NSB is a self-starting, do-it-yourself, sort-of religion. No one seeks approval from any level of government.

Consider just a few hymns, for example, from **THE UNITED METHODIST HYMNAL** (with page references in parentheses):

o The musical setting of Psalm 24 (King James Version, page 212): The opening line is "Holy, holy, holy, Lord God of Hosts." Change "Lord" to "life's".

o "Come Ye Faithful, Raise the Strain" (page 315): Substitute "God of life" for "God" in line 1; ditch the rest.

o "Come Thou Long-Expected Jesus"(page 196): Substitute "future" for "Jesus" in line 1; eliminate line 2.

o "Love Lifted Me" (Insert, no page): Substitute "soul" for "Master" in line 1; delete the rest.

o Psalm 23: Simply exchange "soul" for "Lord."

o Hymn: "This is my Father's world; substitute "life" for "Lord."

The most important consideration to keep in mind as we go about design and scheduling of rites, rituals and practices is that of balance – between:

➢ Individuality and Community, or Self and Other;
➢ Thought [attentiveness & mindfulness] and Action;
➢ Everyday life and expectations;
➢ Heroism and "ordinary" life;

On their face, each of these seems to raise issues of how or even whether balance could be achieved. Each suggests trade-offs. Foremost among these is secular vis a vis sacred. As noted in Chapter 10:

1) The sacred is not to be traded off for secular things; it is to be sought in them.

2) Our world has become overly secular; that is, de-sacralized. And so, we need to infuse nearly all that is secular with the spirit of what is sacred. The NSB takes us at least one step above the level of "trade-offs" by enabling us to recognize the positive values of interactivity in each of the paradoxical combinations twinned above.

3) The desire to balance the above duals neither requires, nor does it imply, any sacrifice of the sacred for the sake of things secular.

Nor would it demand that we focus more on ourselves than the communities in which we are members and/or otherwise involved. NPR's "The Hidden Brain," for example, reported results of a study of rituals. It showed that participation in even artificial rituals enhances trust among the participants. The downside is that it may increase distrust towards those not participating. This is not surprising. It supplies an additional positive incentive – to reach out to others to broaden circles of participation.

As for the other dualities, these are also examples of virtuous cycles:

- **Thought and Action** [attentiveness & mindfulness]: Thoughtfulness enables better Action while Action informs thoughtfulness through the (oft hard) lessons of experience.
- **Everyday life and expectations:** Lessons emerging from everyday life enable our expectations to be refined, while the latter help to energize our everyday life. The key qualifier here does not provide a "trade-off"; it rather brings to bear the hope and faith built into a NSB. These help one to deal with inevitable disappointments in everyday life or developments that diminish expectations.
- **Heroism and "ordinary" life:** Built into the NSB is the concept of the "heroes of everyday life."[317] As the recent history of wanton killings has demonstrated, so-called "ordinary folks" are capable of genuine (that is, not just media-generated) heroism. Examples of heroism elevate ordinary life, while the latter provides opportunities for heroism.

---

[317] For more, see the author's first political book, **WE the PEOPLE: A Conservative Populism.** Lafayette, LA: Alpha Publishing.

Chapter 27

Implications of a NSB

and

Its Challenges to Change Throughout Society

Introduction

Though modest in its scope and ambition, a NSB has potentially radical implications that are sure to arouse opposition from many quarters. For the new system not only challenges established religion, it also challenges schools, lawmakers at all levels, and a variety of other secular organizations and institutions to make changes in rules and practices that most would most likely be reluctant to make. Without being able to do justice to these [which would require another book], let's turn to highlight some major types of changes. If some of these seem to overreach the theme of this book, think again: The realm of the human spirit is limitless. Unless it has turned to the dark side, it should never be circumscribed.

The battle for freedom and liberty never ends. Each generation needs to do what it can to broaden and deepen the space for the expression and achievement of the possibilities of human life. And so, please read and consider the following recommendations. Some may appear to reach beyond the scope of this book because, as yet, they have not been specifically addressed separately. Each, however, is consistent with the NSB's focus on the sacred nature and wonderful possibilities of human life. What's to be done to realize these possibilities, and where?, in? or through?...>>

Schools:

- o Where we can and should… Return prayers and blessings [over meals, et al.] to the educational process;
- o Include spirituality and spiritual discipline education from beginning elementary through high school.

Congress: Initiate Constitutional Amendments re:

- o The introduction of National Initiative and Referendum to bring more direct democracy into our representative system.
- o Teaching spirituality without violating the "establishment clause."
- o Broaden support for the 2nd Amendment.

Family:

Abortion: Reverence towards life implies the need to revise Roe v. Wade to accord with what science reveals as to the development of the human fetus. We know that the fetus is indistinguishable from those of other animal species up to the end of week 1 after conception. So, it cannot be said that "human life begins at conception." And yet, a 20-week threshold for abortion is also not scientifically supportable. One could as well say that an abortion should be performed within 1 week. The practicable truth lays somewhere in between.

Divorce: In light of the fact that heterosexual partners are needed for the upbringing of children, divorce laws need to be revised so as to maintain partnerships for their upbringing except in cases where the lives of family members are lost or are in danger from mothers or fathers. This means that divorce would become more difficult whenever young, dependent children are involved. Similar considerations would affect decisions and rules regarding custody. Sole custody should be disallowed except in cases of violent behavior exhibited by one partner or the other. Marriage licenses should not be issued to young couples until they have completed a course on marriage and parenting.

Same-sex marriage, adoption and child-rearing: One cannot equate two things which differ substantially and meaningfully. Thus, same-sex marriage cannot be equated with heterosexual marriage as if they were both essentially similar forms of "marriage." The prime raison d'etre of heterosexual marriage is the procreation and nurture of human life newly conceived by its marital male and female partners. Same-sex marriage clearly does not qualify. To say "marriage" is a simple matter of "choice" is to denigrate the institution as well as misuse the word. Within the frame of the institution of marriage, the prime focus is on the well-being, nurture and development of children. But for situations where a couple has suffered the loss of his or her marital partner, human children should not be raised by single parent or same-sex couples without the children's frequent interaction with an adult friend or relative of the opposite sex. Any parent will testify that men and women bring different resources to children's upbringing. Thus, children need both male and female sources of guidance. Another implication is that fathers need to spend more time with their babies, not leaving early childhood child care solely to mothers. These considerations imply some significant changes in adoption law.

1st & 2nd Amendments: Consistent with the previous section, questioning same-sex marriage would not qualify the questioner to be labeled homophobic. As for the 2nd Amendment, reverence for human life suggests that any adult person trained in the use of a firearm should be able to carry a firearm for self-defense.

Law and criminal justice:

Death penalty: Imposition of the death penalty is tantamount to government playing God, but human justice is imperfect and too often biased. Also, the death penalty can be viewed as an easy way out of facing tough questions of both justice and punishment. Life at hard labor without parole including victims' compensation would be more appropriate as punishment for a capital crime. Law should not be grounded in lust for vengeance. This would as well be more just to victims. Failing to take a murderer's life would allow that life to be studied. Such studies would help the justice system to understand, and thereby remedy or ameliorate, the causes of violent crime.

Solitary Confinement: Only the "worst of the worst" are supposed to be subject to this form of punishment, but the fact of the matter is that "solitary" is overused and counter-productive. It is too often employed, for example, to punish inmates for ordinary in-prison infractions. Solitary confinement sentences are often too long – for months and years, even though criminal justice experts recommend no more than 15 days. Some court cases on solitary confinement have found that its use is also un-constitutional because it amounts to "cruel and unusual punishment." Whether or not this is true in any specific case, we have learned that most of those who have been subjected to solitary confinement are also subject to mental health problems that such confinement worsens.

Torture: This is unquestionably cruel and unusual punishment and should be banned outright.

Poverty: We no longer live in an equal opportunity society. Inequality continues to worsen in terms of both income and wealth. So, yes, "poverty is always with us" still, even though it should not be. Poverty debilitates. There is little or no dignity in poverty. Lest poverty become intergenerational (as it has become with some families in some locations), we need to focus on the children in poverty-laden families.

The problem here is that the public-school system has become part of the system's engine of inequality. Healthful school lunches need to be maintained, not cut back. Increased funding of mentors, tutors and coaches is required. After school programs that include nutritional supplements are needed if not already provided. Kindergarten classes should be mandatory, also to include nourishing food.

The thorniest part of the poverty issue, however, is lack of resources for children from birth through kindergarten. Many more pre-school programs are needed. More training, education and help for prenatal and new mothers is required. Why? – Because we now know, on the basis of many years of research, that the period of birth through preschool are the most critical years of brain development, lacking which young children may become disadvantaged for life.

A focus sufficient to the gravity of the issue should begin with recognition of a sad fact: The U.S.A. is no longer the land of equal opportunity. The unprecedented jump in indices of inequality of income and wealth since 1975 should have amounted to a huge red flag to those in all sectors of the economy and society – that they should identify and offset anything that aggravates inequality.[318]

Especially in education, where the charter school movement has come to largely represent privatization of public schools that had been founded to generate equal opportunity. Educational unequal opportunity is remarkably evident early-on – in kindergarten and pre-school. Thus, even in a society that looks to education to solve social problems, inequality threatens to become a vicious circle.

What is the "bottom line" on poverty? (no pun intended) It is that poverty is a primarily structural issue, not one of individuals' skills or willingness to work. In other words, poverty is built into the socio-economic and institutional structures of American society. We cannot abolish it. We can only rid ourselves of poverty by engaging in the struggle to revolutionize parties, incentives and institutions. The struggle is fundamentally political.

Politics and Government

Spirit of Democracy & Government of "We the People"

We need to spur a truly "bottom up" approach. As Jefferson wrote: "The only solution to the problems of democracy is more democracy, not less." Thus, we need to introduce elements of direct democracy into our representative system. An organization to advance this goal was founded in 2014, called A

---

[318] For more on this, see this author's essay titled "Inequality" in **ADVANCES IN POLITICS and ECONOMICS** (March, 2019).

People's and Citizens' Congress [APaCC].[319] Democracy also needs to be extended to the economic sector, including governance of both for-profit and not-for-profit organizations. Employee and Consumer Stock Ownership Plans [ESOPs and CSOPs, respectively] that include employee participation in business' governance and distribution of a portion of profits from sales of consumer goods to consumers, for example, should be required for all but the smallest, start-up or early-stage firms. Economic and political democracy are linked. Unfortunately, the linkage is not always made effective in either ESOPs or CSOPS. Too many are subject to un-democratic forms of management.

Federal Government

❖ The Executive Branch: The U.S. Constitution provides for a powerful President, but there has been a steady and increasingly dangerous agglomeration of power in an executive branch governed by the Office of the President. As a result, our federal government is becoming what some have labelled an "Administrative State."[320] Others call it an "oligarchy." This trend has been aggravated by Congressional laziness – a tendency to pass legislation full of good intentions but leaving too much of the drafting of effective law, that governing implementation of legislative intent, to unelected officials (a.k.a. Bureaucrats).

A major part of the solution to the overconcentration of power and money in Washington would be decentralization of the federal government. Ideally, more power and money and accompanying responsibilities should be passed on to localities. Unfortunately, the only intervening powers recognized under the Constitution are states even though, increasingly, solutions to major

---

[319] For more information, go to www.peoplesandcitizenscongress.com, or write to: apeoplesandcitizenscongress2@gmail.com.

[320] For example, see: Postel, Joseph (2012), From Administrative State to Constitutional Government," Washington, D.C.: Heritage Foundation (December 14).

problems fall on the shoulders of local governments.[321]Thus, a serious move towards decentralization (not just "devolution") has to deal with the fact that many state legislatures have been acting so as to diminish the powers of local government, treating the latter as mere "creatures" of the states.[322] This runs askew of a countervailing fact – that most citizens trust their local authorities more than state or federal. We need to try harder to uphold the spirit of local democratic self-governance, an important foundation of "the spirit of America."

❖ **The Congress:** Government by "We the People." Start by promoting realization of which is at stake. After all, the Congress is the only leg of the 3-legged federal stool that is devoted, under the Constitution, to work for and with "We the People." For this to be fulfilled, the institution is in need of major reforms. Two major ones were mentioned earlier. Two others are: (1) At least one Constitutional Amendment needed to get big money out, and people back into, politics; and (2) Reformation of the Congressional committee system to enable a greater and more effective focus on issues with long-term consequences. Like that of global warming/climate change – the poster child of issues with terribly long-term impacts.

Community: Valuation of "community" is another part of the spirit of America. At stake is the quality and accessibility of services to help people to help themselves. Trouble is, too many human service providers confuse their overflow of good intentions with expectations of good consequences from their services. The latter need to be focused on helping people to help themselves within a matrix of community interrelationships.

---

[321] See, for example: Bloomberg, Michael (2017), **"Why Municipalities are the Key to Fighting Climate Change," FOREIGN AFFAIRS** (September/October).

[322] For example, see: Graham, David A. (2017), "Red State, Blue City: The U.S. is coming to resemble two countries, one rural and one urban. **What happens when they go to war?," THE ATLANTIC** (March).

The key concern here has been how to translate spirit and its correlates into reality, else "spirit" comes to be associated with vacuous expression of good intentions and fine feelings. Clearly, the consequences of not making the translation – and so effectively not grounding the spirit in real problems (and vice-versa) – are really quite dire. If such translations are not made, then the "spirit" is effectively empty. If they are, the good works that emerge elevate one's spirit to a higher level of spirituality; indeed, to and of soul and soulfulness.

A New System of Belief to sustain Human Life, individually and collectively, can spread and be nurtured to help transform and sustain the spirit of, yes, truly "We the People".

Chapter 28

Summary Conclusions and Final Words

Introduction

Depending on where one is starting out in their spiritual journey, this book can be viewed as either revolutionary or evolutionary. Ironically, since an overriding concern throughout has been on the nurture of spirituality, the truly religious soul may be the most jolted. The shift in focus from external to internal and from a God-in-heaven to a God of Life amounts to a sea-change. Rooting oneself in reality is most difficult for those who relish cherished myths. Whatever your current standpoint, the choice of change is yours. A spirituality that can grow and be maintained by and for the sustainability of life is at stake.

It's time to recall the main observations and findings that have arisen in our journey. Let's recap and then see how they hang together (or not). They fall into five major categories: Needs, Basis, Opportunities, Practices and Consequences. Consider each in turn.

Needs to change

These arise from our time-limited lifetimes. They also emanate from evidence contrary to the two major beliefs that sustain Christianity and some other major religions: resurrection and life-after-death (LaD). We all live lives that are at least partly sustained by illusions. Some are relatively harmless. Some are not, the two cited above among them. LaD is an especially vain and dangerous illusion to the extent that it enables religious fanatics to rationalize their killing of innocents -- as noted at the outset of this book. Realization that this life is all we've got snaps us to attention -- to not only cherish life but to try to live it to the max. Banishing the vain hope of LaD also eliminates "heaven". We have no place else to go other than back to earth, the depths of the sea or up a chimney.

Bases for change

These rest on the evidence we reviewed that the spiritual emanates from the physical, not the other way around. The consciousness and mindfulness of the human mind is emergent from the brain. They are not supplied by external, supernatural forces. As a higher-level realization, spirituality is emergent from consciousness and mindfulness.

We followed the trails of neuron firings, interactions and chemicals in the brain to identify the major paths and patterns of influence. Both counterpoint and addend, however, came from learning that reductionism is dead – that one cannot trace cause-and-effect in a complex adaptive system (CAS) as convoluted as the human brain. Thus, we found that the human brain enables a creative, learning organism and mindfulness from which spirituality can emerge.

Along the way, we found recent research capable of detecting and crudely measuring our spirituality and identifying segments of the brain more significant as sources of consciousness than others. We also learned of the factors promoting "emergence." Review of attempts to build computer models of the brain led to another insight: That the human brain is not and can never be viewed as a computer. Processes of creativity, imagination and integration are not "algorithmic."

Another important finding led us further away from dependence on the supernatural. It is too much a variegated, veritable rats' nest of influences, including tendencies on the "darkside" of human nature. By resting incarnation on one person and the unreality of "virgin birth" and "resurrection" of that one, it deters realization of incarnation in human life more generally. Human life provides the true opportunity for incarnation of the holy spirit, both individually and collectively, as the basis for a deeper, richer realization of the potential of human life.

Opportunities for change

One of the major and most powerful venues for change is the arena of work, where most of us spend most of the years of our lives. Many of the opportunities here have already been recognized and implemented by enlightened organizations of all types, private and public. Documentation and leads for follow up were provided.

A large amount of ink in the book, however, was devoted to the identification of opportunities to infuse spirituality into things and activities of everyday life. These include sports and other activities where "spirit" is already celebrated. There were deliberate attempts to bridge the gaps between large and small, higher and lower, and "micro"- and "macro"-level activities.

<u>Practices for Change</u> (including rites and rituals)

A large amount of attention was paid to spiritual features already prevalent in major religions. We recognized that most could be adapted for use by a NSB. They include prayer, devotionals, hymns and select practices of religious services. It is this flexibility and adaptability that helps to make a NSB evolutionary.

Prayer is at least as important in the NSB context, but instead of looking upward in prayer, we would send our prayers outward towards other human lives. We would seek offering more than supplication. We would come to realize that soul-building is a process Soulfulness is a product of spiritual work. With practice, spirituality becomes a good habit. The powers of hope, love and faith are suffused with a holy spirit that can be with us at any moment. Meditation and other practices start "physical" and emanate spiritual.

As for "institutionalization" of a NSB, such a reification is really unnecessary and may be undesirable. A NSB will live on to the extent that it does so in the minds and spirits of people, whether or not the NSB becomes an organized religion, legal entity and/or a church. Institutions that survive tend to take on a life of their own. If not governed by an activist, high-energy democracy, that "life" could cease to resonate with the spirit that a living NSB faith represents.

Consequences of change

The NSB offers many potentially beneficial outcomes, few of which as yet have been realized. These include eleven in number (cited in no special order or priority):

> Assisting the generation of a more democratic society whose basis is person-to-person participation in a politics of "We the People," plus broader influence of the public-at-large on systems of governance that, after all, should be theirs. This would result from an increased focus on interpersonal and intergroup relationships and greater appreciation of the interdependencies of "our lives, fortunes and sacred honor." Also, from the realization that the cost of freedom is the responsibility of citizenship.
> Better understanding of how our individual and group behaviors can generate either "virtuous" or "vicious" cycles.
> More appreciation of how our souls and spirituality have been, and continue to be, diminished by the steady secularization and desacrilization of our society.
> Enabling a synthesis of body, mind and soul, "a penultimate yearning" of human beings" along with our search for matter and meaning in all things.
> Helping us to understand that the "dynamic of soul-building lies at the self/other interface.
> Also helping us to understand suffering, that: "to live is to suffer (but) we have the freedom to choose (how to act) with respect to our responsibility to live..."
> The need to shift fights for power into more spiritual domains along with changes in language.
> Contra Humanism, "mysteries and miracles" are not banished.
> A better appreciation of the interdependencies of space and time and of ourselves vis a vis others in the management of our lives.
> A stronger basis for a spiritual, entrepreneurial, learning and service society.

➤ A NSB better suited to aid and abet a more peaceful society and world.

Thus, richer and deeper mines of human lives and their inter-relationships would be brought forth, sufficient to sustain human life on planet earth.

APPENDIX 1

The Vocabulary of Spirituality

A NSB also calls for a vocabulary and a set of sayings that, much like any religion, could be called "sacred." In addition to the latter, these include incarnation, spirit, sacrament(al), holiness, reverence, birth, life, death, marriage, conception, gestation, being, becoming, blessed, awe, wondrous, godlike, heaven(ly), infinitude, marvelous, miraculous, sanctification, baptism, discipleship and resurrection. All of these need to be redefined to incorporate the fullness of their meaning with respect to their intimate connections with the sacred procreation and nurture of human life. "Holiday" should be returned to its original "holy day."

Note how "awe" has been replaced by a word, "awesome" that, bandied carelessly about as it is, has come to be practically meaningless by connoting all or nothing at all. The full meaning of "resurrection" needs to be rescued from its unfortunate association with life-after-death. For, as Emily Dickenson expressed in her poetry [which continues to live and inspire us long after her passing], "Among those things that cannot return are...the dead."

According to the **CONCISE OXFORD ENGLISH DICTIONARY [OED],** resurrection means restoration to life, or revival of a practice, use or memory. Its meaning of as "life-after-death" appears only in Christian belief. Other synonyms independent of the latter are other 'r' words, including renewal, revival and restoration. Even though "resurrection" is not mentioned in his seminal final work, Maslow helps us to connect it to transcendence. One source of the latter is "peak experience" whereby individuals are transformed by an event, crisis or realization that forces them to confront their humanity in relationship to life, to others and to life with others at various levels of community – indeed, world-wide and even unto the cosmos.[323]

In effect, this democratizes resurrection and opens it to each of us without reference to a hypothetical supreme being or life-after-death. A revamped educational system could also help convey how such a profound rush can be realized. This broader (and deeper) view of resurrection also connects intimately with the incarnate.

Once again, incarnation is as fundamental to NSB as to Christianity. Why? – Because it recognizes that Christ brought explicit recognition of the higher consciousness of mankind to us in the form of the Holy Spirit: God-in-Man. This need not, however, rest on an unbelievable myth, that of a virgin birth. Here is one of many topics where science has quite demolished myth. We all know that conception occurs only when sperm enters an egg to begin the process of cell divisions, multiplications and body parts-in-formation that is more miraculous in reality that any myth in our imagination.

Insofar as human gestation is concerned, science also reveals that the blob of fast-dividing cells first emergent cannot be deemed "human" until a week after conception. According to the OED, the term "fetus" does not apply to the human embryo until up to eight weeks have passed.[324]

---

[323] Maslow, Abraham H. (1971), **THE FARTHER REACHES of HUMAN NATURE.** New York: Viking Press. Such experiences should not be confused with those brought about through drugs, especially since drug users are usually despairing loners but for the occasional, mutually destructive company of fellow addicts.

[324] It never ceases to amaze me how these facts are not recognized [or, at least, to my knowledge, not cited], even by those "pro-life" forces on the abortion issue, which continues to excite internecine battles over whether abortion should be banned or significantly limited as late as 20 weeks after conception, as well as by those who claim that human life begins at conception.

It is sufficient to surmise that Christ was conceived in love, then grew -in stature and wisdom to bring a message of love to the world. According to Leo Sauerby's hymn: "Love Came Down at Christmas." The fact that Christ's birth is still celebrated over more than two millennia since his passing is sufficient demonstration of the true meaning of life-after-death, for the meaning of his life and sacrifice and its relevance to humankind will endure for time immemorial.

Christmas could be viewed more generally, for the birth of every baby is a sacred moment worthy of celebration by both parents and community. Yet the holy day is desecrated by graven images promoting commercialism. The holiness of a local crèche, for example, is diminished by its juxtaposition with Santa Claus. And what of the incarnation?

It continues to challenge us to raise ourselves up to attain realization of the god of life that is within us all – the highest awareness of the full meaning of our life force and what each of us can contribute to the nurture, advancement and enrichment of human life on planet earth and even beyond – true transcendence. [This paragraph was written the day after Christmas, 2016.]

Three other keywords in the vocabulary of spirituality go together: spirit, holiness and reverence. "Spirit" is in most common use. We often hear of "team spirit," "company spirit" and "spirit of the season" among a host of similar usages. A critical view of such usage might lead one to believe that, like "awesome," the word has come to mean nearly everything spirit(ual), or airily something akin to nothing.

Yet the word is rooted in the reality of human experience. The fact that it is so widely shared is another indication of how widespread are feelings of "spirit." So, what is the underlying "something"? The fast developing science of brain research enters here as elsewhere. The locus of spirit lies in the prefrontal lobes of the brain.[325] Ironically, the prefrontal locus of exhilarating spirit is the same area that is the source of debilitating depression –

"an area on the lower part of the internal surface of the prefrontal cortex – the ventromedial or subgenual cortex. This...is the brain's emotional control center. It is exceptionally active during bouts of mania, and inactive...during depression."[326]

Please understand here than the term "mania" is not to mean crazy. Again, Carter:

"...those in a state of mania see life as a gloriously ordered, integrated whole. Everything seems to be   connected to everything else, and the smallest events seem bathed in meaning. A person in this state is euphoric, full of energy and flowing with love. They are also in a state of high creativity – the connections they see between things...are often invisible or overlooked by others...The connections between this region and the limbic system beneath it are very dense, closely binding the conscious mind with the unconscious..."[327] (and the mind with emotions)

Thus, a healthy mind in a healthy body is the source of spirit and genuine spirituality, not a revelation brought to us from 'on high' (even though some may (still?) believe it so). And so, too, it seems that I delight in "mania" as well, at least from 1982 when I began my business, Development Strategies

---

[325] Here and earlier [Chapter 3], we have relied on a fine but dated reference, **MAPPING of the MIND**, by Rita Carter (1998). Berkeley, CA: University of California Press. "Locus" does not designate an exclusive place, for the brain draws on many parts to construct images and evoke spirituality, as noted earlier.

[326] Carter, op. cit., p.197.

[327] Ibid., p. 197.

Corporation. Its logo is the both ancient and modern icon of the 8-fold knot, which represents that everything is related to everything else.

In any case, however, we have not yet sufficiently accounted for the influence of the context in which any individual human being is brought up, live and grows (or not). The story of human development is not written by nature alone; there are substantial contextual factors to consider, too, such as familial nurture, frameworks of opportunity (or lack there-of), circumstances (adverse or otherwise), and more as we have observed in several earlier chapters.

Have a Heart

References to "heart" as if it is the center of spirit and joy as well as strength reflects usage from ancient times. The latter was originally based on mythical and other misunderstandings of the biological role of the heart. A dictionary definition of "heart" has seven variants, the first of which is: "A hollow, muscular organ that pumps the blood through the circulatory system by rhythmic contraction and dilation." The second is: "The central, innermost or vital part of something."[328] The latter is metaphorical. In so much of common as well as usage older than any of us, "heart" harkens to the mythical or romantic. Such associations more or less describe the tenor of the non-biological meaning of "heart" to most, consistent with conventional usage.

These misunderstandings, however, continue to be propagated by many religions which also employ the heart as an emblematic symbol. As described in **WIKIPEDIA**, the heart signifies:

> "the temple or throne of God in Islamic and Judeo-Christian religions; the divine center...and the 3rd eye   of transcendent wisdom in Hinduism; the diamond of purity and essence of the Buddha; the Taoist centre of understanding...In the Hebrew Bible, the word for heart...is used...as the seat of emotion, the mind..."

---

[328] **CONCISE OXFORD ENGLISH DICTIONARY** , 11th Edition (2008, p.658).

One needs to go back to ancient Egypt to find a time and place when the heart was (first?) thought to be an important part of the soul. It's high time to update our language as to "heart," "heartfulness," "heartfelt," et al. to reflect true meanings that are soundly knowledge-based. It would be right, proper and meaningful to substitute "soul" for "heart."

Not that there aren't some overlaps. At its best, for example, love-making not only raises heart and breathing rates, it produces feelings of euphoria, joy, fulfillment, transport, rapture and ecstasy. All this may seem to center, if not arise from, the resonance of two hearts even though, in fact, it owes to sexual arousal, the flow of chemicals from the pineal gland to heart and brain, and a growing sense of both sexual and sacred union. One can be forgiven for attributing love to the heart in moments of passion.

"Knowledge-based", however, doesn't quite cut it as a sufficient justification for substituting "soul" for "heart." Too much habitual usage and emotional freight is attached to the use of "heart." The main point is that the usage detracts from recognition of that which is far more profound – soul and soulfulness. One can't imagine raising the level of spirituality country-wide, let alone world-wide, by singing "You gotta have heart," even "lots and lots and lots of it." We need to face a simple fact of human behavior – the overwhelming force of habit. Repeated references to the heart owe to this. We can at least hope that, once the greater soulfulness of soul is recognized, "soul" will come to replace "heart" in much of our language.

APPENDIX 2

Glossary of Terms

❖ **NOTE:** Unless otherwise indicated, the following definitions have been drawn from Oxford English dictionaries.

Alpha-helix: One of the two common conformations of the secondary structure of proteins, in which the polypeptide chain assumes the form of a straight, tightly coiled helix, stabilized by hydrogen bonding between carbonyl and amide groups in the peptide linkages of the chain.

Autocatalytic: Catalysis caused by a catalytic agent formed during a reaction.

Catalysis: The acceleration of a chemical reaction by a catalyst.

Chaos: Merriam Webster definition /

1a: A state of utter confusion; e.g., the blackout caused chaos throughout the city.

b: A confused mass or mixture; e.g., a chaos of television antennas.

2a: A state of things in which chance is supreme; especially, the confused unorganized state   of primordial matter before the creation of distinct forms in the cosmos.

3: The inherent unpredictability in the behavior of a complex natural system (such as the atmosphere, boiling water, or the beating heart)

Complexity: Merriam Webster definition

1: Something complex; e.g., the complexities of a murder trial.

2: The quality or state of being complex; e.g., the complexity of a contract.

Conformation: The shape or structure of something; e.g., with respect to an animal, "the judges run their hands over the dog's body and legs, checking its conformation."

Cybernetics (treated as singular): The science of communications and automatic control systems in both machines and living things.

Cytoplasm: Material or protoplasm within a living cell, excluding the nucleus.

Cytoskeleton: A microscopic network of protein filaments and tubules in the cytoplasm of many living cells, giving them shape and coherence.

DNA [Deoxyribonucleic acid]: A self-replicating material which is present in nearly all living organisms as the main constituent of chromosomes. It is the carrier of genetic information.

Each molecule of DNA consists of two strands coiled round each other to form a double helix, a structure like a spiral ladder. Each rung of the ladder consists of a pair of chemical groups called bases (of which there are four types), which combine in specific pairs so that the sequence on one strand of the double helix is complementary to that on the other. It is the specific sequence of bases which constitutes the genetic information.

Dynamic: (of a process or system) characterized by constant change, activity, or progress.

Emergent:

1. In the process of coming into being or becoming prominent: "the emergent democracies of eastern Europe" (Synonyms: emerging, developing, rising, dawning, budding)

2. Of or denoting a plant that is taller than the surrounding vegetation, especially a tall tree in a forest. As a noun: An emergent property, tree or plant.

Enzyme: A substance produced by a living organism that acts as a catalyst to bring about a specific biochemical reaction.

Hexamers: Polymers formed from six molecules of a monomer. A structural subunit that is part of a viral capsid and composed of six subunits of similar shape.

Hierarchical: Of the nature of a hierarchy; that is, arranged in order of rank; e.g., 'the hierarchical bureaucracy of a local authority.

Incarnation: A person who embodies in the flesh a deity, spirit, or abstract quality; e.g., "Rama was Vishnu's incarnation on earth" / Synonyms: embodiment, personification, exemplification, type, epitome.

Indeterminate: Not exactly known, established, or defined; e.g., "The date of manufacture is indeterminate"/ Synonyms: uncertain, unknown, unspecified, unstipulated./ Antonyms: known, definite, clear

Ion: an atom or molecule with a net electric charge due to the loss or gain of one or more electrons.

Kinetic: Of, relating to, or resulting from motion.

Lipids: Any of a class of organic compounds that are fatty acids or their derivatives and are insoluble in water but soluble in organic solvents. They include many natural oils, waxes, and steroids.

Mapping: An operation that associates each element of a given set (the domain) with one or more elements of a second set (the range).

Liposomes : Biochemistry / A minute spherical sac of phospholipid molecules enclosing a water droplet, especially as formed artificially to carry drugs or other substances into the tissues.

Materialism:

1. A tendency to consider material possessions and physical comfort as more important than spiritual values.

2. The doctrine that nothing exists except matter and its movements and modifications.

Metabolic: from Dictionary.com

   1. Of, relating to, or affected by metabolism.

   2. Undergoing metamorphosis.

Neurological: Relating to the anatomy, functions, and organic disorders of nerves and the nervous system; e.g., "neurological diseases like dementia."

Non-linear: Not arranged in a straight line.

   1.1 Mathematics: Denoting or involving an equation whose terms are not of the first degree.

   1.2 Physics: Involving a lack of linearity between two related qualities such as input and output.

   1.3 Mathematics: Involving measurement in more than one dimension. Not sequential or straightforward.

Noumenal: from Farlex Partner Medical Dictionary, © Farlex 2012.

Intellectually, not sensuously or emotionally, intuitional; relating to the object of pure thought divorced from all concepts of time or space; perceived – to perceive, think.

Nucleon: Physics; A proton or neutron.

Open Systems: Those not closed to external sources of influence.

Organelle: Any of a number of organized or specialized structures within a living cell.

Organometallic: (of a compound) containing a metal atom bonded to an organic group or groups.

Peptides: A compound consisting of two or more amino acids linked in a chain, the carboxyl group of each acid being joined to the amino group of the next by a bond of the type OCNH.

Polarization:

1. Division into two sharply contrasting groups or sets of opinions or beliefs; e.g., "the polarization of society between rich and poor"

2. The action of restricting the vibrations of a transverse wave, especially light, wholly or partially to one direction; e.g., "changes in polarization of light passing through the atmosphere"

Polymerase: An enzyme that brings about the formation of a particular polymer, especially DNA or RNA.

Probabilistic: Based on or adapted to a theory of probability; subject to or involving chance variation; e.g,, "The main approaches are either rule-based or probabilistic."

Protoplasm: The colorless material comprising the living part of a cell, including the cytoplasm, nucleus and other organelles.

Qualia: The internal and subjective component of sense perceptions, arising from stimulation of the senses by any phenomenon.

Recursive: Characterized by recurrence or repetition.

    1.1 Mathematics: Relating to or involving the repeated application of a rule, definition, or procedure to successive results.

    1.2 Computing: Relating to or involving a program or routine of which a part requires the application of the whole, so that its explicit interpretation requires in general many successive executions.

RNA [Ribonucleic acid]: A nucleic acid present in all living cells. Its principal role is to act as a messenger carrying instructions from DNA for controlling the synthesis of proteins, although in some viruses RNA rather than DNA carries the genetic information.

Sacramental:

1. Relating to or constituting a sacrament or the sacraments.

2. An observance analogous to but not reckoned among the sacraments, such as the use of holy water or the sign of the cross.

Sacred: Connected with God or a god or dedicated to a religious purpose and so deserving veneration.

    1.1 Religious rather than secular.

    1.2 (of writing or text) embodying the laws or doctrines of a religion.

    1.3 Regarded with great respect and reverence by a particular religion, group, or individual.

    1.4 Regarded as too valuable to be interfered with; sacrosanct.
    1.5 Connected with God or a god or dedicated to a religious purpose and so deserving veneration.

    1.6 Religious rather than secular; e.g., 'sacred music'

    1.7 (of writing or text) Embodying the laws or doctrines of a religion.

    1.8 Regarded with great respect and reverence by a particular religion, group, or individual e.g., in Hinduism, cows are sacred and the eating of beef is taboo.'

Self-organization: A process in which some form of overall order arises from local positive feedback. The result is a robust organization, decentralized and distributed over the system. Chaos theory treats self-organization in terms of predictability in an otherwise chaotic situation.

Synergy: The interaction or cooperation of two or more organizations, substances, or other agents to produce a combined effect greater than the sum of their separate effects.

Template:

1a: Gauge, pattern, or mold (such as a thin plate or board) used as a guide to the form of a piece being made.

1b: A molecule (as of DNA) that serves as a pattern for the generation of another macromolecule (such as messenger RNA).

2: Something that establishes or serves as a pattern to distribute its weight or pressure (as over a door).

Thermodynamic: The branch of physical science that deals with the relations between heat and other forms of energy (such as mechanical, electrical and chemical energy) and, by extension, with the relationships between and among all forms of energy.

Transcendence:- Existence or experience beyond the normal or physical level; e.g., "the possibility of spiritual transcendence in transcendence of the modern world." / Synonyms: excellence, supremacy, incomparability, matchlessness, peerlessness.

Vesicles: Merriam Webster definition /

1a: A membranous and usually fluid-filled pouch (such as a cyst, vacuole, or cell) in a plant or animal.

b: A small abnormal elevation of the outer layer of skin enclosing a watery liquid.

c:: A pocket of embryonic tissue that is the beginning of an organ.

2: A small cavity in a mineral or rock.

APPENDIX 3

BIBLIOGRAPHY

Anderson, Marianne, & Louis M. Savary (1972), **PASSAGES: A Guide for Pilgrims of the Mind.** New York: Harper and Row Publishers.

Baker, Mark, and S. Goetz (2011), **THE SOUL HYPOTHESIS**: **Investigations Into the Existence of the Soul**. New York, N.Y.: Continuum International Publishing Group.

Bard, Alexander, and J. Soderqvist (2014), **SYTHEISM: Creating God in the Internet Age**. Stockholm: Stockholm Text.

Bearse, P.J. (2004), **WE THE PEOPLE: A Conservative Populism**. Lafayette, LA: Alpha Publishing. This is the first of a trilogy, the other two of which are accessible as Kindle Books via Amazon.com.

Bronowski, Jacob (1977), **A SENSE of the FUTURE**. Cambridge: MIT Press.

(1956), **SCIENCE and HUMAN VALUES**. New York: Harper & Row. (1973), **THE ASCENT OF MAN**.

Carr, Bernard, ed. (2007) **UNIVERSE OR MULTIVERSE**? Cambridge University Press.

Carter, Rita (1999), **MAPPING the MIND**. Berkeley, CA: University of California Press.

Corning, Peter A. (1983), **THE SYNERGISM HYPOTHESIS: A Theory of Progressive Evolution**. New York: McGraw Hill.

Dawkins, Richard (2009), **THE GREATEST SHOW ON EARTH: The Evidence for Evolution.** New York, N.Y.: Free Press.

D'Souza, Dinesh (2009), **LIFE AFTER DEATH: The Evidence**. Washington, D.C.: Regnery Publishing.

Eccles, John, and Karl R. Popper (1977), **THE SELF AND ITS BRAIN: An Argument for Interactionism.** Springer.

Emerson, Ralph Waldo (1841), **ESSAYS: First Series.**

Feynman, Richard (1985), **SURELY, YOU'RE JOKING Mr. FEYNMAN!** New York: Norton.

Friedman, Thomas (2005), **THE WORLD IS FLAT**. New York: Picador.

Fuller, Buckminster (1976), **AND IT CAME TO PASS, NOT TO STAY**. New York: Macmillan.

Gorga, Carmine (2017), **THE ECONOMIC PROCESS: 3rd edition**. Lanham, MD: University Press of America.

Graves, Mark (2016), **MIND, BRAIN and the ELUSIVE GOAL: Human Systems of Cognitive Science and Religion**. New York: Routledge, Ashgate Science and Religion Series.

Gruden, Robert (1982), **TIME and the Art of Living,** New York: Harper & Row.

Hitchens, Christopher (2007), **GOD IS NOT GREAT: How Religion Poisons Everything.** New York: Hachette Book Group USA.

Hofstadter, Douglas (2007), **I AM A STRANGE LOOP**. New York: Basic Books.

Holland, John H. (1998), **EMERGENCE: From Chaos to Order. Reading,** MA: Addison-Wesley Publishing.

Hunter, Sam, & J. Jacobs (1976), **MODERN ART.** Italy: Helvetic Press.

.Jaynes, Julian (1976), **THE ORIGIN OF CONSCIOUSNESS IN THE BREAKDOWN OF THE BICAMERAL MIND**. Boston: Houghton Mifflin.

Jackson, Phil, and H. Delehanty (2013), **ELEVEN RINGS: The Soul of Success.** New York: Penguin.

Johnson, Robert (1998), **BALANCING HEAVEN and EARTH**. San Francisco: Harper.

Johnson, Paul (2007), **HEROES: From Alexander the Great and Julius Caesar to Churchill and De Gaulle.** New York: Harper Collins Publishers.

Kauffman, Stuart A. (1993), **THE ORIGINS of ORDER: Self-Organization and Selection in Evolution.**" New York: Oxford U.P.

Kauffmann, Stuart (2000), **INVESTIGATIONS.** New York: Oxford University Press.

Kauffman, Stuart A. (2008), **REINVENTING THE SACRED**. New York: Basic Books.

King, B.B., **BLUES ALL AROUND ME: The Autobiography of B.B. King.** New York: Avon Books.

Lelyveld, Joseph (2011), **GREAT SOUL: Mahatma Gandhi and His Struggle With India**, New York: Alfred A. Knopf.

Mandlebrot, Benoit (1986), **THE FRACTAL GEOMETRY OF NATURE**. San Francisco: W.H. Freeman.

Maslow, Abraham H. (1971), **THE FARTHER REACHES of HUMAN NATURE**. New York: Viking Press.

Moreira-Almeida, Alex, & F. Santana-Santos (eds., 2012), **EXPLORING FRONTIERS of the MIND-BRAIN RELATIONSHIP**, especially Chapter 6: "Neurological Correlates of Meditation & Mindfulness."

Muller, Richard A. (2016), **NOW: The Physics of Time.** New York: W.W. Norton & Company

Musolino, Julian (2015), **THE SOUL FALLACY: What SCIENCE Shows We Gain by Letting Go of Our Soul Beliefs**. Prometheus Books, Amherst, N.Y.

McLellan, Scott, **CHURCH on SUNDAY, WORK on MONDAY: The Challenge of Fusing Christian Values with Business Life.**

Palmer, Parker (1976?), **"Servant Leadership,"** unpublished pamphlet, and (1980), THE PROMISE of PARADOX.

Penrose, Roger (1994), **SHADOWS OF THE MIND: A Search for the Missing Science of Consciousness.** New York: Oxford University Press.

Pirsig, Robert, **ZEN and the ART of MOTORCYCLE MAINTENANCE.**

Rapp, Don (2007), **ON BALANCE: Mastery of Physical Balance for Life.** Tallahassee, FL: Fulcrum Press, p.47.

Rees, Martin (1999), **JUST SIX NUMBERS**. New York: Harper Collins Publishers.

Rees, Martin, and J. Gribbin (1989), **COSMIC COINCIDENCES**: Dark Matter, Mankind, and Anthropic Cosmology. New York: Bantam.

Robinson, Marilynne (2015), **THE GIVENNESS OF THINGS.** London: Farrar, Straus and Giroux.

Schweitzer, Albert (1988), **A PLACE FOR REVELATION**: Sermons on Reverence for Life. New York: Macmillan Publishing.

Senge, Peter (1994), **THE FIFTH DISCIPLINE FIELDBOOK**. New York: Doubleday.

Sims, Bennett J. (1997), **SERVANTHOOD: Leadership for the Third Millennium.** Boston: Cowley Publications.

Smolin, Lee, **THE LIFE of the COSMOS.**

Sole', Richard & B. Goodwin (2000), **SIGNS of LIFE.** New York: Basic Books.

Steinbeck, John (1962), **WINTER of OUR DISCONTENT.**

Swami Prabhupana, A.C. Bhaktivevedanta (2007), **SRI ISOPANISAD.** Los Angeles: Bhaktivevedanta Book Trust (p.89).

Unger, Roberto Mangabeira, & Cornel West (1998), **THE FUTURE of AMERICAN PROGRESSIVISM: An Initiative for Political and Economic Reform.** Boston: Beacon Press.

APPENDIX 4

INDEX

WORD LIST:

- Soul
- Humanism
- life-force
- spirit
- spirituality
- being
- becoming
- religiosity
- religion
- extra-terrestrial
- supernatural
- atheist
- agnostic
- meaning, system
- external
- EG
- Internal
- Sustain
- Sustainability
- God
- NSB
- God-of-Life
- Creative
- Imagination
- Nature
- Earth
- mindfulness

- Nurture
- Roots
- Rootedness
- Suicide
- Christ
- Christianity
- Buddha
- Buddhism
- Tao
- Taoism
- Hinduism
- Bahai
- Material
- Immaterial
- Materialism
- Descartes
- Terrorism
- Immortality
- Embodied
- Disembodied
- self
- selfhood
- sacrilegious
- fundamental
- truth
- truthfulness
- empirical
- illusion
- functionalism.

- delusion
- replicable
- discovery
- science
- intelligent
- intelligence
- church
- myth
- mythical
- resurrection
- cycles
- stars
- cyclical
- world
- universe
- Catholicism
- Protestantism
- building blocks
- irreducibility
- reductionism
- carbonaceous
- membranes
- parallel processing
- peptides
- linear
- dualism

Also By Peter Bearse PhD

All books available on Amazon.com

A Truly Revolutionary: New American Revolution

Made in the USA
Columbia, SC
18 February 2021

32407973R00213